CHARACTER AS MORAL FICTION

Everyone wants to be virtuous, but recent psychological investigations suggest that this may not be possible. Mark Alfano challenges this theory and asks, not whether character is empirically adequate, but what characters human beings *could* have and develop. Although psychology suggests that most people do not have robust character traits such as courage, honesty, and open-mindedness, Alfano argues that we have reason to attribute these virtues to people because such attributions function as self-fulfilling prophecies – children become more studious if they are told that they are hard-working, and adults become more generous if they are told that they are generous. He argues that we should think of virtue and character as social constructs: there is no such thing as virtue without social reinforcement. His original and provocative book will interest a wide range of readers in contemporary ethics, epistemology, moral psychology, and empirically informed philosophy.

MARK ALFANO is Postdoctoral Research Associate at the Center for Human Values, Princeton University, and Assistant Professor of Philosophy at the University of Oregan.

CHARACTER AS MORAL FICTION

MARK ALFANO

CAMBRIDGE
UNIVERSITY PRESS

CAMBRIDGE
UNIVERSITY PRESS

University Printing House, Cambridge CB2 8BS, United Kingdom

Cambridge University Press is part of the University of Cambridge.

It furthers the University's mission by disseminating knowledge in the pursuit of education, learning and research at the highest international levels of excellence.

www.cambridge.org
Information on this title: www.cambridge.org/9781107538122

First published 2013
First paperback edition 2015

A catalogue record for this publication is available from the British Library

Library of Congress Cataloguing in Publication data
Alfano, Mark, 1983–
Character as moral fiction / Mark Alfano.
p. cm.
Includes bibliographical references (p.) and index.
ISBN 978-1-107-02672-8 (hardback)
1. Character. 2. Virtue. 3. Normativity (Ethics) I. Title.
BJ1521.A44 2013
179′.9–dc23
2012029713

ISBN 978-1-107-02672-8 Hardback
ISBN 978-1-107-53812-2 Paperback

for my wife, who tells me what I need to hear,
and for my parents, who always kept an eye on me

"*Only as creators!* – This has caused me the greatest trouble and still does always cause me the greatest trouble: to realize that *what things are called* is unspeakably more important than what they are. The reputation, name, and appearance, the worth, the usual measure and weight of a thing – originally almost always something mistaken and arbitrary, thrown over things like a dress and quite foreign to their nature and even to their skin – has, through the belief in it and its growth from generation to generation, slowly grown onto and into the thing and has become its very body: what started as appearance in the end nearly always becomes essence and *effectively acts* as its essence! What kind of a fool would believe that it is enough to point to this origin and this misty shroud of delusion in order to *destroy* the world that counts as 'real', so-called 'reality'! Only as creators can we destroy! – But let us also not forget that in the long run it is enough to create new names and valuations and appearances of truth in order to create new 'things'."

Friedrich Nietzsche, *The Gay Science*, 58. Translated by Josefine Nauckhoff, edited by Bernard Williams. Cambridge University Press, 2001.

"Sir Walter [... had] been flattered into his very best and most polished behavior by Mr. Shepherd's assurances of his being known, by report [...] as a model of good breeding."

Jane Austen, *Persuasion*, edited by Janet Todd and Antje Blank, Cambridge University Press, 2006, p. 34.

Contents

Acknowledgments   *page* viii

Introduction: tripartite naturalistic ethics   1

PART I   FACTITIOUS MORAL VIRTUE

1   Identifying the hard core of virtue ethics   17

2   Rearticulating the situationist challenge   35

3   Attempts to defend virtue ethics   62

4   Factitious moral virtue   82

PART II   FACTITIOUS INTELLECTUAL VIRTUE

5   Expanding the situationist challenge to
     responsibilist virtue epistemology   111

6   Expanding the situationist challenge to
     reliabilist virtue epistemology   139

7   Factitious intellectual virtue   157

PART III   PROGRAMMATIC CONCLUSION

8   To see as we are seen: an investigation of social
     distance heuristics   183

References   206
Index   225

Acknowledgments

Nothing of value is accomplished alone. First in these acknowledgments and first in my heart is my brilliant wife, Veronica. She somehow managed to keep both of us sane while we simultaneously wrote books in the same 60-square-foot office. My parents, Ronald and Marjorie, my in-laws, Mary and David, and my dwarf silver marten, Nori, all provided moral support.

I would also like to thank the many people who helped in many ways during the planning, research, writing, and revision of this manuscript. The vagaries of memory may prevent me from thanking everyone who deserves it, but I hope at least to thank everyone I do mention as well as they deserve.

Jesse Prinz advised the writing of my dissertation, on which the first half of this book is based. The dissertation committee also included John Doris, Gilbert Harman, Michael Levin, and Rohit Parikh, all of whom offered useful criticisms and suggestions along the way. Also involved were Graham Priest and Samir Chopra, who served on my prospectus committee.

The dissertation would not have been completed nearly as quickly without the regular feedback of a small group of fellow graduate students: Brian Robinson, Daniel Shargel, Myrto Mylopoulous, and Todd Beattie.

Chapter 8 is very loosely based on my Master's thesis, which was advised by Richard Sorabji and Catherine Wilson. Thanks also to Bernie Frischer for comments on the chapter.

The book manuscript was revised over the course of the 2010–11 and 2011–12 academic years, during both of which I gave a number of invited lectures and conference papers related to the manuscript. During 2010–11, I received incisive criticism and feedback from Gideon Rosen, Daniel Garber, Anthony Appiah, Joshua Knobe, Nickolas Pappas, John Greenwood, Stephen Stich, Nancy Snow, Daniel Russell, Peter Vranas, Christian Miller, Neera Badhwar, James Beebe, Michael Sechman, Rachel

Feddock, Benjamin Morison, Urs Fischbacher, Julia Driver, Chandra Sripada, Christopher Hitchcock, Tamler Sommers, David Wolfsdorf, and Miriam Solomon.

During the 2011–12 academic year, I had the good fortune to be a fellow at the Notre Dame Institute for Advanced Study, where I received plenty of time for research and helpful feedback from Robert Roberts, Vittorio Hösle, Daniel Lapsley, Paul Stey, Anastasia Scrutton, Darcia Narvaez, Robert Audi, Anne Marie Baril, and Paul Stey. In addition, quite a few people asked difficult and helpful questions during conversations, conference presentations, and invited lectures, including: Abrol Fairweather, Heather Battaly, Guy Axtell, Jennifer Lackey, Jonathan Webber, Alvin Goldman, Adam Morton, John Turri, Margaret Cameron, Zachary Horne, Jonathan Livengood, Alex Voorhoeve, Carlos Montemayor, John Basl, Christian Coons, and Nicole Smith.

I owe special thanks to Jonathan Adler, who took the time to send me detailed comments on a chapter despite his diagnosis with terminal leukemia. Special thanks are also due to David Rosenthal, whose wisdom and judgment are unparalleled. And special thanks are of course due to Hilary Gaskin at Cambridge University Press for agreeing to have my manuscript reviewed and working alongside me for the last year as I learned how book publishing works.

Thanks also to Eddy Nahmias, Andrea Scarantino, George Graham, Jessica Berry, and – most of all – AJ Cohen at Georgia State University. They'll know why.

My interest in moral psychology and factitious virtue more particularly stemmed from an interest in the writings of Friedrich Nietzsche, so I suppose I should thank him, as well as Dave Murphy, the high-school English teacher who first introduced me to Nietzsche, and Alexander Nehamas, my undergraduate instructor in Nietzsche.

Introduction: tripartite naturalistic ethics

> To translate humanity back into nature; to gain control of the many vain and fanciful interpretations and incidental meanings that have been scribbled and drawn over that eternal basic text of *homo natura* so far; to make sure that, from now on, the human being will stand before the human being, just as he already stands before the *rest* of nature today, hardened by the discipline of science, – with courageous Oedipus eyes and sealed up Odysseus ears, deaf to the lures of the old metaphysical bird catchers who have been whistling to him for far too long: "You are more! You are higher! You have a different origin!"
>
> Friedrich Nietzsche, *Beyond Good and Evil*, 230

I VIRTUE AND VICE TODAY

In *Ethics and the Limits of Philosophy*, Bernard Williams complains that the word 'virtue' has "acquired comic or otherwise undesirable associations" (1985, p. 9). Yet even the twenty-first century is rife with talk of virtues and vices.

On January 2, 2007, Cameron Hollopeter suffered a seizure and stumbled off the platform of the 137th-Street subway station in Manhattan. One bystander, Wesley Autrey, noticed the emergency and dove onto the tracks to save him from an oncoming train. Lacking time to lift the victim back onto the platform, he pinned Hollopeter in the drainage trench between the rails while the train straddled them. It came so close to crushing Autrey that it left grease on his cap. News of his deed spread quickly: two days later he was awarded the Bronze Medallion – New York City's highest award for exceptional citizenship and outstanding achievement – by Mayor Michael Bloomberg; he was an honored guest on a number of television shows; his daughters were given scholarships and free computers; on January 23, he appeared at the State of the Union address, where President George W. Bush praised him as a "brave and humble" man.

On December 11, 2008, Bernard Madoff was arrested and charged with securities fraud. For decades, Madoff – a revered member of the New York financial elite – had been running a Ponzi scheme, deceiving his clients and investigators alike. Though the damage he wrought is difficult to assess, the total loss to investors has been estimated in the tens of billions of dollars – probably the largest fraud in the history of money. In the aftermath, his son and at least two of his clients committed suicide, and many charitable organizations, his favorite marks, were forced to close.

In January 2009, New Yorkers heeding President Obama's call for a new era of responsibility donated a record 925,000 pounds of food to the *Daily News*-City Harvest feed-the-hungry campaign. Approximately one million needy residents of the city benefited from these donations, which were distributed by 600 community organizations. During the worst economic conditions since the Great Depression, and at a time when New York City in particular was suffering job losses, this display of generosity impressed and encouraged.

On March 3, 2011, Karl-Theodore zu Guttenberg resigned from the Bundestag after a month-long public outcry over the plagiarism of his doctoral dissertation. He had cribbed whole passages from newspapers, editorials, speeches, undergraduate term papers, and even his own supervisor's research, filling about half of his dissertation with unattributed material. The University of Bayreuth revoked his degree. Over fifty thousand doctoral students and professors signed an open letter to Chancellor Angela Merkel to protest her dilatory handling of the controversy. The German author Peter Schneider went so far as to draw a parallel with the impeachment of American President Bill Clinton over sexual improprieties. Why? Because both cases involved "the same question of honesty."

Why did Autrey risk his life to help a stranger? Why did Madoff steal from his clients? Why did New Yorkers succor their neighbors? Why did Guttenberg plagiarize his dissertation?

One way to answer these questions and others like them is by appeal to character traits. Autrey exhibited courage by intervening even at high potential cost to himself. Madoff was greedy and dishonest, manifesting a shocking inclination to deceive and defraud. Ordinary New Yorkers were generous and humane, choosing to forgo their own material benefit in order to help those in need. Guttenberg lacked integrity; he preferred to violate German law, academic standards, and perhaps even his own conscience to save himself effort and time. Traits like callousness, courage, greed, dishonesty, generosity, and tact are dispositions to act and react in characteristic ways. The callous person sniffs at the suffering of others; the courageous person braves dangers to secure something valuable.

The fully virtuous person possesses all or at least a critical mass of the virtues, and so is disposed to do the appropriate thing in a wide range of circumstances. Such a disposition has counterfactual heft: the generous person, for instance, gives when presented with the opportunity, and she *would* give *were* she presented with a similar opportunity. This metaphysically robust property underwrites both the prediction and explanation of her behavior. It is therefore a presupposition of theories of virtue that moral agents have – or at least could have – counterfactual-supporting dispositions.

At first blush this presupposition is uncontentious. How could one deny that people are, or at least could be, just, sincere, compassionate, chaste, considerate, trustworthy, courteous, diligent, faithful, tactful, valorous, and humble? We seem to understand ourselves and one another in terms of such character traits. Bernard Williams (1985, p. 10, n. 7) goes so far as to say that objecting to the notion of character amounts to "an objection to ethical thought itself rather than to one way of conducting it." Yet skeptics such as John Doris (1998, 2002) and Gilbert Harman (1999, 2000, 2001, 2003, 2006) argue that situational influences swamp dispositional ones, rendering them predictively and explanatorily impotent. It's but a single step from such impotence to the dustbin.

Are individual dispositions really so frail? Are circumstances really as powerful as skeptics suggest? This book aims to articulate naturalistic answers to these and related questions.

2 WHAT IS NATURALISTIC ETHICS?

The word 'natural' and its derivatives can be used with both evaluative and descriptive force. Saying that a musician plays naturally means that her playing is graceful, unforced, and so on. Playing naturally is playing *well*. Saying that a dancer waltzes unnaturally means that he moves awkwardly, clumsily, and so on. Dancing unnaturally is dancing *poorly*. But saying that cats naturally have four legs simply means that cats have four legs ordinarily, genetically, or something like that. Naturally having four legs is neither *good* nor *bad*, despite what the pigs in Orwell's *Animal Farm* might have decreed. Similarly, humans do not naturally have four legs, which means that humans do not have four legs ordinarily, genetically, or something like that. Naturally not having four legs is neither *good* nor *bad*.

This book is a project in naturalistic ethics, which prompts the question whether 'naturalistic' is being used with descriptive or evaluative force. I hope that you will be inclined to think that the answer is *both*, for this book is deeply entrenched in descriptive naturalism, and I believe such naturalism is appropriate, fruitful, and thus evaluatively natural.

Three key distinctions will help to explain what I have in mind by descriptively naturalistic ethics.

First, a theory can be *methodologically* or *substantively* naturalistic. *Methodological naturalism* involves using only methods consonant with the natural sciences, such as physics, chemistry, biology, and psychology. Since the sciences would be impossible without the resources of mathematics and logic, methodological naturalism uses methods consonant with them as well. An ethical theory would fail to be methodologically naturalistic if it employed methods that are not only outside the sciences' stable but incommensurate or incompatible with the sciences, such as divination, dowsing, and scriptural interpretation. Much contemporary ethics, especially in the Kantian tradition but also in some of the virtue ethical tradition, has been brazenly methodologically non-natural. I will not argue against such an approach between the covers of this book, but I do hope to show by example that one need not abandon naturalism to engage in a deep and fruitful way with ethics.

Substantive naturalism is a stronger stance, of which the varieties are arranged in a sort of spectrum. At one end of the spectrum, substantive naturalists commit themselves to the existence only of those entities quantified over by the best-established sciences. At the other end, I still consider it substantively naturalistic to commit oneself to the existence only of those entities that enjoy sufficient empirical support from the respectable sciences, or the respectable districts within each science. There is plenty of dissent within each scientific discipline, as the recent controversy over Daryl Bem's (2011) unreplicable attempt to argue for paranormal psychology demonstrates. A type of entity or phenomenon does not become empirically admissible simply in virtue of being suggested by a single study, nor does it become empirically inadmissible simply in virtue of being inconsistent with a single study. As with anything of this sort, the key to interpretation is to generate several explanatory hypotheses that fit the overall pattern of evidence. Since evidence radically underdetermines theory, a unique explanation cannot be expected, but further argumentation, new research, and attention to theoretical strengths such as plausibility, simplicity, consilience, and so on, may tell for or against each of the potential explanations. In this book, I subscribe to a quite permissive substantive naturalism that countenances everything from quarks and ribosomes to expectations and preferences. A theory fails to be substantively naturalistic even on my relaxed view if it purports to refer to entities recognized by none of the sciences, such as deities, immaterial souls, or group minds.

The theory I will adumbrate here is both methodologically and substantively naturalistic. I employ only methods consonant with those used in the sciences and refer only to entities countenanced by the sciences.

Second, a theory can be *merely consistent with* the natural sciences, *abductively suggested by* the natural sciences, or *outright derived from* the natural sciences. This distinction has to do with the logical relation of the ethical theory T_e to the conjunction of scientific theories T_s. If it's not the case that $T_s \rightarrow T_e$, then the ethical theory is consistent with the sciences. This is a much weaker relation than outright derivation, where $T_s \rightarrow T_e$. Between these two extremes lies the type of ethical theory that is an inference to the best explanation of what the (relevant portion of the) conjunction of scientific theories says. An inference to the best explanation is not merely consistent with what it is meant to explain, nor is it logically derived from what it is meant to explain. While an outright derived ethical theory would be interesting, I cannot imagine what one would even look like. My project is not that ambitious. Instead, I want to articulate an ethical theory that is abductively related to the rest of the sciences. What I propose here is the best explanation I can muster for the relevant evidence, taking into account as best as I can the philosophical arguments that have been made for and against various views in the last twenty-five centuries.

Third, a theory may be naturalistic in a *hard* sense if it draws only on the hard sciences, such as physics and chemistry. By contrast, a theory may be only *softly* naturalistic if it draws on both the hard sciences and the soft sciences, including anthropology, psychology, behavioral economics, and biology.[1] While hard naturalistic theories are fascinating and allow for more certain predictions and explanations than their soft counterparts, physics and chemistry give us no grasp of what the good, the right, and the virtuous are. I think, and will attempt to show, that the social sciences to some extent do. Again, then, my project is less than maximally ambitious: I aim to present a softly naturalistic ethical theory.

---

[1] Presumably there is also room for theories that draw *only* on the soft sciences, but I can see no reason to restrict oneself in this way.

In short, I aim to promulgate an ethics that systematically explains as much as possible of two bodies of evidence: the relevant scientific data and theories, and philosophical intuitions and theories about moral conduct. The data are sometimes murky. Some scientific theories are inconsistent with themselves, or with other well-supported theories, or with relevant data. Philosophical intuitions and theories may be unfalsifiable (a direction in which much recent virtue ethics has sadly moved), easily falsified, inconsistent with other philosophical intuitions and theories, or inconsistent with well-supported scientific theories. There is no unique way to handle this cacophony. I will propose one that I believe harmonizes as much as possible of the evidence. Other, incompatible, explanations are surely possible, and in the spirit of collaborative inquiry I invite them. That said, the fact that such explanations are possible, and that for all anyone knows one might be better than the one proposed here, is not itself an objection. Theories are never defeated so easily. The only thing that can truly kill a theory is another theory.

To summarize, the theory to be presented in this book is descriptively naturalistic in four ways. It is methodologically naturalistic because it uses only the methods consonant with those of the sciences; it is substantively naturalistic because it purports to refer only to entities recognized by the sciences; it is abductively related to the rest of the sciences; and it draws on the soft sciences. I think that these four ways of being naturalistic are also theoretically desirable, so I contend that my view is evaluatively natural as well. I will not try to convince you of this now, but the hope is that as you proceed through the chapters you will recognize the value of my approach.

The remainder of this chapter grounds the rest of the book in a partition of ethics into three interrelated projects: normative theory, moral psychology, and moral technology. Normative theory identifies what would be good and bad, right and wrong, warranted and unwarranted. It tells us what may and should be, and (in its more ambitious moments) why it may and should be. Moral psychology explains and predicts how actual human agents conduct themselves in the moral domain, which includes how they see, construe, feel, think, deliberate, desire, act, refrain from acting, and fail to act. It identifies how we function and what we're capable of, morally speaking. Moral technology attempts to bridge the gap between moral psychology and normative theory by recommending ways in which we, as moral psychology describes us, can become more as we should be, as normative theory prescribes. Hitherto, ethicists have primarily concentrated on normative theory and moral psychology. By emphasizing moral technology as well, this project serves as a useful corrective.

2.1 *Naturalistic normative theory*

According to this way of carving up the ethical domain, normative theory is the project of identifying what, both in particular cases and in general, would satisfy the evaluative predicates ('good,' 'bad,' 'better,' 'worse,' 'best,' and 'worst'; 'right' and 'wrong'; 'impermissible,' 'permissible,' and 'obligatory'; 'virtuous,' 'vicious,' 'admirable,' 'exemplary,' and 'flourishing,' to name a few). Different theories answer in different ways. In caricature at least, consequentialism grounds the deontic terms ('right,' and 'wrong'; 'impermissible,' 'permissible,' and 'obligatory') and the aretaic terms ('virtuous,' 'vicious,' 'admirable,' 'exemplary,' and 'flourishing') in the state-based terms ('good,' 'bad,' 'better,' 'worse,' 'best,' and 'worst'). Actions are right because they lead to the best consequences. People are virtuous because they tend or intend to bring about good consequences. Kantian ethics grounds the state-based and aretaic terms in the deontic terms. Good consequences are the sorts of results aimed at by obligatory actions; bad consequences are the sorts of results aimed at by impermissible actions. A person is virtuous if she tends to act from duty. Virtue ethics – at least the agent-based virtue ethics of Slote (2001, p. 7) and Russell (2009, p. 74) – grounds the state-based and deontic terms in the aretaic ones. Actions are right because the virtuous person would do or recommend them, wrong because the virtuous person would avoid or recommend against them. Consequences are good because they are what a virtuous person would aim at when acting in character, bad because they are what a virtuous person would avoid when acting in character (or what a vicious person would aim at when acting in character).

Ordinarily, this part of the ethical project stratifies into three levels. At the most general level, meta-ethics provides an account of the meaning of the various evaluative terms. At the most specific level, applied ethics attempts to answer thorny questions about fraught issues like abortion, euthanasia, suicide, and so on. Between these two lies normative ethics, which provides a more substantive account than meta–ethics without descending to the nitty-gritty of applied ethics. All three levels are part of normative theory, however. While I do engage in much normative theory in this book, much of what I have to say is also about moral psychology and moral technology.

2.2   Naturalistic moral psychology

Unlike normative theory, which attempts to explain what makes things good, right, and virtuous, moral psychology enables us to describe, explain, and predict human thought, feeling, and action in moral contexts.[2] I'll use 'conduct' as an umbrella term to cover many aspects of the moral life, including seeing, construing, feeling, thinking, deliberating, desiring, acting, refraining from acting, and failing to act. All aspects of conduct are important. John Doris has been taken to task for often eliding the internal aspects of moral psychology and focusing on behavior; he, in turn, seems inclined to turn the tables and criticize his opponents for ignoring the external aspects of moral psychology. While I agree that behavior is important, I also recognize that what goes on inside counts. In this book, I try to give sufficient weight to the inside, the outside, and especially to their interaction.

This aspect of the ethical project is at least as old as the normative part, and perhaps older. In the *Nicomachean Ethics*, Aristotle seems to presuppose that his audience recognizes his catalogue of virtues, which does not stand in need of further justification. He devotes much of his effort to developing a rich moral psychology based on emotions, sensitivity to reasons, deliberation, and action. Other philosophers throughout history have articulated their own moral psychologies. In the *Science of Virtue*, Immanuel Kant frames his moral psychology in terms of the will, obedience to the moral law, and the sense of duty. In *A Treatise of Human Nature* and *An Enquiry Concerning the Principles of Morals*, David Hume grounds his moral psychology not so much in reasons and the rational will as in sentiments and feelings. Friedrich Nietzsche attacks his predecessors precisely on the adequacy of their moral psychologies throughout his oeuvre, and especially in the *Genealogy of Morals*, where he claims that the basis of most moral conduct since the rise of Christianity is a distilled and disguised sense of dudgeon and a delight in tormenting people, including oneself.

More recently, interest in moral psychology among analytic philosophers revived with the birth of neo-Aristotelian virtue ethics, non-cognitivist theories of the meaning of moral thoughts and statements, and worries about moral character.[3] This project deals at length with that last issue, which has been raised most trenchantly by John Doris, Owen

---

[2] Some useful introductions to moral psychology include Doris et al. (2010) and Sinnott-Armstrong (2008).
[3] See Anscombe (1958), Blackburn (1998), Gibbard (2003), and MacIntyre (1984).

Flanagan, Gilbert Harman, Christian Miller, and Peter Vranas. All five question – in different ways and with different conclusions – whether people have the traits of character traditionally identified as virtues by normative theory. The worry is that if normative theory positively evaluates ways of being and behaving that are exceedingly demanding or perhaps even impossible for human agents to embody, then either we are doomed to inevitable moral failure or normative theory should rethink its prescriptions. One of the aims of this book is to adjudicate this dispute by weakening the stringency of normative ethical prescriptions while co-opting aspects of our moral psychology, an aim that falls squarely in the third branch of the ethical project: moral technology.

2.3 Introducing naturalistic moral technology

Normative theory identifies what would be good, right, and virtuous. Moral psychology describes, explains, and predicts human conduct in moral contexts. What more could there be to the ethical project? I believe that one key aspect remains. Namely, moral technology. This part of the ethical project is not about *identifying* the good and the right, nor is it about *describing*, *explaining*, and *predicting* how people will think, feel, and act when the good and the right are at stake. Instead, moral technology attempts to bridge the gap between moral psychology and normative theory by proposing ways in which we, as moral psychology describes us, can become more we should be, as normative theory prescribes for us. Moral technology isn't about describing, explaining, or predicting what we are and do from a moral point of view, but about *controlling* or *guiding* what we are and do from a moral point of view. Moral technology subsumes the familiar field of moral education. Whereas moral education aims at, for example, inculcating outright virtue, moral technology aims at that in addition to mere action in accordance with virtue. Whereas moral education is typically reserved for the young or the novice, moral technology is for everyone.

In particular, I shall argue that though most people do not think, feel, and act in ways that traditional normative theory would describe as virtuous (or, for that matter, vicious), we should still attribute the virtues (but not the vices) to one another because these attributions tend to function as self-fulfilling prophecies. Calling someone honest – especially when he has just done something that could be construed as honest – will lead him to think, feel, and act more honestly in the future. Calling someone compassionate – especially when she has just done something that could be construed as compassionate – will induce her to think, feel, and act more compassionately in the future. Caveats and clarifications abound, of course, but the plausible, public attribution of virtues (including, as I shall show, intellectual virtues such as curiosity) tends to lead the target of the attribution to live up to the way she's been described. Furthermore, this effect is robust in at least two senses: it induces behavior in accordance with the attributed trait in a variety of circumstances (thus exhibiting cross-situational consistency) and it is long-lived, inducing behavior in accordance with the attributed trait for hours, days, even months (thus exhibiting temporal stability).

There is a near-universal presumption that if people are not virtuous, then they should not be told that they are virtuous. I shall argue on pragmatic grounds that we should, in the right circumstances and in the right ways, attribute virtues to people even if they might not have them. Aristotle thought that people became courageous by acting courageously; I contend that they become courageous (or near enough) by being called courageous. Aristotle claimed that people become courteous by acting courteously; I contend that they become courteous (or near enough) by being called courteous. Aristotle believed that people become creative by acting creatively; I contend that they become creative (or near enough) by being called creative. When this happens, I call it *factitious virtue*.

2.3.1   Does moral technology need an introduction?

I've claimed to be introducing moral technology, but it might seem that this aspect of the ethical project is as old as the rest. In one sense, I agree, as the examples adduced below will show. In another sense, however, I think that moral technology has gotten such short shrift, especially in recent analytic philosophy, that it can hardly be said to constitute a continuous thread of the ethical project in the way that moral psychology and normative theory can.

Most contemporary students of moral technology are not philosophers but marketers, charity workers, politicians, and pedagogues. Moral technology was not always so atrophied. In the *Republic*, for instance, Plato described in (from a contemporary perspective, incredible) detail how to train the guardians of the ideal city, going so far as to say that an entire society would unravel if the wrong musical modes came into vogue.

In Chapter 8, I will show that Epicurus and his followers deployed a finely designed piece of moral technology in the Garden. Epicurus is reputed to have told his followers to behave at all times as if he were watching – a prescription of his normative theory. I will argue at some length that his materialist metaphysics led him to think that his followers would satisfy this prescription best if they always felt as if he were watching. To bridge the gap between how they were according to Epicurean moral psychology and how they should be according to Epicurean normative theory, he had a statue of himself erected in the Garden.[4] I will suggest that Epicurus in fact hit on a powerful way to decrease the social distance people perceive among themselves. Recent work by behavioral economists shows that the feeling of being watched, even by a statue or a photograph of a face, induces other-regarding preferences and behavior of diverse sorts, from generosity to eco-friendliness.

2.3.2   *Is moral technology paternalistic or manipulative?*

In their recent book, *Nudge*, Richard Thaler and Cass Sunstein (2008) defend what they call libertarian paternalism, the attempt by governments and other institutions to design the choice architectures of environments in such a way that people in those environments freely choose what their own better angels would want them to choose, even if they would not so choose were the environment slightly different. For instance, placing nutritious food at eye level in cafeterias leads people to consume it rather than the fattening foods placed above or below eye level.

It might seem that moral technology is just a recapitulation of libertarian paternalism, with all its attendant defects. I think otherwise, for several reasons.

First, moral technology is politically neutral. It is about people's interactions with one another. The interventions recommended by libertarian paternalists are often made not to individuals but to governments or other institutions. They deal with tax law, charitable organizations, and the licensing of motorcyclists. Moral technology deals with what we say to each other, what we say about each other, and what sorts of decorations we put on our own walls. Libertarian paternalism is therefore the political cousin of moral technology, which is limited to the ethical domain. Someone inclined to accept one may have a penchant for the other, but they come neatly apart.

Second, and relatedly, libertarian paternalism primarily concerns itself with third-personal interventions. Paternalism essentially involves one person facilitating another's well-being. It hardly makes sense to say that

---

[4] Another, closely related, example of moral technology is Jeremy Bentham's Panopticon, a design for a jail in which the prisoners feel watched by the warden at all times. This parallel is discussed at more length in Chapter 8.

someone could treat *herself* paternalistically. This is presumably one of the reasons people find paternalism, even the libertarian paternalism espoused by Thaler and Sunstein, worrisome. Moral technology, by contrast, can be practiced on oneself. You can decorate your study with images of faces rather than images of flowers. I can ask people to call me industrious, conscientious, and punctual. (They may not oblige, but that's a different problem.) Thus, there is in principle no reason why moral technology cannot be *reflexive* and *symmetric*, whereas libertarian paternalism is essentially anti-reflexive and asymmetric.

Finally, libertarian paternalism is solely about human behavior: as long as the right behaviors are manifested, libertarian paternalists do not care how they were brought about. This is, of course, not to say that they deny the existence of thoughts, feelings, and emotions. It's just that they don't care as such about *how* those thoughts, feelings, and emotions conspire to bring about the desired behavior, only *whether* they bring it about. Moral technology is stricter in this regard: because having certain thoughts, feeling certain emotions, and deliberating in certain ways are themselves morally good (in addition to the behaviors such mental phenomena result in), the moral technologist aims (among other things) to generate the right sorts of thoughts, emotions, and cognitive processes. Doing what the open-minded person does is admirable, but thinking as the open-minded person thinks is too. Acting as the encouraging person acts is praiseworthy, but feeling as the encouraging person feels is too. Investigating as the curious person investigates is excellent, but wanting what the curious person wants is too. This means that moral technology must concern itself more than libertarian paternalism with the mind and the heart.

One of the problems with paternalism, even libertarian paternalism, is the connotation of manipulation and manipulativeness that it carries. "Don't worry your pretty little head about it," says the paternalist, "I've got it all figured out for you." Someone engaged in moral technology of the sort that I recommend in this book needn't take up such an attitude. I take it that Marcia Baron (2003, p. 47) is on the right track when she says that the ills of manipulation and manipulativeness include "arrogating to oneself decisions that are not one's to make" and "putting undue pressure on others." The person involved in manipulation is too inclined "*to steer others*" (p. 48). Telling someone that she is honest, at least when it's done in the way I will argue, may be an attempt to steer her, but it is not an attempt to steer her *too much*.

3 A ROADMAP

The key concept of this book is factitious virtue. I call it 'factitious' because the moral technology I am advocating results in artificially virtuous conduct. From the Latin verb for doing or making, 'factitious' suggests both the careful calibration and skill of an artist and the technological know-how of an artificer. The aural resemblance to 'fictitious' is an added bonus. Although we may not be virtuous in *fact*, tactically deployed *fictions* result in *factitious virtue*.

Hitherto, it's been unclear whether empirically minded critics of virtue ethics were successful because it was unclear what their target was, so in Chapter 1, I identify what I consider the "hard core" of virtue ethics. In Chapter 2, I rearticulate the situationist challenge and attempt to bring some order to the many situational factors that influence moral conduct. Chapter 3 canvasses existing attempts to defend virtue ethics from the situationist critique; most of these attempts turn out to be unsound or to give up some of the "hard core" of virtue ethics. Then, in Chapter 4, I articulate my own response to the challenge: factitious virtue.

The second half of the book introduces a parallel critique of virtue epistemology, the family of views that defines justification and knowledge in terms of personal traits or dispositions. Chapter 5 expands the situationist challenge to so-called responsibilist virtue epistemology, which countenances motivational intellectual virtues such as open-mindedness, creativity, and intellectual courage. Chapter 6 expands the challenge to so-called reliabilist virtue epistemology, which countenances purely cognitive intellectual virtues such as deduction, induction, and inference to the best explanation. Chapter 7 explores the extent to which the factitious virtue response articulated in Chapter 4 can be modified to respond to epistemic situationism. In the final chapter, I show another way in which moral technology may be used to respond to the trouble that moral psychology often makes for normative theory.

To the extent that this is possible, I have tried to make the chapters modular. I'm not so narcissistic as to think that every reader will read from cover to cover; four other sensible paths through the book are:

- The *virtue ethics* path: Chapters 1, 2, 3, 4, and 8
- The *virtue epistemology* path: Chapters 5, 6, and 7
- The *pessimistic empirical* path: Chapters 2, 5, and 6
- The *optimistic empirical* path: Chapters 4, 7, and 8

Researchers interested in virtue ethics but not virtue epistemology will find the *virtue ethics* path congenial. It should also be possible to use the *virtue ethics* path in a graduate or upper-level undergraduate seminar. Similarly, researchers in virtue epistemology should find the *virtue epistemology* path congenial, as should teachers of graduate or upper-level undergraduate seminars in epistemology. I also realize that virtue theorists may be eager to refute my arguments against traditional virtue ethics and virtue epistemology; for them, the *pessimistic empirical* path might be most appropriate. And for anyone who wants to use my work as a springboard to further research in moral technology, the *optimistic empirical* path would be congenial.

PART I

Factitious moral virtue

CHAPTER I

Identifying the hard core of virtue ethics

He has all the virtues I dislike, and none of the vices I admire.
Winston Churchill, apocryphal

I   THE VIRTUES OF VIRTUES

The clarion call of the revival of virtue ethics was Elizabeth Anscombe's feisty "Modern Moral Philosophy" (1958). She claimed that it is not worthwhile to do ethics until we possess a proper philosophy of psychology – one that provides a theory of reasons, motives, and dispositions inter alia. According to Anscombe, the discipline of moral philosophy has been led down the garden path by the seeming generality of terms like 'ought,' 'should,' 'right,' and 'good.' These terms are too abstract and thin to be of much use in reasoning about our actual moral conduct, and they derive from an outmoded theory of divine command. Furthermore, they shift the focus of moral attention away from agents and whole lives onto particular actions; morality thus devolves into picayune casuistry.

While one might be inclined to contest these points, Anscombe's emphatic return to Aristotle made its mark on value theory. For the last five decades now, a sizeable contingent of moral philosophers has paid close attention to such notions as *eudaimonia* (translated variously as 'happiness,' 'flourishing,' and 'well-being'), character, and virtue, in addition to the more common modern focal points of goodness, rightness, and obligation.[1] Virtues became such a hot topic that even those outside the tradition felt it incumbent upon themselves to address it. For instance, John Rawls (1971, p. 436) glosses virtues as "strong and normally effective desires to act on the basic principles of right."

Philosophers of science such as Imre Lakatos (1995) distinguish between the "hard core" of a research program and its "protective" or "auxiliary

---

[1] See, for instance, Hursthouse (1999, p. 74) and Kupperman (1995, p. 7; 2001, p. 250).

belt." The phrase "hard core" refers to the conjunction of claims that the research program must defend at all costs. Other claims made by researchers in the program are considered auxiliary hypotheses intended to form a "protective belt" around the hard core. For instance, Newtonian astronomers allowed themselves to posit new heavenly bodies and tweak the gravitational constant G in light of new data, but they could not allow themselves to give up the inverse-square law. A theory is not falsified until its hard core can no longer be protected by new auxiliary hypotheses, or until such hypotheses grow so ad hoc that researchers abandon it and seek an alternative.

Naturalistic ethics is a research program, just like Newtonian physics. To see whether the situationist challenge truly threatens virtue ethics, then, we must determine which propositions constitute its hard core. In this chapter, I canvass the raft of metaphysical, conceptual, methodological, and empirical arguments that have been advanced for preferring virtue ethics, from which I cull ten central tenets of virtue ethics. These tenets are candidates for inclusion in the hard core. I argue that seven should be accepted unrevised, two should be weakened, and one should be relegated to the auxiliary belt. The remaining seven, along with the revised pair, constitute the hard core of virtue ethics.[2]

The arguments are:

(1) The proper objects of moral *contemplation* are not deeds or occurrent motives, but something broader – either behavior-producing traits of character or character as such.

(2) The proper objects of moral *evaluation* are not deeds or occurrent motives, but something broader – either behavior-producing traits or character as such.

(3) Theorizing about virtues and character transports moral discourse from the rarified air of abstract principles into the evaluatively and descriptively 'thick' realm of motives and reasons.

(4) Reflecting on the virtues is a better guide to action than reflecting on abstract principles.

(5) The conceptual apparatus of virtue ethics helps to bridge the 'is'–'ought' gap.

(6) Moral cultivation or education is more effective when the focus is on virtues and character than when it is on the application of abstract rules.

---

[2] This chapter is based in large part on my (forthcoming b) article.

In this section, I expand on these arguments in dogmatic fashion, not so much to convince you of their soundness as to motivate the virtue ethical approach. The aim is to show that virtue ethics has prima facie strengths that consequentialism and deontology arguably do not possess – strengths that together merit serious consideration.

1.1　Virtue and moral contemplation

The first point can be construed as methodological. When we think about morality, we most fruitfully ask "How should one live?" rather than "What is our duty?" or "How may we be good?" or even "How can we be happy?" (Williams 1985, p. 4).[3] This dilation of focus enables one to engage in long-term projects, which such ethicists as Peter Geach (1977, p. 16) have argued are necessary for a fulfilling life.

In his reflections on *eudaimonia*, Aristotle makes a similar point: "the happy person is the one who, adequately furnished with external goods, engages in activities in accordance with complete virtue, not for just any period of time but over a complete life" (1101a). There is certainly something right about this argument. Flitting from moment to moment without long-term projects is no way to live. Fulfillment derives at least in part from major accomplishments, which take planning and protracted effort.

The virtue ethical approach seems well suited to such long-term contemplation. It focuses on habitual sensitivity to reasons and stable motivational structures. Whereas consequentialism (or at least act consequentialism) and theories that focus on following rules will tell us what to *do* (here, now), virtue theory may help provide answers about what and how to *be*.

1.2　Virtue and moral evaluation

Furthermore, virtue ethicists sometimes point out that when we approve or disapprove (and when we express these attitudes in praise or blame), the object is often not (or not only) what someone does. Instead or in addition, it is either the robust motive or trait from which the action flowed, or the person herself. Even such a committed utilitarian as John Stuart Mill admitted, "It really is of importance, not only what men do, but also what manner of men they are that do it" (1859/2010, p. 64). One of the reasons we care about what people do, on this view, is that their actions

---

[3] See also Crisp (1996, pp. 1–2) and Slote (1992, pp. 3–8).

afford glimpses of their character. Conduct is an expression – and therefore an indicator – of character. While the actions themselves and the consequences they produce may be good or bad, what interests the moral evaluator are the inferences that can be drawn about people's character on the basis of these actions and consequences. A jilted lover is upset about what her paramour *did*, but even more upset about what that shows him to *be*. The violation of trust is one thing, the trait of dishonesty another. Critics of Karl-Theodore zu Guttenberg were appalled by his action, but even more distraught over the implication that he could not be trusted to act honestly in political negotiations and decisions about the nation's military forces. Those who praised Wesley Autry were of course impressed by his rescue of Cameron Hollopeter, but they celebrated him as a hero for what that brave deed showed about his character.

On this understanding of moral evaluation, actions receive their moral flavor at least in part from the dispositions that lead to them. A noble act is one such as the noble person would perform, and (some such as Slote 2001, p. 7 and Russell 2009, p. 74 even add) it is noble because the noble person would perform it. N. J. H. Dent (1975, p. 319), for instance, argues that temperance is (but justice is not) a virtue because "the temperance of acts is dependent on the temperance of men," whereas the justice of acts is not.

This theory of the relation between virtuous acts and virtuous traits has its discontents, of course, most notably Thomas Hurka (2001, pp. 3–28, 2006) and Judith Jarvis Thomson (1996). For them, the direction of analysis runs in the opposite direction: a virtuous trait is whatever disposition leads (in the right way) to virtuous acts, which are taken as primitive. Should we say that "T is a virtue because T leads in the right way to actions of type A," or that "Because T is a virtue, T leads in the right way to actions of type A"? This is a deep metaphysical question, and one I will not attempt to adjudicate here, or for that matter elsewhere in this book. For my purposes, the explanatory connection may not matter so long as the following biconditional is true: "T is a virtue if and only if T leads in the right way to actions of type A."

1.3 Moral schizophrenia versus virtue as a 'thick' concept

Next, while moral theory needs to distinguish between right-making properties and motivating properties, allowing too great a rift between them amounts to a sort of "moral schizophrenia." This moniker was coined by Michael Stocker, according to whom one "mark of a good life is a harmony between one's motives and one's reasons, values, justifications"

(1976, p. 453). This line of argument holds that even if consequentialism (or deontology) were true and even if people somehow brought their behavior in line with its precepts, either they would not be motivated to maximize utility (or act from universalizable maxims) as such, or their having such motivation would be incompatible with what otherwise seems like genuinely moral motivation. The contents of their motives and of their reasons might coincide extensionally, but not intensionally, or if they did coincide intensionally, the agent would seem cold, detached, even immoral. Hence, either the justification or reason for their behavior would differ from the motive driving their behavior, or it would be the same but appear immoral.

The urinal fly nicely illustrates the dissociative side of the argument from moral schizophrenia. Not long ago, Schiphol airport in Amsterdam had a problem in its male restrooms: travelers failed to aim properly, leaving the walls and floor a slippery, reeking mess. Signs encouraging patrons to be considerate had no effect. A clever inventor realized that if men simply had a target they would regulate their behavior in the desired way, so he created a sticker depicting a lifelike horsefly that could be affixed to the optimal zone of the urinal. The change was immediate and complete; Schiphol now has some of the cleanest bathrooms in any airport. The men using these urinals exhibit some moral (or at least social) schizophrenia. The reason they keep the restroom pristine (consideration for fellow-travelers) has nothing to do with their motive for keeping the bathroom clean (wanting to piss on a fly). While the consequences of this intervention are undeniably good, the conduct of the urinal users might not be aptly described as virtuous: they behave as they do, not out of consideration for other travelers or for the janitors who have to clean up after them, but in order to piss on a fly.

Another example illustrates the other side of the argument from moral schizophrenia. Imagine that you've just completed a marathon, at the age of 50. Someone you take to be your friend waits at the finish line, gives you a big hug, and gushes with what seems like heartfelt congratulations. Later you discover, however, that he did so only out of a sense of duty. He wasn't impressed with your accomplishment. He wasn't happy for you. He just felt obligated to congratulate you. Or perhaps he thought it would promote overall happiness to congratulate you. Such motives seem to detract from the sincerity of the congratulations, perhaps even making your alleged friend immoral.

Since virtue ethics advises one not only to do the right thing but to do it for the right reason, it arguably avoids the theoretical mediation that plagues its competitors.[4] Virtuous agents deliberate and act on 'thick' reasons, which fuse together the motivational and evaluative components that are divorced in cases of moral schizophrenia. The thick/thin distinction is due to Bernard Williams, who says that thick concepts "seem to express a union of fact and value. The way these notions are applied is determined by what the world is like (for instance, by how someone has behaved), and yet, at the same time, their application usually involves a certain valuation of the situation, of person or actions" (1985, p. 129). The use of such concepts fuses together right-making properties and motivating properties, potentially obviating concerns about moral schizophrenia.

1.4   Virtue as action-guiding

Related arguments have been levied to show that virtue ethics enjoys other advantages over alternative theories. One such argument is that focusing on virtue concepts provides a better guide to action than focusing merely on good and bad, right and wrong, obligatory, permissible, and forbidden. For instance, Anscombe (1958) claimed that asking whether a particular action is morally wrong may leave one dumbfounded, but that asking whether it was unjust would often make the answer "clear at once."

The thickness of virtue concepts and their usefulness in guiding action are directly connected. Whereas 'right' and 'wrong' are purely evaluative, 'unjust' is both evaluative and descriptive, giving us a better handle on when it is applicable. If asked what a good or bad person typically does, we find ourselves nonplussed. There are so many possible answers. But if asked what a scrupulous or unscrupulous person typically does, answers readily spring to mind. In the same way, when considering whether some proposed course of action would be good or bad, one may feel puzzled. But when considering whether the course of action would be dignified or undignified, the answer (and, by extension the answer about what to do) is often clear.

1.5   Virtue and the 'is'–'ought' gap

Another argument has it that the thick concepts of virtue ethics (e.g., prudence, charity, modesty) capture intuitive moral psychology better than the thin concepts of consequentialism and deontology (e.g., goodness,

---

[4] See Annas (1993, p. 70), Audi (2001, pp. 82–83), Foot (1997, 2001, p. 9), Hudson (1980), McDowell (1979, p. 88), Wallace (1974, p. 193), and Williams (1985, p. 19).

rightness, obligation), and that these thick concepts help to bridge the 'is'–'ought' gap. Philippa Foot (2001, p. 7), for instance, points out that resolving virtue notions such as *honest* into their descriptive and normative components is nigh impossible. An honest person is one who tells the truth, perhaps even because it's the truth, but an honest person is praiseworthy insofar as she is honest.

This fusion of explanatory and evaluative properties separates virtue ethics from consequentialism and deontology. While consequentialists can easily say that a benevolent person is someone who does (or tries to) maximize the good (or the expected good, or whatever), they are not in the habit of committing themselves to there actually *being* lots of benevolent people. Though Kantians can of course say that the rational person is someone who acts from a universalizable motive (or a good will, or whatever), they typically do not go on to assert that many people *are* in point of fact rational. Indeed, Kant seems to have thought it was outright impossible to say of any given act whether it was done from a universalizable motive.

Virtue ethicists are different. At least in their more optimistic moments, they do say that a critical mass of people really are virtuous. As Alasdair MacIntyre (1984, p. 199) puts it,

> to identify certain actions as manifesting or failing to manifest a virtue or virtues is never only to evaluate; it is also to take the first step towards explaining why those actions rather than some others were performed. [... W]ithout allusion to the place that justice and injustice, courage and cowardice play in human life very little will be genuinely explicable.

If one knows that Albert is honest, one can predict his behavior (truthtelling), but one can also justly praise him. This egalitarian attitude toward the virtue of ordinary people is heartening, and it may go some way toward bridging the 'is'–'ought' gap, but it only does so if MacIntyre and his fellow-travelers are right (a presumption that, as we shall see, situationists attack).

1.6 Virtue and moral education

Finally, according to proponents of virtue ethics, moral education is most effective when the teacher appeals not to abstract principles but to thick virtue terms. As a matter of empirical fact, exhortations to maximize happiness or to do one's duty fall flat, whereas encouragements to act courageously and prudently catch the audience's attention and imagination. Martha Nussbaum (1995, p. 10) takes this argument a step further, saying that literature is an ideal medium of moral education because narratives use thick concepts to describe, explain, and evaluate behavior, leading empathetic readers to follow suit. Given that so many of our stories are about angels and demons, saints and sinners, heroes and villains, messiahs and scapegoats (often embodied by the same individual), thick, narratological terminology is an ideal medium for moral education.

To answer the question, "Why should I do the right thing?" by saying, "Because it produces good consequences" or "Because it's in accordance with the rules," would not motivate the moral acolyte. To answer it by saying, "Because you're honest [or respectful, or diligent, or whatever]," would motivate.

As I mentioned above, this one-sided presentation is intended not as a decisive argument in favor of virtue ethics but as motivation for the thought that virtue ethics has much to offer, perhaps even more to offer than its competitors. The question remains, though, whether virtue ethics is empirically and theoretically adequate. Perhaps it is merely the best of a bad lot. To answer that question, we must identify the minimal commitments of virtue ethics, then assess them in light of evidence and arguments in both philosophy and the sciences.

2   LIMNING THE HARD CORE

The alleged strengths of virtue ethics help us to identify its hard core: whatever is presupposed or entailed by those strengths is a candidate for inclusion in the hard core. In the remainder of this chapter, I consider ten such candidates, two of which are revised and one of which is rejected. The remaining seven, along with the weakened two, constitute the hard core of virtue ethics. These ten claims are:

> (*acquirability*) It is possible for a non-virtuous person to acquire some of the virtues.
>
> (*stability*) If someone possesses a virtue at time t, then *ceteris paribus* she will possess that virtue at a later time t'.
>
> (*consistency*) If someone possesses a virtue sensitive to reason r, then *ceteris paribus* she will respond to r across contexts.
>
> (*access*) It is possible to determine what the virtues are.
>
> (*normativity*) *Ceteris paribus*, it is better to possess a virtue than not, and better to possess more virtues than fewer.

(*real saints*) There is a non-negligible cohort of saints in the human population.

(*explanatory power*) If someone possesses a virtue, then reference to that virtue will sometimes enable one to explain her behavior.

(*predictive power*) If someone possesses a virtue, then reference to that virtue will sometimes enable one to predict her behavior.

(*egalitarianism*) Almost anyone can be virtuous.

(*integration*) Possession of the virtues is positively correlated; in other words, if someone possesses one virtue, she is more likely to possess other virtues as well.

The balance of this chapter adjudicates the arguments for including these ten candidates in the hard core of virtue ethics.

2.1 Acquirability

If virtues were innate and immutable dispositions, virtue ethics would be a strange theory indeed. It would be puzzling to encourage people to be or behave in a certain way if they *must* be or behave that way or *cannot* be or behave that way. So if the virtues could not be acquired, it would be senseless to recommend being virtuous or behaving virtuously. Praising people for their beauty troubles us for precisely this reason. While it is of course good to be beautiful, and while beauty itself merits praise, it seems odd to praise *people* for having it.

Furthermore, if *ought* really does imply *can*, and if virtue ethics is right in saying that people ought to be virtuous, it follows that they can become virtuous or, if they already are virtuous, remain so.

Finally, if virtue-possession is praiseworthy and people are only (or most) legitimately praised for what they are responsible for, virtue-possession is something one can be responsible for. *Mutatis mutandis* for vice and blame. It seems hard to imagine, however, that one could be responsible for an innate trait. Someone born with sociopathic tendencies is more to be pitied than censured, whereas someone who becomes a sociopath through habituation is presumably more blameworthy. Similarly, while being born with a genetic defect such as blindness is pitiable, and we pity people who have such a defect, it would be odd – even inhumane – to blame them for the defects. By contrast, if they were to acquire similar defects through their own intentional action (say, by self-mutilation) we would be more willing to cast aspersions on them, or at least to pity them less.

2.2   Stability

Once acquired, virtues should be hard to lose. If Benny acts courageously one minute and rashly the next, it would hardly do to say that he really was courageous but became cowardly in the course of a few seconds. Virtue attribution would then be a post hoc mug's game. If they pick out anything, virtue terms designate psychological structures that are more than ephemeral.

I also prefer to distinguish between stability of virtue-possession and stability of virtue-expression. Though these two are tightly connected, it is possible for someone possessing the relevant trait to fail to express it in some circumstances. Aristotle (1095b) himself makes this point when he says that the virtuous person is still virtuous when asleep, and when he claims that some things are beyond human endurance, such that even the virtuous person should not be expected to hold up under such strains. Nevertheless, Aristotle argues that virtues are stable, saying that "actions done in accordance with virtues are done in a just or temperate way not merely by having some quality of their own, but rather if the agent acts [...] from a firm and unshakeable character" (1105b). The vast majority of virtue ethicists since Aristotle have concurred.

2.3   Consistency

A related idea is that if someone possesses a virtue responsive to reasons of type r, she will exhibit responsiveness to all such reasons. As N. J. H. Dent puts it, virtue causes appropriate behavior in "ever-various and novel situations" (1975, p. 328). For instance, the generous person countenances the well-being of others as a reason to share resources beyond what he merely owes them. And he continues to countenance this reason regardless of virtue-irrelevant (i.e., reason-irrelevant) features of his beneficiaries (age, sex, attractiveness, ethnicity, and ability to reciprocate), himself (mood, state of hurry), and his environment (ambient noise, ambient smells, and presence of bystanders).

The rider about normatively irrelevant features is crucial. The generous person should not be expected to give when able in all circumstances. Aiding and abetting criminals is not generous. Donating one's last penny is foolish. Attempting to help someone who wants to be left alone is rude. Nevertheless, if a man shared only with Bibi Andersson lookalikes who gave him come-hither looks he would be at best imperfectly generous.

A virtue's characteristic reason is typically cited in explanations of virtuous actions of the form, "He φ'd because p." For instance, a characteristic reason of honesty is non-deception; the characteristic reason of temperance is moderation; and the characteristic reason of justice is desert:

(Q-Honesty) Why did Albert admit that he didn't enjoy dinner?
(A-Honesty) Because he saw that otherwise his interlocutor would have been deceived.
(Q-Temperance) Why did Beatrice have water rather than wine?
(A-Temperance) Because she realized it would have been immoderate to have another glass of wine.
(Q-Justice) Why did Carlos concede the game?
(A-Justice) He saw that his opponent deserved to win.

Each of these mini-explanations is couched not merely in terms of beliefs and desires, but in terms of the reasons the protagonist has to act. Albert is worried about deceiving others; Beatrice watches out for extreme behavior on her own part; Carlos wants the best man to win. It would seem that virtue-referencing explanations typically take this form.

Like the stability requirement, the consistency requirement is not exceptionless. Someone can be temperate even if she occasionally fails to countenance moderation as a reason. Also like the stability requirement, the consistency requirement is not tied directly to action. Someone can be sensitive to a reason without always acting on that reason, but such failure should be the exception rather than the rule.

2.4 *Access*

Any normative theory worth its salt should hold out at least the possibility of identifying its norms. Utilitarianism, however, is often thought to stumble on the access requirement, since the computational complexity involved in determining what would maximize happiness (or goodness, or utility) is arguably beyond our ken. In fact, consequentialist theories that identify right action as maximizing *expected* good consequences or *direct* good consequences have been formulated at least in part as a reply to this objection. Similarly, it may seem difficult to decide whether a motive is genuinely universalizable – who really knows what the world would be like if people lied to murderers on the hunt? Kant seems to have thought we'd end up in a real pickle, but someone more cynical (and reasonable) would suggest that we're already in that pickle, and it's not really so bad.

For virtue ethics, the access requirement comes down to being able to know what the virtues are and what they call for. As Aristotle puts it, actions "are called just and temperate when they are such as the just and the temperate person would do" (1105b). Knowing whether any particular action is virtuous, then, presupposes knowing what the virtuous person would do in the circumstances, and knowing in general what makes an action virtuous presupposes knowing either what the virtues are and how to balance them against each other from one case to the next, or what the virtuous person would do in any circumstances. Thinkers as diverse as Robert Audi (2001), Philippa Foot (1997), and Jesse Prinz (2009) all endorse this requirement.

2.5   Normativity

Virtue theorists differ on whether the virtues invariably lead to right action or good consequences but, with the possible exception of Nietzsche, they agree that having a virtue is better than not having it, having more is better than having fewer, and having all is better than having only some. According to Philippa Foot (1997, p. 3), "virtues are in general benefi-cial characteristics, and indeed ones that a human being needs to have, for his own sake and that of his fellows." Judith Jarvis Thomson (1997, pp. 282–84) likewise argues that virtuous individuals are good for their communities, and that virtue-possession is also (though perhaps not exceptionlessly) good for the possessor himself.

2.6   Real saints

One way to insulate virtue ethics is to say that there need not be real saints, or fully virtuous people. On this view, which was recently artic-ulated at great length by Daniel Russell (2009), virtue ethics erects a regulative ideal of the saint, rather than identifying actual individuals to emulate. A more sanguine virtue ethicist should accept *real saints*, however, and anyone tempted by Linda Zagzebski's (2010) attempt to ground the meaning of virtue terms in real moral exemplars must accept it.

At this point, it might be useful to introduce what I call the *saturation metaphor* to help explain what's meant by being fully virtuous.[5] Many properties are gradable. For instance, a piece of paper can be ultramarine, baby blue, powder blue, and so on. At the same time, the paper needn't be all the same hue. It could be ultramarine in some areas, baby blue in others, powder blue in still others, and splotched with white here and there. The paper's saturation with blue has both a depth dimension (how deep is the blue?) and a breadth dimension (how deep is the blue in each region?). From a normative standpoint, the property of being virtuous admits of the same two distinctions. Someone may be a saint, deeply virtuous through and through; this would correspond to the paper's being ultramarine from edge to edge. Someone may, however, be mostly virtuous through and through; this would correspond to the paper's being baby blue from edge to edge. The breadth metaphor applies as well: someone may be deeply virtuous in some respects but continent, incontinent, or vicious in others. This corresponds to the paper's having splotches of ultramarine cheek by jowl with splotches of baby blue, powder blue, and white. Just as it's assertible, even true, to say of a piece of paper that it's blue even if it has a few splotches of white, so it may be assertible, even true, to say of a person that she's virtuous or even a saint despite the fact that she is not robustly virtuous through and through.

I worry, however, about debating *real saints* given the constraints on psychological research. A scientific study to determine whether a given individual is a saint would require systematically tempting and tormenting the poor person. This is hardly something a human subjects committee would look favorably upon. Suggestive evidence, however, is available. In a fascinating study, Jeremy Frimer et al. (2011) interviewed twenty-five "moral exemplars" (recipients of a national award for extraordinary volunteerism) and twenty-five demographically matched ordinary people. They found that the exemplars exhibited higher levels of commitment to the promotion of their own interests, to the promotion of the interests of their communities, and, crucially, to the integration of their interests with those of their community. These "moral giants," as Frimer and his colleagues call them, may have managed to exemplify complete virtue because they managed to identify (or at least reconcile) their narrow self-interest with the interest of their fellows.

---

[5] Thanks to David Rosenthal for discussing this metaphor with me. This metaphor is closely related to what Swanton (2003) has in mind by calling virtue a "threshold concept" and what Russell (2009, pp. 112–26) has in mind by calling it a "*satis* concept."

Especially since the situationist challenge does not apply to *real saints*, I am willing to accept this condition tentatively into the hard core of virtue ethics.

2.7   Explanatory power

Many of the advantages claimed for virtue ethics above relied on the assumption that virtues are explanatory as well as normative. In other words, in explaining why someone performs an action, it should often be necessary to appeal to her possession of a virtue. Alasdair MacIntyre (1984, p. 199) says that much of human behavior would be "genuinely inexplicable" without appeal to virtues.

Explanatorily powerful properties support lawlike generalizations, i.e., generalizations that are confirmed by observation of their instances and can be projected to novel observations. The property of *being green* is explanatorily powerful because the fact that all observed emeralds have been green supports the generalization that all emeralds are green. The property of *being grue* (green if observed before time *t* but blue otherwise), by contrast, is not only unprojectable but counter-projectable. The fact that all observed emeralds have been grue supports the generalization that no emeralds are grue.

Explanatorily powerful properties are typically understood as natural kinds, and it is contemporary orthodoxy that natural kinds are metaphysically robust properties that can and should be investigated a posteriori. Furthermore, I follow David Lewis (1986) and Wesley Salmon (1984) in thinking that explanatory power is grounded in causal mechanisms. Most virtue theorists who commit themselves to the explanatory power requirement do so by saying that virtues are causally efficacious.[6] The best way to show that virtues have explanatory power would be to demonstrate that they cause (or prevent) behavior. The next best way is to demonstrate their correlation with behavior. Since much of psychology has yet to graduate to the level of demonstrating causal mechanisms, virtue ethicists and their critics should be content for now if it can be shown that virtue-possession is reliably correlated with behavior and that a plausible functional story connecting virtue-possession to behavior can be told.

---

[6] See Annas (2011, pp. 8–10) Dent (1975, p. 328), Hudson (1980), MacIntyre (1984, p. 199), and Wallace (1974, p. 193).

2.8   Predictive power

The social sciences obviously do not formulate exceptionless laws consonant with the deductive-nomological model. Economists do not predict recessions with probability 1.0. Political scientists do not forecast elections with certainty. Psychologists do not predict human behavior or mental states with anything approaching the rigor of the hard sciences.

Nevertheless, if virtue ethics is to have explanatory power, it stands to reason that it should have predictive power as well. How much? The minimal metric is doing at least as well as would have been expected without the trait. For example, if a randomly chosen person can be expected not to lie in a given context with probability 0.7, then an honest person can be expected not to lie in the same context with probability greater than or equal to 0.7. Still, this constraint is disappointingly weak. Beefing up the requirement with a strict inequality seems only trivially better. Anything else, though, feels ad hoc. Perhaps all can agree, however, that acting in accordance with virtue at a significantly better rate than could be expected without it is a fair requirement.

Robert Merrihew Adams (2006, p. 124) makes a useful distinction in this regard. He distinguishes virtues related to imperfect duties, such as generosity, from virtues related to perfect duties, such as chastity. A person can be generous if he gives to charities only occasionally. Someone can be helpful even if she doesn't always help her friends carry boxes when they move. A person simply does not count as chaste if she refrains from violating her wedding vows only sometimes (Doris 2010, p. 139, n. 5). Someone hardly counts as temperate if he only goes on one bender a week.

It seems to me that Adams may be moving too far from the notion of virtue when he introduces the notion of duties, but a related distinction between high-fidelity and low-fidelity virtues would do most of the same work. A high-fidelity virtue requires near-perfect consistency, whereas a low-fidelity virtue requires much higher consistency than one would expect without the trait in question. The high-fidelity virtues include chastity, fairness, fidelity, honesty, justice, and trustworthiness. If someone acts in accordance with chastity in 80 percent of the opportunities he has for cheating on his partner, that hardly makes him chaste. If someone doesn't steal in 70 percent of the cases where she could, that doesn't make her honest. Speaking in terms of the saturation metaphor, high-fidelity virtues are only attributable to someone who has the property in both its full depth and breadth dimensions. By contrast, low-fidelity virtues include charity, diligence, friendliness, generosity, industry, magnanimity, mercy, tact, and tenacity.[7] Again using the saturation metaphor, low-fidelity virtues may be attributable even to someone who has the property in some depth and breadth, but nowhere near full depth and breadth. If someone gives to charity 20 percent of the time (assuming the sums are sufficient), that could count as charitable. If someone shows mercy even occasionally, that might qualify him as merciful. While it's more difficult to argue against the low-fidelity virtues using the sorts of psychological studies currently available, it's not nearly so difficult to argue against the high-fidelity moral virtues, a point I discuss in more detail below.

2.9   Egalitarianism

Another way to insulate virtue ethics from empirical critique is to say that most people could never become virtuous. Only an elite cadre – owing to their genes, upbringing, drive, or luck – can ever become virtuous. If this is right, then psychological experiments showing that two-thirds of people will comply with an authority figure in administering what they take to be potentially deadly shocks to an innocent victim (Blass 1999) can be shrugged off.

Such an attitude, though plausible for Plato, Aristotle, and Nietzsche, rubs our democratic ethos the wrong way. The saturation metaphor is helpful here as well. *Egalitarianism* could mean that anyone could reach the normative ideal of sainthood. This would amount to a universalization of the *real saints* condition, and is obviously implausible even without empirical investigation. Various weaker interpretations of *egalitarianism* are, however, available. Keeping in mind that this notion springs from the tendency of virtue ethicists to say that much of human behavior would be inexplicable and unpredictable without reference to virtues and vices, the idea seems to be that for any given virtue, a sizeable plurality, though perhaps not a majority, of people will be sufficiently saturated with it as to make the attribution of the virtue conversationally permissible. A large proportion of people are close enough to being fully honest that it's assertible, even true, to say that they're honest. A large proportion of people are close enough to being fully generous that it's assertible, even true, to say

---

[7] These lists aren't meant to be comprehensive or uncontroversial, but I hope they at least point in the right direction.

that they're generous. The devil is of course in the details. What's a large enough proportion? Over half? Nearly half? More than a third? And what does it mean to be "close enough to being fully honest" (or generous)?

These are difficult questions that I will only attempt to answer over the course of the book, not in this chapter. For now, I will merely gesture at a weaker version of the *egalitarianism* condition that I think is at once sufficiently contentful and minimally plausible: almost anyone can act in accordance with virtue; indeed, almost anyone can reliably act in accordance with virtue. This relaxed condition does not go so far as to require that anyone can be virtuous, just that almost anyone can be brought reliably to do what the virtuous person would do.

2.10   Integration

The integration condition is a weaker version of the unity of virtue thesis, according to which someone (fully) possesses any particular virtue if and only if she possesses all virtues (Aristotle 1144b33–1145a2). To defend this prima facie implausible thesis, one may point out that the courageous person is not rash, and so does not enter into dangerous situations without a little prudence. Similarly, the honest person is not tactless, and therefore does not blurt truths better left unmentioned. Integration requires less; on this theory, someone is more likely to be just given that she is courageous, more likely to be temperate given that she is humble, more likely to be honest given that she is faithful. The most recent sustained treatment of the unity of virtue thesis is in Daniel Russell's excellent monograph, *Practical Intelligence and the Virtues*. There, he distinguishes the purely normative interpretation of the thesis from its thick interpretation (2009, pp. 335–73). On the purely normative understanding, in order for some agent *fully* to possess a given virtue, she must fully possess practical wisdom. We measure our progress and regress from the normative ideal of full virtue by our closeness to fully integrated practical wisdom. On the thick understanding of the unity thesis, someone's even partially possessing a given virtue makes him more likely to possess all the others. This normative-cum-descriptive interpretation is the one in Doris's sights, but Russell does not endorse it. He says, for instance, that no particular agent we may consider possesses all of the virtues (p. 336).

Like Russell (2009) and Badhwar (1996), I find the thick version of the integration thesis heroic but implausible. Furthermore, since the normative version is not implicated in any of the arguments for virtue ethics discussed above, it seems to be outside the hard core of virtue ethics.

To sum up then, the following set of claims constitutes what I consider to be the hard core of virtue ethics:

(*acquirability*) It is possible for a non-virtuous person to acquire some of the virtues.

(*stability*) If someone possesses a virtue at time t, then *ceteris paribus* she will possess that virtue at a later time t'.

(*consistency*) If someone possesses a virtue sensitive to reason r, then *ceteris paribus* she will respond to r across contexts.

(*access*) It is possible to determine what the virtues are.

(*normativity*) *Ceteris paribus*, it is better to possess a virtue than not, and better to possess more virtues than fewer.

(*real saints*) There is a non-negligible cohort of saints in the human population.

(*explanatory power*) If someone possesses a virtue, then reference to that virtue will sometimes help to explain her behavior.

(*predictive power**) If someone possesses a high-fidelity virtue, then reference to that virtue will enable nearly certain predictions of her behavior; if someone possesses a low-fidelity virtue, then reference to that virtue will enable weak predictions of her behavior.

(*egalitarianism**) Almost anyone can reliably act in accordance with virtue.

In the next chapter, I rearticulate the situationist challenge in light of this analysis.

CHAPTER 2

Rearticulating the situationist challenge

We are best punished for our virtues.
Friedrich Nietzsche, *Beyond Good and Evil*, 132

I   MOTIVATING THE CHALLENGE

I have set high but I hope not unreasonable standards for a plausible theory of virtue ethics, requiring a theory that conforms to the *acquirability, stability, consistency, access, normativity, real saints, explanatory power, predictive power**, and *egalitarianism** conditions. Now I turn to the broadside attack mounted by philosophical situationists. It seems to me that this is best understood as a challenge to the conjunction of *consistency, explanatory power, predictive power**, and *egalitarianism**. To motivate the critique, I begin with a discussion of a few illustrative experiments. The factors that interfere with virtue can seem unmanageably diverse, so I next attempt to taxonomize these factors into *bad reasons, situational non-reasons,* and *non-moral individual differences.* Each of these factors is then further subdivided, with illustrative studies and meta-analyses cited along the way. Finally, I explain how, despite these interfering factors, it feels so natural to think that virtue is quite common; in other words, I explain away intuitions about traits.

The first illustrative experiment is John Darley and Daniel Batson's (1973) Good Samaritan study, which was conducted with subjects from the Princeton Theological Seminary. Participants filled out a questionnaire to determine whether they related to religion as a means, an end, or a quest. They were then asked to prepare a talk either on job prospects for seminarians or on the New Testament parable of the Good Samaritan, in which a robbed and beaten man is ignored by a priest and a Levite but helped by a lowly Samaritan. The moral of the story is of course that one should emulate the compassionate Samaritan, not the sanctimonious clergy. Presumably the seminarians knew this, and presumably each of them wanted to follow Jesus' advice.

To test whether the seminarians would act on the lesson they were about to teach, Darley and Batson arranged for each of them to encounter a distressed confederate slumped on the ground along the path from the questionnaire station to the speech station. Some were told that they had time to spare, others that they were just on time, and still others that they were running late. The experimenters covertly observed whether the subjects stopped to help like the Good Samaritan about whom they were to sermonize. Before reading the next paragraph, ask yourself: which of the treatment conditions influenced their behavior? Was it their view of religion, the topic of their talk, or their degree of hurry?

If you predicted that their view of religion or the subject of their talk made the difference, you are like most people – attributing behavior to internal variables. And like most people you are mistaken. Subjects' religiosity and speech subject were uncorrelated with their helping behavior, but their degree of hurry made all the difference. Despite the fact that they were reenacting the very parable about which they were to lecture, a huge majority (90 percent) of the rushed participants failed to show compassion; by contrast, those without a sense of hurry helped 63 percent of the time. Since the treatments were randomly assigned, we must assume that the same subjects who failed to help when rushed would have helped had they been unrushed, and conversely.

Next, in a pair of famous experiments, Alice Isen and Paula Levin (1972) varied subjects' mood by giving them cookies or arranging for them to find a dime in the coin return of a public payphone. Those in the cookie experiment were then prompted to help a classmate. When their moods were elevated by the unexpected cookies, participants were more willing to help. Similarly, in the dime experiment, subjects who found the spare change were much more willing to spontaneously help a confederate who 'accidentally' dropped a sheaf of papers in their path. Had subjects in these experiments been benevolent or compassionate in the way required by virtue ethics, most would have done the same thing: helped unless they had a strong or overriding reason not to. What we find instead is that their mood largely determined whether they helped.

It's important to note that these experiments also suggested that the subjects were not vicious. Vices are character traits just as much as virtues are; the difference lies not in their consistency, but in their moral valence. Not all subjects in these experiments failed to intervene, and presumably those who did help did so in part (though not wholly) because they wanted to help. This result, however, is in perfect harmony with the situationist message that most people lack traditional character traits – good, bad, and indifferent.

The situationist critique of virtue ethics proceeds by pointing out that if people are unconsciously susceptible to such seemingly trivial and normatively irrelevant influences as their degree of hurry, receiving cookies, and finding dimes, one can only infer that they would also be swayed by major temptations. Situationist experiments suggest that most people do not even have flimsy virtues, let alone robust ones. Experiments like Stanley Milgram's (1974) obedience study (in which participants put what they thought was 450 volts of electricity through another human being on the say-so of the experimenter) and the Haney, Banks, and Zimbardo (1973) prison simulation (in which participants labeled 'guards' became monstrously cruel while those labeled 'prisoners' internalized the label almost completely) elicited such appalling behavior in response to seemingly insubstantial situational pressures that Doris and Stich (2005, p. 119) feel certain in saying that people do not merely "fall short of ideals of virtue and fortitude, but that they can be *readily* induced to *radically* fail such ideals."

What I want to argue in this chapter is that it may not be possible to defend the conjunction of *consistency, explanatory power, predictive power**, and *egalitarianism**. People can be expected to behave the same way in iterations of the same situation. If Zena contributes money to a good cause when the sun shines on Monday, she would most likely contribute to the same cause when the sun shines on Friday. People do not exhibit cross-situational consistency, however, even when the difference in situation is minor and normatively irrelevant. Their future behavior cannot be predicted with sufficient certainty on the basis of previous behavior. Zena might be a fair-weather benefactor, failing to give when the sun hides its face. As I discuss in more detail in the next chapter, Doris's solution to this sort of inconsistency is to use a more fine-grained vocabulary of local traits: he might argue, for instance, that Zena lacks the global trait of charity but possesses the local trait of *fair-weather-charity*. While there may be a few people who exemplify the global traits lionized by virtue ethics, there is little reason to think that others could follow in the footsteps of such saints even if they do exist. Empirical results cannot show that virtue is an unachievable ideal for every single person, but as Doris and Stich have argued, "the burden of argument has importantly shifted: The advocate of virtue ethics can no longer simply assume that virtue is psychologically possible" (2005, p. 121).

Harman (1999) goes further in attacking virtue ethics, arguing both that there may be "no such thing as character, no ordinary character traits of the sort people think there are, none of the usual moral virtues and vices," and that the local traits countenanced by Doris are so different from what we intuitively count as virtues that they may not count as traits at all.

Helping behavior is but one possible manifestation of virtue, though one would expect it from people who are generous, compassionate, altruistic, benevolent, considerate, courteous, friendly, or humane. The difficulty with testing other virtues is that they are harder to operationalize. How does one experimentally test subjects' courage without violating their rights?

One virtue that has been investigated systematically is honesty, and it too has been found to be highly sensitive to seemingly trivial and normatively irrelevant situational variables. In one of the largest (n = 10,865) studies of character ever conducted, Hartshorne and May (1928) tested students' propensity to cheat (as exhibited on in-class tests, homework, athletic contests, parlor games), steal (as exhibited in play situations and classroom situations), and lie (either to escape disapproval or to gain approval).

A naive believer in traits would expect the students to fall into one of three groups: inveterate deceivers, middling opportunists, and upstanding truth-tellers. Inveterate deceivers have the consistent vice of dishonesty; they deceive whenever it would benefit them. Opportunists deceive only occasionally, when the benefit is great and the potential of being caught is minimal. Upstanding truth-tellers never deceive, or only when some other ethical concern overrides the impetus not to deceive. That is what one might expect. Hartshorne and May found, however, a mean intercorrelation between different pairs of situations presenting opportunities for deception or honesty of only 0.23. They summarized their results in the following way:

[N]either deceit nor its opposite, 'honesty,' are unified character traits, but rather specific functions of life situations. Most children will deceive in certain situations and not in others. Lying, cheating, and stealing as measured by the test situations used in these studies are only very loosely related. Even cheating in the classroom is rather highly specific, for a child may cheat on an arithmetic test and not on a spelling test.

Children who cheated on one spelling test were likely to cheat on another, but their cheating on a spelling test was only weakly correlated with other cheating behavior, and even less correlated with other types of dishonesty like stealing and lying. This local consistency supports Doris's claim that attributions of global traits like honesty are likely to fail, while attribution of local traits like *in-class-spelling-test-honesty* may succeed.

More recently, the behavioral economist Dan Ariely (2008) conducted a series of honesty experiments with Harvard and Massachusetts Institute of Technology students. Participants at Harvard took a trivia quiz and were rewarded monetarily for each correct answer. Ariely enabled cheating for some of the students by allowing them to grade their own tests, rather than having the proctor grade them. Like Gyges with his ring of invisibility, their honest behavior ceased as soon as they were not watched. On average, students in the experimental condition claimed to have correctly answered 10 percent more questions than the control group. Participants at MIT took a math quiz, but this time there were three experimental conditions. Some were asked before the quiz to write down the names of ten books they had read in high school, others to write down as many of the Ten Commandments as they could remember, and the rest to write, "I understand that this study falls under the MIT honor system." Those in the experimental conditions claimed to have solved 33 percent more questions than those in the control group – despite the facts that almost no one could recall all ten commandments and that MIT has no honor system. Such results are of course grist for Doris's mill: people are not honest, but they may be Ten Commandments-primed honest and non-existent-honor-code-primed honest.

In another study, Ariely asked MIT students to solve as many equations as they could in a short time. There were two experimental conditions in which cheating was possible. In the first, like the previous study, subjects graded themselves. These students claimed to have solved 77 percent more equations than those in the control group. In the second experimental treatment, not only did participants grade themselves, but instead of being paid directly with cash they were first paid with non-monetary tokens, which they exchanged for cash. These students claimed to have solved 184 percent more equations than the control – more than double the cheating found in the first experimental condition. Are people non-monetary-currency dishonest? Ariely's studies suggest that the answer is yes.

If similar results hold for other virtues, which we should accept as a default assumption barring strong evidence to the contrary, then we have reason to worry that little human conduct is explicable or predictable by reference to the virtues. This is inconsistent with the conjunction of *consistency, explanatory power, predictive power*, egalitarianism**.

2   INTERFERING FACTORS

Although the litany of variables – degree of hurry, cookies, dimes, spelling tests, priming the Ten Commandments, imaginary honor codes, non-monetary currency – seems unmanageably diverse, a careful review of the literature suggests a way of unifying and systematizing many situational influences on behavior. In this section, I attempt to taxonomize these interfering factors into *bad reasons, situational non-reasons*, and *non-moral individual differences*. I will argue that the most normatively troubling of these three types of interfering factors are situational non-reasons.

2.1   Bad reasons

Someone could fail to be virtuous because he is too easily swayed by bad reasons. What is a bad reason? It's useful in this context to distinguish between *a* reason and *all-things-considered* reason for conduct. What you have all things considered reason to do, avoid, believe, and feel is presumably a function of the various, often incompatible, reasons you have to do, avoid, believe, think, and feel. For instance, an athlete has a reason to take steroids: doing so will make him stronger, faster, and more competitive. But he also has a reason not to take steroids: doing so is unsportsmanlike, possibly illegal, and potentially damaging to his health in the long run. What he has all things considered reason to do is a function of these and any other relevant reasons. In this section, I will construe bad reasons quite broadly to be any reasons that go against the conduct supported by all things considered reason. Bad reasons come in at least two varieties: *temptations* and situational *demand characteristics*.

2.1.1   Temptations
We're all familiar with temptations. You want to eat healthy food, exercise regularly, stop slouching, and drink less beer. And yet, the burger is so tasty, the couch so inviting, good posture so forgettable, and the India Pale Ale so hoppy. The situationist critique has little, if anything, to do with such temptations, which, after all, are completely familiar to

virtue ethicists and slot nicely into their scheme of virtue, continence, incontinence, and vice.

2.1.2 Demand characteristics

Situational demand characteristics are more insidious than temptations. They comprise the subtle features of situations that either give people bad reasons without their realizing it or induce them to attend too much to bad reasons and too little to good reasons. They tend to influence behavior on the sly, as it were. Two such demand characteristics are the presence of bystanders and social distance cues.

On March 13, 1964, Kitty Genovese was raped and stabbed in the Kew Gardens neighborhood of Queens. Although dozens of neighbors heard her cries for help, no one called the police until at least half an hour after the assault began. In addition to decrying her murderer as a vicious killer, the public responded to the event with outrage at the apathetic witnesses.[1] After this horrific event, a slew of social scientists began to theorize about and experiment with the so-called unresponsive bystander effect. In situations where it is known that multiple people may intervene, helpful responses to emergencies are less frequent than in situations where only one person can intervene (or where several may intervene but none knows about the others). From a naive dispositional point of view, this phenomenon is quite strange. One would expect the probability that someone helps to increase monotonically with the number of potential helpers. In fact, however, it seems to *decrease* monotonically with the number of potential helpers. Bibb Latané and John Darley (1970) hypothesized that the presence of other potential helpers reduces the probability that at least one of them comes to the victim's aid for two reasons. First, the presence of other people leads to a "diffusion of responsibility." Each person feels only partially responsible for what happens because he is in a position to know that others could intervene instead, and to know that others know that he knows they could intervene, and to know that others know that he knows that they know that he knows they could intervene, and so on.

---

[1] There is some controversy over the details of this case, but for my purposes here, that is irrelevant. The research on bystander interventions was spurred by what people thought had happened to Genovese, even if what people thought was incorrect. Furthermore, further such cases crop up in the newspapers on a regular basis. In October 2011, for instance, *The New York Times* ran a piece titled "Bystanders' Neglect of Injured Toddler Sets off Soul-Searching on Web Sites in China," after Wang Yue, a two-year-old on a busy street in Guangdong Province, was struck by two different trucks and ignored for seven minutes by at least eighteen passers-by.

Without further argument, however, the diffusion of responsibility might be expected simply to cancel any increase in helping behavior as the number of bystanders increases. But the unfortunate fact remains that helping is not constant but monotonically decreasing with the number of potential helpers. Latané and Darley's second hypothesized cause of decreased helping may enable us to save the phenomena. They argued that in addition to the diffusion of responsibility, when bystanders are able to observe each other they rely on what they perceive others to think in construing ambiguous stimuli. As I discuss in more detail below, moral psychologists neglect the power of attention and construal at their peril. When one sees that others do not intervene, one tends to assume that they have disambiguating information that the situation in fact is not an emergency. Everyone mistakenly takes everyone else's inaction as expressing knowledge that action is unnecessary, so everyone concludes that action is unnecessary.

Experiments have borne out these two explanatory factors. Latané and Darley (1968) found that 75 percent of solitary bystanders in a simulated fire emergency intervened, while only 10 percent intervened when two impassive confederates were present. Latané and Rodin (1969) similarly found that 70 percent of solitary bystanders intervened when they heard what sounded like a bookshelf collapsing on someone in the adjacent room, whereas only 7 percent helped when a phlegmatic confederate sat beside them. And in a study conducted by Darley and Latané (1968), subjects who heard a confederate in another room endure a simulated epileptic seizure were most likely to intervene when alone (85 percent), next most likely when there was one other bystander (62 percent), and least likely when there were four other bystanders (31 percent). What's more, reaction times were inversely correlated with the number of bystanders. These results are extremely robust, as Latané and Nida's (1981) meta-analysis shows; moreover, they have stood the test of time, as Schwartz and Gottlieb's (1991) more recent replication indicates. The more people who might help, the lower the probability that anyone will help and the longer one has to wait for help if it comes at all.

A third potential explanatory factor for the unresponsive bystander effect invokes attentional focusing. People in groups tend to look at the floor and avoid eye contact, but people who (think they) are alone let their eyes and attention wander over everything in their vicinity. In group contexts, therefore, people are less likely to notice cues of trouble because they do not attend to as many cues as they otherwise would.[2]

---

[2] One final partial explanatory factor may be the fear of embarrassment, which would place bystander effects in the category of temptations rather than situational demand characteristics.

Since I devote most of Chapter 8 to social distance, I merely mention it here. The interested reader can jump directly to Chapter 8 for a detailed investigation of the power of social distance and the heuristics we use to track it.

Situational demand characteristics may also help to explain the infamous Milgram (1974) studies in obedience and the Haney, Banks, and Zimbardo (1973) prison simulation. In the former, participants acted on bad reasons for juicing an innocent, non-consenting individual with hundreds of volts of electricity. The fact that the experimenter in these studies said to go on was *a* reason to go on, but a bad reason, since the participants clearly had, all things considered, reason to stop. The carefully designed experimental setting, however, made it difficult for participants to recognize what they had all things considered reason to do, which induced them to act on bad reasons.[3] Similarly, in the Zimbardo prison simulation, the arbitrarily assigned social roles of the 'prisoners' and 'guards' were bad reasons for them to behave in the astonishing ways they did. Being designated a guard gave participants *a* reason to lord it over the prisoners, but a bad reason, since they clearly had, all things considered, reason to behave humanely.

The better we come to understand situational demand characteristics, the more they transform into temptations. A demand characteristic is, if you like, a temptation in disguise. Hence, both temptations proper and demand characteristics should be handled straightforwardly by virtue ethics. Just as there is a virtue of temperance that relates to sensuous temptations, we can baptize the virtue of social temperance, which would relate to social temptations that often overpower people in the case of bystander apathy and may even lead to Milgram and Zimbardo-esque results. Temptations make it hard to be virtuous, but this isn't news. Perhaps the psychological evidence shows that temptations are even stronger than we tend to assume, but that is merely a matter of degree. If bad reasons were the only difficulty raised by situationism, it wouldn't be a devastating challenge. In the next section, I discuss situational non-reasons, which I take to be the heart of the situationist challenge.

2.2 *Situational non-reasons*

While it may be possible for virtue ethicists to find a place for temptations and situational demand characteristics in their moral psychology,

---

[3] For a more detailed analysis of the Milgram studies in obedience, see Chapter 8.

situational non-reasons such as ambient sensory stimuli, mood elevators, and mood depressors present a harder problem. Unlike bad reasons,
non-reasons don't even provide the agent with *a* reason for conduct contrary to her all things considered reason. They're merely causal influences
on moral conduct, and yet they are hugely and secretly influential. This
is why I take situational non-reasons to be the heart of the situationist
challenge. The point here is not the familiar platitude that it's hard to be
good, that temptations and other counterincentives lead people from the
straight and narrow path of virtue. Mood effects and ambient sensibilia
are not temptations. In *Lady Windermere's Fan*, Oscar Wilde's avatar, Lord
Darlington, quips that he can resist anything but temptation. If the situationist critique succeeds, even that may be too sanguine. The idea is not
that people easily succumb to temptation, but that *non-temptations* play a
surprisingly large role in moral conduct, including both external behavior and more internal phenomena such as thought, feeling, emotion, and
deliberation. In this section, I discuss some of the relevant psychological
findings on situational non-reasons, many of which can be united under
the headings of *attentional focusing* and *openness to new experiences*.

2.2.1 Ambient sounds

The volume of ambient sounds influences both helping behavior and
physical aggressiveness. People subjected to sounds at high volume
(> 80 dB) consistently help less – both in emergency and non-emergency
situations – than those subjected to sounds at low volume (< 80 dB). For
example, Matthews and Cannon (1975; see also Boles and Haywood 1978,
Korte et al. 1975, and Page 1974) found that fewer subjects were willing
to help a confederate who 'accidentally' dropped a belonging when background noise levels were at 85 dB than when they were at 65 dB. High
ambient sound levels seem to cause attentional focusing: people attend
only to the one or two most salient features of their environment. This
entails an overemphasis on the focal points and an underemphasis on all
else. Focusing has been successfully used to explain the effects of ambient noise both on helping behavior and on non-moral behavior, such as
noticing unusual elements of one's surroundings (Cohen 1978; Cohen and
Lezak 1977; Korte and Grant 1980).[4] This is a phenomenon understood
by iPod users in cities; an easy way to ignore beggars and cat-callers is to
turn up the volume so that one does not even notice them.

---

[4] This point will become especially pertinent when I introduce the situationist challenge to virtue
epistemology.

High levels of ambient noise have also been tied to aggressive behavior. While loud noises are generally insufficient to cause aggression, people already disposed to aggress do so more frequently and more violently in the presence of high-volume sounds. Donnerstein and Wilson (1976; see also Geen and O'Neal 1969, and Konecni 1975) found that subjects given a chance to electrocute a confederate who had angered them did so more often and with higher voltages when ambient noise was loud than when it was soft. Noise had no effect on subjects who were not angered and thus not disposed to aggress. Attentional constriction helps to explain this behavior as well: when angered in high-volume contexts, people focus their attention only on the object of their rage, leading to more aggressive behavior.

2.2.2 *Ambient smells*
Like ambient sounds, ambient smells have a significant effect on helping behavior. Robert Baron (1997) showed that people engage in more helping behavior when exposed to pleasant smells than to no smells. Experimenters solicited help from passers-by in a mall. In one condition, they asked for help in front of a bakery or coffee shop; in the other, they requested help in front of a dry goods store. Subjects in the first condition were more likely to help than those in the second.

Why do pleasant smells have this effect? One plausible explanation is that they directly cause a dilation of attentional focus. Baron and Thomley (1994) conducted an experiment to investigate the effects of pleasant fragrances and direct mood elevation on both task performance and helping behavior. They found that both exposure to pleasant fragrances and receipt of a small gift (the mood elevator) improved performance on an anagram task. In addition, both factors increased participants' willingness to volunteer. Another potential explanation of the connection between pleasant odors and helping behavior is that pleasant smells cause positive moods, which are independently connected to dilated attentional focus, a point I discuss in more detail below. In either case, the end of the causal chain is broader attentional focus, which is strongly tied to noticing features of one's environment, including whether someone needs help.

2.2.3 *Other sensibilia*
I will not go into the evidence that other sensibilia influence conduct just like ambient sounds and smells, though there is plenty of such evidence. Chen-Bo Zhong, Vanessa Bohns, and Francesca Gino (2010), for instance, found that people are more inclined to cheat in a dimly lit room

than a brightly lit room, and that people wearing sunglasses behave more selfishly than those wearing clear glasses.

2.2.4 *Mood elevators and depressors*

While moods are not situational in the same way that ambient smells and sounds are, they form a valid part of the situationist critique because they are *morally irrelevant* and because they are *easily induced* by seemingly trivial situational factors (mood elevators and depressors). A number of studies have connected mood and emotion with helping behavior.[5] Emotions and moods are difficult to tease apart, but arguably emotions have intentional content (either propositional or sub-propositional) whereas moods do not. Emotions both positive and negative have been shown to lead to heightened helping behavior. Apsler (1975), for instance, found that embarrassed subjects were more willing to help than unabashed ones. Carlsmith and Gross (1968) used guilt to induce help, as did Regan (1971), who found that subjects made to feel responsible for a mishap in the lab were more willing to help in a seemingly unrelated task.

The question of emotional influences on motivation has been addressed in the economics literature as well. Loewenstein (2000), for instance, points out that emotions lead to preference-dynamism, contrary to classical decision- and game-theory. This dynamism is not the same phenomenon as unpredictability or uncertainty. Rather, the effects of emotions and moods are systematic, including an overvaluation of the object of emotion, as well as overvaluation of the present and immediate future.

James Weyant (1978) complicates the picture somewhat by showing that the effect of mood interacts with both the cost to oneself and the perceived benefit to the other. His $3 \times 2 \times 2$ analysis is summarized in Table 2.1.

Note that while positive mood induced elevated levels of helping regardless of benefit and cost, negative mood was sensitive to both benefit and cost. This supports the attentional focusing and openness to experience hypotheses. Those in a positive mood are open to new experience and fail to focus on the cost–benefit ratio. By contrast, those in a negative mood are averse to new experiences and focus carefully on a single factor, the cost–benefit ratio; thus, when it is high their helping behavior is depressed below baseline, but when it is low their helping behavior

---

[5] See Isen, Clark, and Schwartz (1976) and Isen, Shalker, Clark, and Karp (1978). Isen (1987) reviews much of this literature.

Table 2.1 *Effect of mood, cost, and benefit on helping behavior*

Benefit to others	Cost to self	**Positive mood**	**Neutral mood**	**Negative mood**
High	*High*	Elevated	Baseline	Baseline
	Low			Hyper-elevated
Low	*High*			Depressed
	Low			Baseline

is elevated even above that of subjects in a positive mood. Schaller and Cialdini (1990) argue that happy individuals differ from unhappy ones in their:

1. *Access to affect-related memories and thoughts*, with positive recollections, attributions, and cognitions more accessible to elated than to saddened persons.
2. *Attention/orientation to the environment*, with elated individuals showing a greater tendency to attend to and make contact with external stimuli in a broad, encompassing fashion, and saddened individuals showing a greater tendency to attend to the self and to make contact with the environment only in a most selective manner.
3. *Level of arousal and physical activity*, with happy persons demonstrating greater than normal levels of physiological arousal and behavioral activity, and saddened persons demonstrating reduced arousal and activity.
4. *Process of decision-making*, with elation leading to a less controlled, more heuristic decision style, and sadness leading to a more controlled, highly considered approach.
5. *General motivational drive*, with elated individuals striving for a counterhomeostatic enhancement of higher-order goals (e.g., affiliation, attachment, competence, achievement) and saddened individuals striving primarily for the homeostatic restoration of affective equilibrium.

All of these differences, especially attention/orientation to the environment, corroborate the thesis that good mood does not lead directly to helping behavior, but rather enables one to notice opportunities to help and encourages one to engage in new activities, including but not limited to altruistic ones.

Furthermore, good mood and sexual arousal both seem to lead to openness to new experiences. Dan Ariely (2008) induced sexual arousal in 20-year-old male subjects by asking them to masturbate while watching pornographic videos. While in a 'hot' state, they filled out a questionnaire, the results of which were compared with questionnaires they had completed while in a 'cold' state. Questions covered subjects' willingness to engage in a variety of sexual activities that would be considered disgusting, illegal, or immoral. Questions included the following:

- Can you imagine being attracted to a 12-year-old girl?
- Could it be fun to have sex with someone who was extremely fat?
- Could you enjoy sex with someone you hated?
- Would it be fun to watch an attractive woman urinating?
- Can you imagine getting sexually excited by contact with an animal?
- Would you tell a woman that you loved her to increase the chance that she would have sex with you?
- Would you slip a woman a drug to increase the chance that she would have sex with you?

Men in the 'hot' state were uniformly more willing to engage in these activities, often by huge margins. Thus, while openness to new experience may lead to increased helping behavior, it may also lead to increased behavior of a morally problematic kind. Fair moods do not make us fair. Nor do foul moods make us foul. Instead, positive moods and emotions induce dilated attentional focus and openness to new experiences. Negative moods and emotions induce constricted attentional focus and avoidance of new experiences. Whether moods and emotions effect good or bad behavior, then, depends on what we focus on and what new experiences lie open to us.

2.2.5   *A note on empathy*

Empathy has been classed variously among the moods, the emotions, and even the moral virtues. I should think that it is none of these, but rather a tendency to enter both cognitive and affective states roughly congruent to those one perceives, believes, or imagines others are in.[6] In any event, empathically induced emotion has been shown to induce helping behavior

---

[6] It may, however, be an intellectual virtue, since it presumably enables a kind of vicarious introspective knowledge of others' affective states. Even this is unclear, however, since empathy may also make it difficult to admit hard truths about other people.

in a variety of situations.[7] Daniel Batson (1991; see also 2002) argues for the empathy-altruism hypothesis, according to which "empathic emotion (an other-oriented emotional response congruent with the perceived welfare of another individual) evokes altruistic motivation (a motivational state with the ultimate goal of increasing the other's welfare)." The idea is that, when Nora empathizes with Oscar, she has an incentive to act as if she regards his well-being as her own. Since she feels (perhaps in an attenuated, approximate way) whatever he feels, she does best if she also sees to it that he feels good. To avoid this entanglement with another's well-being, Nora could break her empathic connection with Oscar, thereby avoiding the ill-effects of empathizing with an unfortunate. Batson's (1991, 2002) studies show that, like the iPod users mentioned above, people sometimes do break their connection with others in just such situations, corroborating the empathy-altruism hypothesis.[8]

Since almost any mental state can be the object of empathy, however, one wants to know whether empathy as such influences helping behavior, or merely empathically induced emotions. The answer to this question is unclear, so I prefer not to count empathy as a situational non-reason in its own right.

2.2.6 *Attentional focus and openness to new experiences*

Attention is an important but neglected topic in moral psychology. As evidence from the social sciences indicates, people's values, perceptions, and objective situations alone do not constitute a sufficient basis for the explanation of human conduct, including moral conduct. Diverse situational factors cause our attention to constrict or dilate and our willingness to engage in new experiences to decrease and increase. Broadened focus enables us to attend to more stimuli, while constricted focus allows us to look intensely at normatively relevant (or irrelevant) features and ignore irrelevant (or relevant) ones. Arien Mack and Irvin Rock's (1998) work on the power of inattentional blindness emphasizes this point. They point to the now-famous study in which participants watched a video of six people passing a basketball. Asked to count the number of passes, about half of the participants failed entirely to notice that around two-thirds of the way into the short film a woman in a gorilla suit walks on to the screen, turns to face the camera, beats his chest in a threat display, and ambles

---

[7] See Batson, van Lange, Ahmad, and Lishner (2003) for a comprehensive if partisan state-of-the-art essay.
[8] Goldman (1993) and Miller (2009) also discuss empathy in this vein.

off. Since they were paying attention only to the number of passes, they missed entirely this seemingly conspicuous element of the film.

Above, I discussed the emblematic Isen and Levin (1972) dime study, which found subjects were significantly more willing both to help and to learn general-interest information after finding a dime in a payphone's coin return. Batson et al. (1979) replicated this result. They hypothesize that good (bad) mood is not especially moral (immoral), but that it makes people more (less) willing to engage in all kinds of new behaviors. The Darley and Batson (1973) Good Samaritan study corroborates this speculation: presumably subjects in the hurried condition not only would have failed to help the distressed confederate but also would have declined to learn general-purpose information. They were less open to new experiences of all sorts – selfless and selfish – than were their unhurried counterparts.

Quite recently, Krupka and Weber (2006) conducted an experiment to investigate the interaction of social norms and attentional focusing with pro-social behavior. Eliminating strategic influences by having participants play a one-shot economic game, they showed that "thinking about or observing the behavior of others produces increased pro-social behavior." If people do not focus on others in this way, pro-social norms they themselves countenance are not triggered and hence do not lead to behavior they themselves would prefer. Pablo Brañas-Garza (2007) corroborated these results with a dictator game experiment. The control condition was a standard dictator game. The experimental condition differed only in one respect; dictators' instructions included the sentence, "Note that the recipient is in your hands." Simply drawing dictators' attention to this fact induced greater allocations to the recipient. It seems, in a way, that Socrates may have been right: much evil is committed and good omitted not so much out of ill will but out of ignorance of and lack of attention to morally relevant cues.

Because situational non-reasons such as sensibilia and mood effects are both seemingly trivial and normatively irrelevant, and because they exert a great deal of influence on people's morally relevant conduct, I consider them to be the heart of the situationist challenge. Bad reasons are bad, but it may be possible to handle them. Non-reasons are hugely influential, typically unnoticed, and provide no reason for the conduct they induce.

2.3 *Non-moral individual differences*

One last class of influences that has sometimes been considered in the context of the situationist challenge is individual differences of a non-moral variety. It's been argued that such demographic and temperamental char-acteristics as culture, gender, and the so-called Big Five personality vari-ables influence moral conduct. Since these characteristics are difficult, if not impossible, to modify, they challenge the acquirability condition on virtue ethics. However, I remain unconvinced of the influence of these characteristics on moral conduct. They occasionally correlate with moral outcomes, but the correlation tends to be weak and ambivalent.

2.3.1 Culture and gender

In a recent article, Jesse Prinz (2009) makes a case for including culture and gender as variables that influence both acts of compassion and giving behavior. He cites cross-cultural replications of the Milgram experiment where obedience rates differed from the baseline established by Milgram (1974) of 65 percent. For instance, in Germany, 85 percent of subjects were fully obedient (Mantell 1971). In Australia, by contrast, overall compli-ance was a mere 28 percent (Kilham and Mann 1974), with women show-ing significantly greater defiance than men. This leads Prinz to suggest that both *gender* and *national character* are causal determinants of behav-ior; for instance, Americans are hyperindividualistic, Germans extremely obedient, and Australians resolutely anti-authoritarian. He may be right, but his argument is dubious, as closer attention to Thomas Blass's (1999) meta-analysis of all replications of the Milgram paradigm shows. What we find is that subjects in the United States, South Africa, Jordan, Spain, Italy, West Germany, and Austria all obey at roughly the same rate. The sole substantial exception is the Kilham and Mann (1974) study in Australia. Instead of spinning off just-so stories about national character, then, the appropriate response is to find a design feature of the Kilham and Mann experiment that explains its outlier status. This study involved a modification of the original paradigm to make it easier for subjects to disobey: the experimenter was replaced by a second confederate who was assumed to be a mere participant in the study. It was also the sole study in which a difference between genders was detected; in all nine of the other studies that compared men and women, no gender differences emerged. For better or worse, it appears that women cannot be expected to defy authority more reliably than men.

Furthermore, two studies conducted only with women participants even point in the opposite direction. Ring, Wallston, and Corey (1970) conducted a Milgram-style experiment with fifty-seven female subjects and found a 91 percent obedience rate – significantly higher than the obedience rate for studies on men. Sheridan and King (1972) ran a similar study in which the learner was replaced by an adorable puppy that yelped and writhed in pain every time it was shocked (unlike Milgram's confederate, the puppy actually had electricity flowing through it). *All* female subjects obeyed to the bitter end.

Prinz (2009) also cites cross-cultural data on helping behavior, most of which uses the Isen and Levin (1972) paradigm. Here he may have scored a point, but the evidence is far from dispositive. Buchan, Johnson, and Croson (2006) and Levine, Norenzayan, and Philbrick (2001) found significant differences in spontaneous non-emergency helping behavior in major cities of different countries. However, both studies suffer from economic confounds. The fact that denizens of Rio de Janeiro were three times as likely as New Yorkers to pick up a pen for a stranger may owe more to the fact that a pen is many times more valuable in Rio de Janeiro than in New York City, where both cost of living and average income are much higher.

Experiments in behavioral economics have largely failed to bear out Prinz's notion that some nationalities are more generous than others. Camerer and Thaler (1995) found negligible differences in giving behavior by participants in the United States, Israel, Slovenia, and Tokyo; Charness, Haruvy, and Sonsino (2007) corroborated these results with participants in Israel, Spain, Texas, and California. Bohnet and Frey's (1999a) Swiss subjects gave about as much as most American subjects. Such studies suggest that we should not be too sanguine about finding important differences in helping behavior across either cultures or genders.

2.3.2   *The 'Big Five' individual difference measures*
Even if culture and gender play less of a role in moral conduct than philosophers such as Prinz have been wont to argue, some individual differences are robustly documented by personality psychologists.

Perhaps the most prominent model in personality psychology is the Five Factor model (also known as the 'Big Five') – openness, conscientiousness, extraversion, agreeableness, and neuroticism (McCrae and John 1996). Someone's personality can be sketched in broad outline by assigning him an ordered quintuple on these dimensions. For instance, someone might be highly conscientious, slightly introverted, rather disagreeable, and quite neurotic. Another person might be somewhat unconscientious, quite extroverted, slightly agreeable, and not at all neurotic. The names for these individual differences may suggest that some of them simply are virtues (e.g., openness, conscientiousness, and agreeableness), or that they at least would have an impact on moral conduct.

These implications cut opposite ways. On the one hand, if agreeableness is a virtue, and agreeableness is well documented in personality psychology, it would seem that (contrary to situationism) some people really are virtuous. On the other hand, since someone's Big Five signature is highly static over the course of decades, these individual differences may be inconsistent with the acquirability of virtue. As I argue in more detail about conscientiousness below, however, the names of these individual differences are misleading. Agreeableness lacks the normative oomph of a virtue, since it easily shades over into being a pushover. The psychologists' conscientiousness is not the moral or intellectual virtue it may seem, as it overlaps to a great degree with compulsivity. What's more, like pretty much all dispositional factors, the Big Five fail to correlate in a robust way with conduct (Mischel and Peake 1982), exhibiting cross-situational consistency coefficients below 0.3 in most cases.

I'm thus inclined to count the Big Five neither as evidence against the hard core of virtue ethics (i.e., against *acquirability*) nor as evidence for it (i.e., for *consistency* and *egalitarianism**). If my arguments in this section have been on the right track, virtue ethicists should worry somewhat about bad reasons and non-moral individual differences, but the real focus of concern should be situational non-reasons. A question remains, however. Namely, given all these influences on moral conduct, why is belief in traits so widespread and intuitive? In the next section, I attempt to answer this question.

3   EXPLAINING AWAY INTUITIONS ABOUT TRAITS

Situationism is an error theory. It claims that people are systematically mistaken in attributing virtues. Error theories owe us an account of why we fall into error, if only to comfort us in our intellectual iniquity. Why do we have so many trait terms, and feel so comfortable navigating the language of traits, if actual correlations between traits and individual actions are undetectable without the use of sophisticated statistical methodologies (Jennings, Amabile, and Ross 1982)?[9]

To answer this question, situationists invoke a veritable pantheon of gods of ignorance and error. Some, like the fundamental attribution error, the false consensus effect, and the power of construal, pertain directly to

---

[9] This section is based in large part on my (2011) article.

trait attributions. Others are more general cognitive heuristics and biases, whose relevance to trait attributions requires explanation. These more general heuristics and biases include selection bias, availability bias, availability cascade, and confirmation bias.

Only three of these phenomena have been addressed in the philosophy literature to date: the power of construal, the fundamental attribution error, and confirmation bias. Somewhat oddly, defenders of virtue ethics such as Sreenivasan (2002, p. 58) have invoked the power of construal in their arguments, but I will show that they are mistaken in thinking that it supports their position. Harman has briefly discussed the fundamental attribution error and confirmation bias (1999, p. 325), but otherwise little attention has been paid to explaining why we might be so prone to attributing character traits despite scant evidence, and, even in the face of contrary evidence.

I aim to fill this void here by exploring the relevance of various phenomena to explaining away intuitions about the existence and robustness of traits. I first discuss the attribution errors, which are peculiar to our folk intuitions about traits. Next, I turn to the heuristics and biases, which – though they apply more broadly than just to reasoning about traits – entail further errors in our judgments about trait-possession. I elaborate all of these biases in a somewhat dogmatic fashion; it is beyond the scope of this chapter to argue in each case that the bias really exists. Instead, I explain what the biases are, cite the relevant authorities, and draw inferences from them in order to show their relevance to the dialectic about virtue ethics.

3.1 Attribution errors

Attribution errors are cognitive biases that have to do specifically with our intuitions about personality traits. They lead to consistent mistakes in one direction or another. This section describes three: the fundamental attribution error, the false consensus effect, and the power of construal.

3.1.1 The fundamental attribution error
According to Lee Ross (1977, p. 183; see also Ross and Nisbett 1991), people are prone to the provocatively named "fundamental attribution error," a tendency to attribute most or all observed behavior to internal, dispositional factors rather than external, situational ones. When we observe others reading a script, for instance, we tend to assume they believe what they are saying, even when we are told in advance that they did not

prepare the script and are merely reading it because they were asked to (Jones and Harris 1967, p. 22). We seemingly cannot help making what James Uleman and his colleagues (1996, p. 211) call "spontaneous trait inferences," which occur "when attending to another person's behavior produces a trait inference in the absence of our explicit intention to infer traits or form an impression of that person."

Why exactly people exhibit this spontaneous reaction has not been fully answered. The problem may be partly perceptual, stemming from the Gestalt phenomenon: we focus on the figure rather than the ground. So when we observe people acting in a situation, the people themselves are our focus and hence the only factor we consider in explaining their behavior (Harman 1999, p. 325; Ross and Nisbett 1991, p. 139). In later chapters, I return to the fundamental attribution error and attempt to explain why it is so robust and how it can even be harnessed for the good through factitious virtue attributions.

The obverse side of the fundamental attribution error supposedly has to do with people's attributions regarding their own behavior. According to Jones and Nisbett (1971, p. 93), the unique breakdown of the fundamental attribution error occurs when we explain what we ourselves have done: instead of underemphasizing the influence of environmental factors, we overemphasize them. Especially when the outcome is negative, we attribute our actions to external factors. This bias seems to tell against situationism, since it suggests that we can recognize the power of situations at least in some cases. However, the existence of such an actor-observer bias has recently come in for trenchant criticism from Bertram Malle (2006), whose meta-analysis of three decades worth of data fails to demonstrate a consistent actor-observer asymmetry.[10] Malle's meta-analysis only strengthens the case for the fundamental attribution error. Whereas Jones and Nisbett had argued that it admitted of certain exceptions at least in first-personal cases, Malle shows their exceptionalism to be ungrounded.

3.1.2 *The false consensus effect*

Ross, Greene, and House (1977; see also Fields and Schuman 1976) were the first to discuss the false consensus effect, which occurs when people assume that their own opinion, desire, or other internal state is representative of the opinions, desires, etc. of a group or population to which they belong. In particular, this effect engenders a tendency to think that one's

---

[10] For more on this controversy, see Malle, Knobe, and Nelson (2007).

own choice in a particular dilemma is the norm, which leads to false trait attributions to others. For instance, Ross and colleagues asked passers-by on the street to carry a sign inscribed "Eat at Joe's!" Those who agreed to help estimated that 62 percent of others would do the same, while those who declined thought others would decline 67 percent of the time. Unless 29 percent of people would both accept and decline the solicitation, something is fishy about these numbers.

The false consensus effect helps explain away intuitions about dispositions in the following way: once we make the fundamental attribution error and attribute a trait, we assume everyone else attributes the trait too, thereby reinforcing our own belief. If we assume that others explain Ignacio's tax evasion as expressing his dishonesty, we are more likely to say so to them, thereby triggering an availability cascade (defined below) about Ignacio, who might be an otherwise upstanding citizen. If, however, we think that tax evasion is patriotic, we may praise him as a civic hero, triggering a different cascade.

Like the fundamental attribution error, the false consensus effect has come in for criticism, and once again I believe this criticism is mostly erroneous. Dawes and Mulford (1996, p. 202), for instance, point out that treating oneself as a sample of 1 means that one should in fact use one's own opinion as a guide to the opinions of others, just as one should use an arbitrary other person's opinion as a guide. Nevertheless, the problem is that a sample of 1 is a scant evidential base. Dawes and Mulford do not dispute the claim that people do treat their own case as evidence; they merely point out that it is not entirely irrational to do so. But since one should be wary of making precise predictions based on any single datapoint, so one should be wary of making such predictions when that datapoint is oneself.

We may explain the relevance of the false consensus effect to the dispute about virtues by pointing out that, since people tend to make such rash inferences, they are prone to over-attributing traits. They could reason as follows: "Well, I helped these strange fellows advertise for Joe's Bar, so almost anyone would do the same. I guess most people are helpful!" Such an inference, however, is at best dubious. Statistical methodologies with sufficiently large and diverse samples should instead be used to assess such general claims, a point to which I return below.

3.1.3   The power of construal

Walter Mischel and Yuichi Shoda (1995, p. 258; see Ross and Nisbett 1991, pp. 59–89) argue that people's subjective construals of their situations account for a lot of the variability in behavior. Ambiguous environmental cues require interpretation. Was John's laugh light-hearted or sadistic? Is that person running down the street panicked or just late for a meeting? Are those cries coming from the apartment next door a plea for help from a battered wife or just the television blaring? What one person sees as an emergency calling for immediate action, another sees as a nuisance or at least as unclear.

The power of construal is relevant to the dispute about traits because, if someone attributes one trait (say, helpfulness) to Jack and another (say, thirst for recognition) to Jill, he will interpret the same objective behavior (going up the hill to fetch a pail of water) differently depending on which person does it. Jack is trying to help out, but Jill just wants to be praised. Jill could not care less about our welfare, but Jack wants to make sure we stay hydrated. Once a trait has been attributed, all ambiguous evidence is interpreted as if it flowed from the trait, an instance of the confirmation bias discussed below.

I have been unable to locate studies that demonstrate such an appeal to construal to massage apparent inconsistencies in trait attributions. Nevertheless, insightful novelists have picked up on the phenomenon, as *Angel* (1957/1984, p. 72) by Elizabeth Taylor (the English writer, not the American actress of the same name) demonstrates. In one particularly striking passage from this novel, Angel, the daughter of the widow Mrs. Deverell, has recently come into money. Angel whisks her mother away from the grocery store she had run for years to live at Alderhurst, a sumptuous mansion. Mrs. Deverell still tries to keep in touch with her working-class friends but they seem changed. I quote at length:

> Either they put out their best china and thought twice before they said anything, or they were defiantly informal – "You'll have to take us as you find us" – and would persist in making remarks like "I don't suppose you ever have bloaters [non-gourmet fish] up at Alderhurst" or "Pardon the apron, but there's no servants here to polish the grate." In each case, they were watching her for signs of grandeur or condescension. She fell into little traps they laid and then they were able to report to the neighbors. "It hasn't taken *her* long to start putting on side." She had to be especially careful to recognize everyone she met, and walked up the street with an expression of anxiety which was misinterpreted as disdain. [...] All of their kindnesses were remembered and brooded over; any past kindness Mrs. Deverell had done – and they were many – only served to underline the change which had come over her.

In this passage, Mrs. Deverell's former friends systematically misconstrue her actions now that she has become rich. In the novel, if any character is virtuous, it is she; none of the others recognize this fact, however, because of the power of construal. By contrast, several of the other characters gain undeserved reputations for their virtue because of converse misconstrual. Such all-too-human tendencies vitiate our ability to detect virtue and vice, leading to over-attribution of both virtues and vices.

3.2   Heuristics and biases

In this section, I discuss several heuristics and biases that – though they apply more broadly than attribution biases proper – are relevant to folk intuitions about traits. In particular, these biases have to do with the inputs to our cognitive processing. The selection bias, for instance, leads us to make inferences on non-representative data. The availability bias leads us to make inferences based on stereotypes and easily recalled examples rather than all the data; availability cascades redouble the problems engendered by the availability bias. And confirmation bias leads us to seek out only evidence that confirms our predetermined opinions.

3.2.1   Selection bias

Though they argue that people are not cross-situationally consistent in the way that talk of traits leads us to believe, situationists usually also admit that, when socially embedded in day-to-day life, our attributions of traits lead to correct predictions of behavior. Like an unsound argument with a true conclusion, our reasoning processes begin with false premises about the existence and robustness of traits and derive true predictions about others' behavior. As Ross and Nisbett (1991, p. 7) put it, "biased processing of evidence plays an important role in perceptions of consistency," yet "the predictability of everyday life is, for the most part, real."[11] We use "fast and frugal heuristics" (Gigerenzer 2007, p. 158; see also Gigerenzer et al. 2000, Kahneman, Slovic, and Tversky 1982, and Sunstein 2005) to make inferences to conclusions that serve our pragmatic needs well enough in the environments we typically inhabit. Such heuristically powered inferences are not deductively valid arguments from true premises nor even sound inductions, and they can go wildly wrong if used in circumstances for which they were not adapted, but they do an adequate job of guiding us in everyday life.

Think of the old yarn about the King of Siam's refusal to believe that water could freeze: he made an inference from the behavior of water in

---

[11] See Doris (1998, p. 508).

typical conditions to the behavior of water in atypical (for him) conditions. We can reconstruct his reasoning as relying on the premise that all water is liquid or vapor. While this premise is false, it led to only true inferences until the king contradicted his Dutch guest. Analogously, we make inferences based on traits about how people will behave in counterfactual scenarios (Edgar is honest; if anyone were honest he would not lie; so Edgar will not lie). Though the trait-invoking premises of such inferences are false, they will not lead us astray if the right social and other environmental influences conspire, like a benevolent Cartesian demon, to make our conclusions true.

3.2.2 Availability bias

When people use the availability heuristic, they take the first few examples of a type that come to mind as emblematic of the whole population. This process can lead to surprisingly accurate conclusions (Gigerenzer 2007, p. 28), but it can also lead to preposterously inaccurate guesses (Tversky and Kahneman 1973, p. 241).[12] We remember the one time Maria acted benevolently and forget all the times when she failed to show supererogatory kindness, leading us to infer that she must be a benevolent person. Since extremely virtuous and vicious actions are more memorable than ordinary actions, they will typically be the ones we remember when we consider whether someone possesses a trait, leading to over-attribution of both virtues and vices.

3.2.3 Availability cascade

An availability cascade occurs when the availability bias goes viral; Timur Kuran and Cass Sunstein (1999, p. 683) define a cascade as "a self-reinforcing process of collective belief formation by which an expressed perception triggers a chain reaction that gives the perception of increasing plausibility through its rising availability in public discourse." In the United States, for instance, it is commonly believed (and, importantly, commonly asserted) that many of Christopher Columbus's contemporaries thought the Earth was flat prior to his famous voyage of 1492. This falsehood has been repeated so many times that people assume it must be true. Similarly, it is commonly believed (and repeated) that Albert Einstein failed at least one of his mathematics classes in grade school. Because this howler is repeated so frequently, it seems plausible to many. Quite recently, Congressman Paul Ryan's budget plan has been publicly called serious by

---

[12] Below, in Chapter 6, I discuss availability in much more detail.

so many people that it seems like it might actually be serious, even though it contains economic howler after economic howler.

This phenomenon is relevant to our belief in traits because cascades about a person's personality are easily triggered. In fact, we already have a word for them: gossip. This is the fate suffered by poor Mrs. Deverell in the passage from *Angel* quoted above. People spread the word that she has become haughty; that lie is repeated and repeated; and eventually it comes to seem plausible, despite the fact that not a single person has witnessed an instance of her acting haughtily.

3.2.4   *Confirmation bias*

Confirmation bias is the tendency to search for, interpret, and remember information in a way that confirms one's beliefs. The bias has a long and distinguished pedigree, having been identified (though not under its current name) by Sir Francis Bacon (1620, p. 79), who said:

> The human understanding when it has once adopted an opinion [...] draws all things else to support and agree with it. And though there be a greater number and weight of instances to be found on the other side, yet these it either neglects or despises, or else by some distinction sets aside or rejects.

Charles Darwin (2009, p. 44) in his autobiography remarks that after years of working as a scientist, he adopted the following "golden rule":

> whenever a published fact, a new observation or thought came across me, which was opposed to my general results, to make a memorandum of it without fail and at once; for I had found by experience that such facts and thoughts were far more apt to escape from the memory than favourable ones.

More recently, contemporary psychology has provided experimental evidence for the confirmation bias and its relation to trait ascription. Mischel and Peake (1982, p. 750) suggest that anecdotal evidence is likely to be biased (or misconstrued) because instances of prototypic trait-relevant behavior are given too much weight in assessments. When once we decide (perhaps because of the fundamental attribution error) that someone is cowardly or temperate or conscientious, all our further observations are guided and colored by that decision. This is precisely the phenomenon dramatized in the passage from Taylor's *Angel* quoted above.

4   THE MISCHELLIAN CONSENSUS

While I have undertaken a more extensive literature review than all other philosophical commentators on the empirical evidence for situationism to date, the psychology and economics journals teem with studies I have not cited. It would take several lifetimes to discuss them all, but I hope that the discussion here makes it clear both that situational non-reasons exert surprising influence on moral conduct and that we should treat intuitions about traits as providing little evidence for the existence and robustness of virtues. Ever since Walter Mischel's (1968) landmark literature review, in which he showed that in nearly every objective study of personality individual dispositions account for at most 10 percent of behavior (and usually between 1 percent and 4 percent), social psychologists have taken a dim view of traitology. Mischel further showed that though cross-situational consistency is not to be had, intra-situational stability does exist, often accounting for at least 20 percent of behavior in iterations of the same situation. As Gordon Allport (1966), himself a friend of traits, aptly put it, "Every parent knows that an offspring may be a hellion at home and an angel when he goes visiting. A businessman may be hardheaded in the office and a mere marshmallow in the hands of his pretty daughter."[13]

With such low correlations, the explanatory and predictive power of trait attributions are severely infirmed. Even Seymour Epstein (1983), a defender of personality theory, agrees with situationists that predicting particular behaviors in particular situations on the basis of trait variables is "usually hopeless." Traits, according to him, are better evaluated by reference to general behavioral trends than particular behaviors. This is the so-called aggregation solution, according to which the proper variables to correlate are traits and behavioral patterns, not traits and individual actions. The aggregation solution, however, admits of at best a Pyrrhic victory for defenders of personality. After all, the *explanatory power* and *predictive power** conditions discussed in the previous chapter apply not just to trends but to individual actions. This, I take it, is the best version of the situationist challenge to virtue ethics to be articulated to date. It may nevertheless fail to convince, so in the next chapter I critique the many responses to situationism that have accrued in the philosophical literature of the last two decades.

---

[13] See Mischel and Peake (1982) for a more recent literature review that comes to the same conclusion, even about conscientiousness, one of the so-called Big Five traits.

CHAPTER 3

Attempts to defend virtue ethics

You rob reality of its meaning, value, and truthfulness to the extent
that you *make up* an ideal world.

Friedrich Nietzsche, *Ecce Homo*, Preface: 2

I   FAMILIES OF RESPONSES TO SITUATIONISM

The situationist challenge is not without opponents. Three primary
responses can be identified:

(*dodge*) Virtue is a rare ideal, so empirical evidence that most people are
not virtuous is irrelevant.

(*retreat*) Although the situationist critique shows that traditional virtues are chimerical, an empirically informed theory of virtue can
still be formulated in terms of virtuous actions or local traits.

(*counterattack*) The empirical evidence does not support the situationist
critique.

In this chapter, I canvass the best versions of all three arguments and
assess them in light of the hard core of virtue ethics. (Readers who are
already convinced by the previous chapter may prefer to skip directly
to the next chapter, where I articulate my own positive response to the
challenge.) Most of these arguments turn out either to be unsound or
to concede part of the hard core. A few developments of the counterattack and retreat look promising, however, and raise two interesting
possibilities. If situationists are right that context determines much
of human behavior, then behavior can be controlled by arranging to
find oneself in the appropriate context. It can also be controlled by
actively producing appropriate contexts instead of submitting to them
passively.

2 THE DODGE

Advocates of the dodge point out that for the ancients, full virtue was a rare last fruit of a lifelong project. That most people are not virtuous is therefore no surprise; in fact, it may be a prediction of a suitably elitist virtue ethics. Myles Burnyeat (1980), for example, discusses the myriad ways in which an aspirant to virtue can go wrong, strongly insinuating the rarity of virtue before philosophers took up the situationist challenge.

Christian Miller (2003, p. 379) fleshes out this argument by drawing on the Aristotelian distinctions among virtue, continence, incontinence, and vice. The virtuous person does the right thing wholeheartedly. The continent person does the right thing, but only conflictedly. The vicious person does the wrong thing wholeheartedly. The incontinent person, like the continent, is conflicted, but his better self loses the battle and he does the wrong thing. Christine Swanton (2003, p. 30) points out that many of the participants in the Milgram studies in obedience, a favorite stalking horse of situationists, displayed intense emotional distress. This is evidence, she claims, of nascent or incomplete virtue, not of lack of virtue. Obedient subjects were incontinent; they wanted to do the right thing but failed.

The dodge may seem promising, but there are reasons to worry. First, it appears to cede the *egalitarianism**, *explanatory power*, and *predictive power** conjuncts in the hard core of virtue ethics. If moral education is as hard as Burnyeat makes it seem, most people could not be brought to behave in accordance with virtue, let alone be virtuous. If most people are non-virtuous, then, *pace* MacIntyre's (1984) claim that much of human behavior would be "genuinely inexplicable" without appeal to virtues, the virtues are loose cogs in our motivational machinery, reliably licensing neither the explanation nor the prediction of behavior.

Second, by referring to the distinctions among virtue, continence, incontinence, and vice, this response constricts the range of situational factors that it can handle. Temptations and situational demand characteristics – what I called bad reasons in the previous chapter – are naturally handled by this response: people do the right thing but not wholeheartedly because they're tempted, or they do the wrong thing because of situational demand characteristics. But situational non-reasons such as ambient sensibilia and mood effects have nothing to do with continence and incontinence. Thus, the dodge at best responds to a sub-class of situational influences, and a sub-class that is intuitively less worrisome anyway.

Finally, if most people are non-virtuous, then moral education may involve the very "moral schizophrenia" that virtue ethicists have criticized in other ethical theories. If moral education takes the form of advising someone to do what the virtuous person would do, learners would be forced to ask "Is what I propose to do what the virtuous person would do [or advise] in my situation?" Such an attempt to emulate (or follow the advice of) an imaginary virtuous person introduces the same rift between reasons and motives that virtue ethics is taken to bridge by its proponents.

3   THE RETREAT

Instead of dodging the situationist charge, some have preferred to retreat and retrench, allowing that much of what situationists say is correct but claiming that despite this, a suitably weakened version of virtue theory is empirically adequate. Two directions for the retreat can be distinguished: the retreat into one-off virtuous acts and the retreat into local virtues.

3.1   *Virtuous acts*

If one agrees that the dodge gives up too much, one might be tempted to retreat to an act-based virtue theory like that of Thomson (1996, 1997). Thomas Hurka (2001, 2006) goes so far as to say that the act-based virtue theory should not be considered a retreat from its dispositional cousin. Instead, he argues, people really recognize only virtuous acts as intrinsically valuable, relegating virtuous dispositions (if there are any) to mere instrumental value. Moving virtue ethics in this direction strips it of much of its appeal, however, since it gives up on the *consistency, stability, explanatory power,* and *predictive power** of virtues.

Situationist critics have explicitly admitted that their arguments do not apply to act-based theories of virtue. Despite this, most responders to the situationist challenge do not follow this route. I take it that their reluctance is best explained by the fact that this way of defining virtue is unattractive to anyone who finds the arguments for virtue ethics canvassed in Chapter 1 compelling.

3.2   *Local virtues*

A less extreme retreat endorses something like Doris's theory of local virtues. If virtues are natural kinds, then they should be discovered a posteriori. Though ethicists may be disappointed to find that the global trait of honesty does not exist, they should be excited to find that there are stable local traits. Parsimonious lists of cardinal virtues notwithstanding, if it turns out that there are hundreds of virtues, so be it.[1] Doris seems inclined, for instance, to distinguish a large variety of local traits that fit within the global virtue of courage. His preferred method seems to be to individuate traits as finely as required for them to actually support counterfactuals and confident predictions. Instead of *courage* or even *physical-courage*, he would have us speak of *battlefield-physical-courage*, of *storms-physical-courage*, of *heights-physical-courage*, and of *wild-animals-physical-courage*. Indeed, he seems inclined even to differentiate between *battlefield-physical-courage-in-the-face-of-rifle-fire* and *battlefield-physical-courage-in-the-face-of-artillery-fire*. Though it might seem that he is being flippant by cutting the fabric of traits so finely, he claims that this principle of individuation "is the beginning of an empirically adequate theory" (2002, p. 62).

Doris's notion of local traits is not entirely unprecedented. As Rachana Kamtekar (2004, p. 479) points out, Aristotle himself paved the way for this idea in the *Nicomachean Ethics* by distinguishing greatness of soul from due pride (1123b) and magnificence from generosity (1122a). If theorists of local traits are on the right track, people should aim not so much to develop robust global traits like courage but to reinforce and amalgamate local traits like *courage-in-the-face-of-physical-danger -while-in-a-good-mood* and *courage-in-the-face-of-social-pressure-while- smelling-coffee*. If one knows the limits of one's local virtues, one could at least in principle aim to ensure that one is called upon to act courageously only when one is in the appropriate circumstances.

One practical problem for the theory of local traits is that, from a normative point of view, virtues are best individuated by their characteristic reasons. The *consistency* requirement implicitly does so because it is formulated in terms of virtues' characteristic reasons. Generosity appeals to the needs of others; courtesy appeals to conventions of society; courage

---

[1] Note, by the way, that a fairly comprehensive list of the cardinal virtues, especially of the virtues of other and past cultures, is by no means parsimonious. Here's a shot: altruism, beauty, benevolence, charity, chastity, cleanliness, compassion, consideration, contentment, cooperativeness, courage, courteousness, dignity, diligence, empathy, endurance, fairness, faith, fidelity, filial piety, forgiveness, friendliness, frugalness, generosity, gravitas, greatness of soul, honesty, hope, humanity, humility, industry, justice, magnanimity, mercy, modesty, obedience, patience, piety, prudence, reverence, severity, sincerity, tact, temperance, tenacity, trustfulness, trustworthiness, and valor. One fun game to try at home is to pick three or four of these at random and then to imagine what a society would have to look like if these were its cardinal virtues.

appeals to threats to valued objects and ends. Local traits, by contrast, are individuated by both their characteristic reasons and the normatively irrelevant causal powers of the situation. *Generosity-while-watched-by-fellow-church-members* appeals to both the needs of others and social pressure; *courtesy-while-in-a-good-mood* appeals to both conventions of society and one's normatively irrelevant subjective state; *battlefield-courage-in-the-face-of-rifle-fire* appeals to both threats against something valuable and the normatively irrelevant type of the threat.

If local traits really are as fine grained and individualized as Doris suggests and Adams concedes (2006, pp. 125–30), then a virtue theory framed in terms of local traits would have to modify the *consistency* condition (since as currently formulated it appeals only to reasons) and possibly reject the *access* condition (since there will end up being so many traits that we could not possibly determine what they are).[2] Perhaps both changes are acceptable, but they do come at a cost.

Another concern raised by the theory of local traits is interpersonal comparison. If we learn moral reasoning at mother's knee, then presumably attributions that apply to one agent could equally be applied to (or denied of) another. The theory of local traits, however, threatens to make interpersonal comparisons of virtues impossible or at least very difficult. This is because local traits are individuated not only by their characteristic reasons but also by situational parameters. While I find it plausible to suppose that we have some way of individuating reasons, the individuation of situational parameters often seems ad hoc. For Doris, the strategy seems to be to assume that someone has the most global version of a trait that one has license to attribute, and then to pare that back as further evidence rolls in. It might at first seem that someone has the virtue of *courage*, but then we find that he caves in to social pressure, so we attribute *physical-courage*. Then we find out that he's great in battle but a quivering mess of fear when he sees a tiger, so we attribute *battlefield-physical-courage*. Then we find out that he's a hero in the face of rifle fire but is reduced to tears in the face of grapeshot, so we attribute *battlefield-physical-courage-in-the-face-of-rifle-fire*. These further distinctions seem increasingly ad hoc, which suggests that different distinctions may have to be made for different people. In the same way that one wants to be able to say (and learn) that *A* and *B* have the same belief, desire, thought, or emotion, one wants to be able to say (and learn) that they

---

[2] It seems to me that this is what Russell (2009) should have said in his articulation of what he calls the *enumeration problem*.

have the same virtue or vice. If, however, local traits are individuated in such an ad hoc, fine-grained way, this may be impossible. The local trait theorist would have to add that the fine distinctions made in one person's case would for the most part apply in another person's case. Else, the traits that *A* has might turn out to be incommensurable with the traits that *B*, *C*, and *D* have.

This concern applies most directly to the *access* condition, as it suggests that, if traits are sufficiently local, their names will be unlearnable. While it would be possible to acquire the names of a few eponymous traits (maverick, quixotic, chauvinistic, sadistic, tawdry, draconian, quisling) by direct ostension, our trait vocabulary must, for the sake of acquirability and interpersonal comparison, be less about Socratizing or Pegasizing than sagacity and pusillanimity.

Another worry about local traits is that their identification may be worryingly post hoc. Consider the local traits of *honesty-towards-one's-brothers* and *honesty-towards-one's-sisters*. Are these two distinct traits? If they are, what about *honesty-towards-one's siblings*? Is it yet another trait, or just the conjunction of the other two? How many honesty-relevant local traits does someone who displays honesty towards her siblings possess? Just *honesty-towards-siblings*? Both *honesty-towards-brothers* and *honesty-towards-sisters* but not *honesty-towards-siblings*? All three? One of the congenial things about individuating virtues by their characteristic reasons is that it gives us a principled way of answering questions about how many virtues someone has.[3] The fear is that because local traits are individuated not only by their characteristic reasons but also by other, normatively irrelevant, situational features, there may be no way to answer the question how many virtues someone has. I take seriously Quine's dictum, "No entity without identity" (1969, p. 23). The theory of local traits seems to run afoul of it.

4 THE COUNTERATTACK

The dodge and the retreat both attempt to make virtues of necessity. Some defenders of virtue ethics, however, want to make a necessity of virtue. They argue that the evidence cited by situationists is unconvincing. The cheekier among them even claim that social psychology supports virtue ethics.

---

[3] Note that this presupposes that we have a way of individuating reasons. I will not take up that matter here, but I hope and trust that meta-ethicists have come up with a way to do so.

4.1   Introspection

The counterattack comprises a slew of independent ripostes. The first I discuss comes from Julia Annas, who claims that the deliverances of introspection confirm the existence of character traits – damn the social scientists' torpedoes, and full speed ahead. She objects to considering character traits primarily "from the point of view of a scientific observer," preferring instead to focus on how "we understand our own dispositions" (2003, p. 23). She then goes on to say, "I don't discover my own generosity or the lack of it by doing correct or faulty probability calculations." Instead, Annas would prefer to determine why someone does what she does by focusing on "her own account of her actions."

It should be plain, however, that introspection cuts no ice, especially in light of my argument in the previous chapter that intuitions about traits are unreliable. The question is not whether people take themselves to have traits or to be motivated by their traits but whether they actually do have these traits. Furthermore, research in moral dumbfounding suggests that the reasons people give for their moral judgments are often confabulated post hoc. Jonathan Haidt (2001), for instance, discusses studies in which participants read vignettes in which the protagonists engage in morally questionable behavior. Participants are asked to make moral judgments about the protagonists, then asked for the reasons supporting these judgments. Even when it should be clear to them that their reasons are invalid, they typically do not revise their moral judgments. In one representative vignette, a brother and sister commit incest. While they have sex only one time, use a prophylactic, enjoy the experience, keep it a secret, and never regret what they've done, the protagonists are nevertheless roundly condemned by most participants. When asked for reasons for this judgment, they cite the dangers of inbreeding, the possibility of emotional harm, and so on, but these reasons are clearly inoperative in the vignette. If experimenters point out the problems associated with these reasons, participants usually respond by getting angry or saying things like, "I don't know, I can't explain it, I just know it's wrong." Such research suggests that the reasons people give for their moral judgments are unreliable. It's only a small leap from confabulation about reasons for judgments to confabulation about reasons for actions. Barring evidence to the contrary, we should assume that the reasons people give when explaining their own moral behavior will be similarly untrustworthy.

Worse still, recent psychological research on the distinction between implicit and explicit moral self-concept (Monin and Miller 2001; Monin,

Pizarro, and Beer 2007) suggests that people's behavioral dispositions and their dispositions to make moral judgments are typically uncorrelated. If you want to know how someone will act or why they behave the way they do, it seems to be better to use what's called an implicit association test than to ask them to respond to moral dilemmas with reasons (Perugini and Leone 2009). The former draws on the same cognitive and affective resources that behavior draws on, whereas the latter seems to draw on a store of explicit rules – rules that people may know in a sense without being in any way disposed to follow them.

4.2 Equivocation

In his defense of virtue ethics against the situationist challenge, Gopal Sreenivasan (2008, p. 604) points out that the meaning of a 'cross-situationally consistent trait' is a function of how one individuates situations into equivalence classes. "In one sense," he says, "a trait is cross-situationally consistent if it is manifested across situations that differ in respect of the kind of feature inviting behavior that manifests that trait," (consistency$_1$) while in another sense, a trait is cross-situationally consistent if it is manifested "across situations in which this feature remains constant, but other features vary" (consistency$_2$). As I understand this distinction, consistency$_1$ allows reasons-providing features of the situation to vary, whereas consistency$_2$ allows non-reasons-providing features of the situation to vary; this seems to be roughly the same distinction I made in the previous chapter between bad reasons and situational non-reasons. According to Sreenivasan (p. 605), virtues are traits individuated by consistency$_1$. I contend that they are individuated *neither* by consistency$_1$ *nor* by consistency$_2$, and that the correct principle of virtue individuation appeals only to reasons (call it consistency$_3$).

A hypothetical example based on the case of Wesley Autrey illustrates this objection. Suppose that Romo is in a good mood, sees a seizure victim lying in the path of an oncoming train, and risks his own life to save the victim. Further suppose that Romo would act as Table 3.1 indicates.

If Romo were in a good mood and saw a victim in the path of an oncoming train, a charging bull, or a knife-wielding murderer, he would recognize that someone was in danger and needed help, which would lead him to save the victim. However, if Romo were in a neutral or bad mood, he would fail to act – perhaps because he would not notice that someone was in danger and needed help, perhaps because he would not care whether the victim needed help, perhaps because he would be frozen with

Table 3.1 *Romo's counterfactual reaction profile*

	Oncoming train	Charging bull	Knife-wielding murderer
Good mood	Saves victim		
Neutral mood	Doesn't save victim		
Bad mood			

fear, or perhaps for some other reason or even no reason at all. According to consistency$_1$, Romo should be considered courageous. Across situations that differ in respect of the kind of feature inviting behavior (the threat), he is disposed to behave in the appropriate way. The fact that his behavior would seem non-virtuous if we looked at possible worlds that differ in another respect, namely his mood, is irrelevant to consistency$_1$. For consistency$_1$, what matters is similarity across the rows of the table.

In contrast, for consistency$_2$, what matters is the columns, not the rows. So, according to consistency$_2$, Romo is not courageous. Holding constant the feature of the situation that invites the behavior (the threat) while allowing his mood to vary, his behavior changes, so he doesn't possess the trait. Also according to consistency$_3$, Romo is not courageous; he has decisive reason to help in all nine permutations but only responds in three of them, so he is not courageous.

Now suppose that another person, Schlomo, is in a bad mood, sees a seizure victim lying in the path of an oncoming train, and risks his life to save the victim. Further suppose that Schlomo would act as Table 3.2 indicates.

If Schlomo were in a neutral or bad mood and saw a victim in the path of an oncoming train, a charging bull, or a knife-wielding murderer, he would recognize that someone was in danger and needed help, which would lead him to save the victim. However, if Schlomo were in a good mood, he would fail to act – perhaps because he would not notice that someone was in danger and needed help, perhaps because he would not care whether the victim needed help, perhaps because he would be frozen with fear, or perhaps for some other reason or even no reason at all.

Is Schlomo courageous? As before, consistency$_2$ and consistency$_3$ deliver negative answers. Using consistency$_1$, however, Sreenivasan is committed to saying that Schlomo is courageous; holding the courage-irrelevant factor of mood constant, he would react appropriately to all courage-eliciting circumstances.

Table 3.2 *Schlomo's counterfactual reaction profile*

	Oncoming train	Charging bull	Knife-wielding murderer
Good mood	Doesn't save victim		
Neutral mood	Saves victim		
Bad mood			

But Romo and Schlomo have precisely opposite counterfactual profiles. It hardly makes sense to attribute the same virtue to both.

Worse still, if cowardice is a trait that entails failing to do the courage-appropriate thing across courage-eliciting situations as individuated by consistency$_1$, and if Romo and Schlomo are placed in courage-eliciting circumstances while in a good mood, Romo is courageous and Schlomo cowardly. But if they are placed in courage-eliciting circumstances while in a bad or neutral mood, the attributions are reversed: Romo is cowardly and Schlomo courageous. Presumably cowardice and courage are contraries, though; the same person cannot possess both traits at the same time. One could get around thinking of cowardice and courage as contraries by speaking not of cowardice but of *cowardice-before-bulls-while-in-a-good-mood* and speaking not of courage but of *courage-before-murderers-while-in-a-bad-mood*. This is the way Doris suggests individuating local traits, as I explained above, but of course Sreenivasan is unwilling to accede to this suggestion.

Evidently, both trait-relevant and trait-irrelevant features of the situation should be allowed to vary if global virtues are being investigated. Being globally courageous means reacting appropriately to all situations that provide decisive reason to protect something even at a risk to oneself. In other words, being courageous means responding appropriately to all situations where the decisive *reason* is courage's characteristic reason.

4.3 Morally unimportant behavior

Next, consider the counterattack according to which situationist experiments do not test morally crucial behavior. As John Sabini and Maury Silver (2005, p. 540) say, "picking up or not picking up" a stranger's papers is not "a very important manifestation of a moral trait." While this is a fair criticism of the Isen and Levin (1972) phone booth experiment, it ignores a large swath of the situationist literature. Consider just the Darley and Batson (1973), Milgram (1974), and Haney, Banks, and Zimbardo (1973) studies. Is the failure to help a distressed man lying by the side of the road morally trivial? Is applying dangerous shocks not morally crucial? Is forcing guiltless fellow-participants in an experiment to clean latrines with their bare hands morally unimportant? While some experiments test for unimportant behaviors, many test important ones.

Moreover, evidence from behavioral economics suggests that people's actions in low-stakes situations reliably predict their actions in high-stakes situations. For instance, Hoffman, McCabe, and Smith (1996) found no significant differences in the behavior of proposers or responders in ultimatum games when the stakes were $10 or $100.[4] Slonim and Roth (1998) found that behavior changed only slightly even when financial stakes were varied by a factor of twenty-five. If these results can be extrapolated to non-economic behavior, then the studies that use trivial actions as independent variables do in fact provide (indirect) support for skepticism about global virtues.

4.4   One-off versus longitudinal studies

Another counterattack claims that one-off experiments cannot provide evidence for or against virtue. Sreenivasan (2008, p. 607) is responsible for this argument as well; he claims that the question of consistency cannot be answered by comparing different cohorts under different experimental treatments. Instead, the only evidence he would accept looks at the same cohort under different experimental treatments over the course of days, weeks, months, or even years. He categorically denies that "any data from a one time performance experiment [can] do anything to establish" the conclusion that the participants in the experiment lack a character trait. Such data are not thick on the ground. However, what little there are (e.g., Hartshorne and May 1928) lend no comfort to this counterattack.

In addition, if the traits in question are high-fidelity virtues, one-off experiments *can* provide strong evidence against (though only weak evidence for) the presence of the traits. Because generosity and beneficence are low-fidelity virtues, it may be that whether someone gives money to a charity is only weak evidence for or against his generosity. But because chastity and most other types of loyalty are high-fidelity virtues, whether

---

[4] For more on this topic, see Camerer and Thaler (1995), Hoffman, McCabe, Shachat, and Smith (1994), and Roth, Prasnikar, Okuno-Fujiwara, and Zamir (1991).

someone cheats on his spouse even once can constitute strong evidence of a lack of fidelity (though perhaps only weak evidence for fidelity).[5]

The issue is more complicated and asymmetric than Sreenivasan realizes. By way of comparison, consider how you might test whether a given coin has the 'virtue' of always landing *heads* or a given die has the 'virtue' of always turning up *ace*. These dispositions require a certain kind of consistency. If you flip a coin once and note that it shows *heads*, you gain only very weak evidence that it is double-headed. If you roll a die once and it turns up *ace*, you should update your confidence in its being loaded only minimally. Many repeated trials would be required to determine or even strongly corroborate that the coin is double-headed or the die loaded. But now consider what you could conclude if the coin turned up *tails* or the die showed *six*. At the very least, you could say that the coin was not double-headed and the die not sufficiently loaded so that it *always* showed *ace*. Virtues – at least high-fidelity virtues – are like being double-headed or maximally loaded. A single test can *disconfirm* someone's possession of a virtue, but it cannot *confirm* the virtue's presence. Since many situationist studies test for high-fidelity virtues, these studies (at least) can in fact disconfirm the presence of the relevant traits.

4.5   *Confounding traits*

The next counterattack argues that situationist experiments are confounded by other, uncontrolled dispositional variables. They presume to test for one virtue, say honesty, but other virtues like prudence kick in and dampen the expression of the target trait. People with multiple, inconsistent character traits are bound to have opposing impulses and must violate at least some of them. Rachana Kamtekar (2004, p. 473; see also Miller 2003, p. 369 and Sreenivasan 2008, p. 607) claims that subjects in the Milgram experiments may have had two contrary virtues: compassion and obedience. Hence, when they did not express compassion it was not because they were the passive pawns of situational influences but because they were expressing the opposing virtue. Obedience may not be a virtue, but it is a trait. A less contentious version of this counterattack would therefore say that tests for trait t_1 may be confounded by the presence of traits $t_2, t_3, \ldots t_n$, which may, but need not be, virtues. The basic idea here is

---

[5] If this is right, it casts doubt on most of Christian Miller's (2003, 2009, 2010) otherwise persuasive arguments, which focus almost solely on helping behavior and thus only on low-fidelity virtue.

that the empirical evidence merely emphasizes how susceptible people are to bad reasons, especially to situational demand characteristics.

As an a priori exercise this argument is valid, but I am unconvinced that it actually applies to the studies on which situationists rely. Milgram varied his experimental conditions to see whether people were simply obedient (as these defenders of virtue now suggest post hoc) or only obedient when certain situational cues were present. His results support the latter thesis. Subjects' maximum obedience rate dropped from 65 percent when the 'learner' was in another room to 40 percent when he was in the same room and 30 percent when they could only shock him by physically placing his hand on the electrode (1974, p. 35). Whether it is compassionate to shock someone does not vary as a function of distance, but subjects' willingness to shock did. Other normatively irrelevant situational influences produced similar effects. When the experimenter delivered his instructions to participants over the phone, their maximum obedience dropped to 20 percent (p. 61). This is, of course, still an appalling result, but it is less than one-third the maximum obedience rate when the experimenter was present. The issue was not just one of obeying the experimenter's authority. When the experimenter demanded that he himself be shocked, maximal obedience plummeted to 0 percent (p. 95). It is simply impossible to explain all of the results of this series of experiments by claiming that subjects were obedient.

4.6　The behaviorism bogeyman

The next counterattack argues that situationist experiments assume a crude – and refuted – behavioristic model of action. Correlations between objective situational variables and behavior fail to take into account subjective construal and deliberation. According to Rachana Kamtekar (2004), Kristjan Kristjansson (2008) and Candace Upton (2009), when this model is replaced by a more sophisticated model that refers to internal states and their interactions, it turns out that the data provided by situationist experiments can be either dismissed or explained away. I fear that this counterattack is not only wrong but wrong-headed.

First of all, situationists do not subscribe to a crude behavioristic model of conduct. They emphasize behavior because it's important, but they have a story to tell about how objective conditions are construed, deliberated on, and reacted to.[6] This model clearly has room for a variety

---

[6] See Anderson and Bushman (2002, p. 34) for an illustrative model and graph.

of stages in decision-making. In fact, it's not so different from the virtue ethicists' own model of conduct, which typically makes reference to objective reasons in the environment, sensitivity to those reasons in the agent, deliberation about conduct based on perceived reasons, and action based on deliberation. In fact, the situationist model is more sophisticated than the virtue ethical model because it finds a place for situational non-reasons.

To see further how this is relevant, recall the tale of Wesley Autrey, who risked his own life to save a stranger from an oncoming train. Now consider several other hypothetical bystanders to Cameron Hollopeter's seizure and fall. The characterization of each of them ends with a sentence beginning, "However...". Let us assume that but for the fact mentioned in this sentence, each hypothetical bystander would have done exactly as Autrey did.

John Doe was also on the platform. However, he was listening to his iPod at maximum volume and did not notice Hollopeter's fall.

Jane Roe was also on the platform. However, she was in a thoroughly dejected mood; her depressed spirits made the whole world seem grey and uninteresting, so she too missed Hollopeter's fall, along with more or less everything else that happened.

Dorian Vivalcomb was there, too. He was in great spirits, having just won a small lottery. His bright mood led him to attend to every feature of his environment, so he immediately noticed Hollopeter's fall. However, Dorian mistook what he saw for performance art and assumed nothing was the matter.

Blavdak Vinomori was also waiting on the platform. He was a visitor in New York City, unsure what to expect. When he saw Hollopeter fall, he looked around to see how others would react. However, none of them seemed concerned, leading him to believe nothing was the matter, so he went back to perusing his tourism guide.

Vivian Darkbloom was waiting for the train as well.[7] She saw Hollopeter fall. However, because she didn't like the cut of his jib, she decided not to help Hollopeter as he lay on the tracks, his body wracked by seizures.

Vivian Bloodmark was yet another commuter on that eventful day. She noticed Hollopeter's fall, realized it was an emergency, and decided that the best course of action would be to rescue him. However, when she heard the oncoming train, she froze in fright.

---

[7] This may seem pedantic, but I feel it necessary to point out that the name 'Vivian' can be used for men and women, and that in recent decades it has been used almost solely for women.

Do John Doe, Jane Roe, Dorian Vivalcomb, Blavdak Vinomori, Vivian Darkbloom, and Vivian Bloodmark share anything of moral value with Wesley Autrey? Which of them, if any, possesses the virtue of courage? To answer these questions, we need to decide which sub-dispositions fall within the scope of being virtuous. To put the same point in a different way, what we need is a principled way of deciding which stages in the production of behavior are implicated in the metaphysics of virtue. On my reading of the virtue ethics literature, all of them are. To be courageous is to have a complex disposition to *notice* when others are in need, to *construe* ambiguous cues well, to *want* to intervene on behalf of threatened values, to *deliberate* soundly about what would in fact be the best way to intervene, and to *succeed* in interventions one decides to make.[8] That's a five-napkin burger of a disposition. If this is the right way to think about virtues, what follows is that simply correlating objective conditions with behavior is *too lenient, not too stringent*. If someone does not intervene when courage is called for, then a fortiori he does not notice, construe, desire, deliberate, and intervene. In addition to doing what the virtuous person would do, one needs to notice what the virtuous person would notice. One needs a kind of moral attentiveness.[9]

4.7 Parity of traits and situations

The penultimate counterattack has two prongs. The first points out that the infamous 0.3 ceiling (Mischel 1968) on correlations between dispositions and behaviors is not a 0.0 ceiling, concluding that 0.3 might just be "sufficient to underwrite some conception of character" (Sabini and Silver 2005, p. 541). While personality variables may be of little use in predicting whether a given agent will act in accordance with a trait on any particular occasion, in the aggregate they turn out to be quite powerful (p. 542). This is a fair point. What this discussion requires, however, is the distinction between high-fidelity and low-fidelity virtues. Aggregation is warranted

---

[8] Rather oddly, Sreenivasan argues that to answer the question of whether someone acted virtuously, we need not take into account the objective conditions, and that we can start at the construal stage. This means that someone counts as virtuous if she does what, by her lights, is the right thing to do, even if her lights are satanically wicked. Anscombe (1958, p. 2) and Foot (2001, p. 75) rightly point out conscience is not a final arbiter, and that it can lead to truly vicious action.

[9] Advocates of the ethics of care have long emphasized such attentiveness, though there exists no small disagreement on how best to attain it. Jane Tronto (1993, p. 128) thinks that passive, non-conative detachment enables one to notice morally salient situational cues, whereas Peggy DesAutels (2004) argues for engaged 'moral mindfulness,' which actively searches for moral and social cues. I am inclined to agree with DesAutels because I think we are more likely to notice what we're looking for than what we're not looking for.

with the latter but, I contend, not the former. In a fascinating series of recent studies, Angela Duckworth and her colleagues have demonstrated that the virtue of grit, which she glosses as "perseverance and passion for long-term goals" (2007, p. 1087), correlates with a variety of behaviors, from educational attainment and grade point average to retention at West Point and success in the National Spelling Bee.[10] Because it has world enough and time, even a small dose of the low-fidelity virtue of grit is enough to produce important behavioral effects. The same does not go for high-fidelity virtues. A small dose of honesty, even if aggregated over time, does not make one an honest person. If the allegations against him are true, the disgraced biologist Marc Hauser, who allegedly fabricated data for his research on primates, arguably lacks the virtues of integrity and intellectual honesty even if he is guilty of only the eight counts of scientific misconduct for which he has been sanctioned. Think about that: just eight failures over the course of a decades-long career may be enough to disqualify Hauser.

The second prong of this counterattack argues that situational influences have a correlation ceiling of their own, at 0.4 (Funder and Ozer 1983), putting the power of dispositions and the power of situations roughly on par. Kenneth Bowers argued decades ago that situationism overstates its case by treating the 0.3 correlation as negligible. Like Doris and Harman in their less provocative moments, Bowers believes that "a position stressing the interaction of the person and the situation is both conceptually satisfying and empirically warranted" (1973, p. 307).

It may be that those toeing the situationist line have taken it for granted that if dispositions explain N percent of behavior then situations explain $(100 - N)$ percent. This is emphatically not the case. What neither explains independently must be attributed to their interaction, to a third factor, or to randomness. Psychologists such as David Funder (2006) and John Jost and Lawrence Jost (2009) argue persuasively that the psychology of the twenty-first century should supplement the recognition of the 0.3 ceiling with another that recognizes the limited power of situations. This new consensus would domesticate the situationist challenge without removing its sting. Combined with the second version of the retreat, however, it opens up the possibility of a virtue ethics couched in terms of the *portability of context* (the degree to which agents may intentionally

---

[10] See Duckworth, Peterson, Matthews, and Kelly (2007); Duckworth and Seligman (2005, 2006); Duckworth, Tsukayama, and May (2010); and Duckworth, Kirby, Tsukayama, Bernstein, and Ericsson (2010).

situate themselves in contexts that encourage conduct in accordance with virtue) and the distinction between *situation-consumerism* and *situation-producerism* (taking an active role in shaping one's own situation and the situations of others, rather than viewing oneself as a passive pawn of situational influences).

4.8   Mischel and Shoda's "cognitive-affective personality system"

The two most recent book-length responses to the situationist challenge are Daniel Russell's (2009, pp. 260–62, 323–31) *Practical Intelligence and the Virtues* and Nancy Snow's (2009, pp. 19–31) *Virtue as Social Intelligence*. They contend that the cognitive-affective personality system (CAPS) model of personality developed by Walter Mischel and Yuichi Shoda (1995) is both empirically adequate, in the sense that it demonstrates the dominant role of personality in driving behavior, and normatively adequate, in the sense of being consilient with the hard core of virtue ethics. There are grounds for concern, however, on both fronts, which seem to arise from Snow and Russell's misunderstanding of the CAPS model.

On the empirical side, both Snow and Russell seem to think that CAPS traits, unlike ordinary dispositions, explain and predict most of the variance in people's behavior. Recall that all of the worry generated so far about traditional traits was due to the fact that they tend to explain, at most, 10 percent of the variance in people's behavior. For CAPS traits to be an improvement on ordinary traits, they should explain a lot more than that. When we turn to Mischel and Shoda's research, however, what we find are correlations such as 0.47 for verbal aggression, 0.41 for compliance, 0.28 for whining, and 0.19 for pro-social talk (p. 250), which means that they explain at most 20 percent of the variance in behavior. These results are perhaps a slight improvement, but only slight. This is not in any way an embarrassment for Mischel and Shoda, of course, as they contend that the CAPS model supports the view that behavior is attributable in part to personality, in part to situation, and in part to the interaction of the two. At best, the CAPS view is one more reason to opt for an interactionist picture of human agency, not a personalist one.

Furthermore, even if the above argument is unconvincing, there is little reason to "understand traditional virtues as a subset of CAPS traits" (Snow 2009, p. 31). This is because CAPS traits are individuated internally. For example, someone would count as having CAPS-compassion if he were reliably disposed to want to help, deliberated well about how to help, and acted successfully on the basis of that deliberation *whenever he thought someone needed or deserved help.* Someone would count as having *CAPS-courage* if they were reliably disposed to want to overcome, deliberated well about how to overcome, and acted on the basis of his deliberation about *perceived* threats. But of course compassion isn't (just) a matter of helping when you *feel* that someone needs or deserves help; it's a matter of helping when someone *does* need or deserve help. And courage isn't (just) a matter of responding to *perceived* threats; it's a matter of responding to *actual* threats. This is the same point I made above in responding to the charge of behaviorism. Virtues as traditionally conceived include a sensitivity to reasons. CAPS traits don't.

5   TOWARDS AN IRENIC INTERACTIONISM

Suppose one has taken the situationist critique to heart, has largely given up on acquiring global high-fidelity virtues, holds out hope of acquiring global low-fidelity virtues, and wishes to find a way to make the best of whatever local virtues one has. What practical strategies might one employ? In this section, I identify two strategies that can be used in tandem to co-opt the power of situations. The guiding insight behind both strategies is to simulate fully-fledged global virtues. The next chapter develops these strategies in greater detail.

5.1   *The portability of context*

One strategy involves the *portability of context*: seeking out situations conducive to one's particular situational susceptibilities. While Doris (2002, p. 147) is right that a romantic dinner with a flirtatious colleague while one's spouse is out of town is an easy sort of temptation to recognize and avoid, what is to be said about situational influences that are not temptations or counterincentives, such as ambient sounds, ambient smells, all-too-mercurial moods, and ever-changing social distance? Should jackhammers be banned? Should people always wear perfume? Should we all take mood-enhancing drugs? Should people make sure always to look one another in the eye? The question is whether (or to what extent) a person can carry her preferred context with her (and to what extent social networks, institutions, and governments may enable and even participate in this process).

Maria Merritt's (2000) theory of the "sustaining social contribution to character" can be read as an implicit endorsement of the portability of context. While her aim is to develop a Humean rather than a neo-Aristotelian theory of virtue, one could reinterpret her argument as saying that people may behave as if they possessed global virtues not because they actually do possess the traits but because they find themselves in virtue-eliciting situations only when they are also in appropriate contexts. For example, she argues that, rather than trying in vain to galvanize your character against all temptations great and small, "a more sensible [project] would be the exercise of care in your choice of [social situations]" (p. 378). The primary difficulty with this theory is that character is not sustained solely through the social contribution; non-social situational factors such as mood elevators and depressors also affect virtue-relevant behavior. Thus, her theory should be considered an essential proper part of a complete response to the situationist challenge.

One pragmatic use of research in social psychology, then, is the identification of such contexts. We may dream, for instance, that some day people will be able to take a virtue-battery, which would say which local traits they have. With this knowledge, they could then plot out a life trajectory that (so far as possible) avoided situations uncongenial to their trait signature. They could carry their preferred contexts with them – making use of the portability of context. Sadly, the current state of psychology is nowhere near realizing this dream. In the meantime, we may want to investigate other ways to encourage action, thought, and feeling in accordance with virtue.

5.2   Situation-consumerism versus situation-producerism

A more active strategy for dealing with the power of situational influences involves the distinction between *situation-consumerism* and *situation-producerism*. The portability response treats situations like restaurants. If Burger King is conducive to health, visit Burger King. If Taco Bell is not conducive to health, avoid Taco Bell. If situation S_1 is conducive to virtue, seek situation S_1. If situation S_2 is not conducive to virtue, avoid situation S_2.

If we think of ourselves not only as situation-consumers but also as situation-producers, the power of situational influences becomes a tool rather than a threat. To continue the health analogy, another way to approach nutrition is to make your own meals. In the same way, rather than simply seeking and avoiding situations based on their virtue-conducive properties, we may take a more active role and create (both for ourselves and for others) situations with an eye to their virtue-conduciveness.

Hagop Sarkissian (2010) seems to have this idea in mind when he argues that "minor tweaks" in someone's comportment may lead to "major payoffs" both for her and her community. This is a promising line of argument, but Sarkissian's development of it leaves much to be desired. Though he is doubtless right that "not only do situations affect our own behavior, but we too return the favor," he provides no warrant for the further, blithely optimistic, claim that "we influence the situations we find ourselves in *as much as* they influence us" (emphasis mine). The fact that there is a two-way street running between situations and persons does not entail that the traffic is equal in both directions. My own view, as I explained in section 4.7 of this chapter, is that situations are more influential than traits, but not overwhelmingly so. Sarkissian also asserts that one particular Confucian virtue (*de*, or moral charisma) enables its possessors "to control situational contexts and influence others through non-coercive means." That may be, but of course like any other global trait, *de* may not be common or even commonly acquirable. Answering the situationist challenge to virtue ethics by baldly asserting the existence of a virtue that gives one power over situations is clearly question-begging.

Instead of trying to instill the mythological virtue of *de* in ourselves, I suggest that we attempt to design our environments in such a way as to encourage action, thought, and feeling in accordance with virtue. Karl Marx famously said, "Philosophers have hitherto only interpreted the world in various ways; the point is to change it" (1845/1998). Echoing that sentiment, I conclude with a maxim of moral technology: situationists and defenders of virtue ethics have hitherto only interpreted situations in various ways; the point is to change them.

CHAPTER 4

Factitious moral virtue

[O]ne man is king only because other men stand in the relation of subjects to him. They, on the contrary, imagine that they are subjects because he is king.

Karl Marx, *Capital: Critique of Political Economy*, volume 1, p. 23, fn. 22. Translated by Samuel Moore and Edward Aveling. Edited by Frederick Engels. Written 1867, translated 1887.

I INTRODUCTION

According to the situationist critique, which I have tried to rearticulate and expand in the preceding chapters, high-fidelity virtues such as temperance, loyalty, and honesty are exceedingly rare, and even low-fidelity virtues such as generosity, grit, and friendliness are quite uncommon. Appeal to these traits underwrites neither the explanation nor the prediction of conduct in a wide variety of contexts. Since virtue ethics presupposes the explanatory and predictive power of the virtues, it rests on a foundation of sand. Let us grant for the sake of argument that the critique succeeds, that virtue ethics is descriptively inadequate, that not enough people do or could possess the sorts of traits virtue ethicists care about. It might seem that the appropriate response would be to reject virtue ethics, perhaps reverting to a theory framed in terms of virtuous acts rather than traits or mere action in accordance with virtue rather than action from virtue. Both of these responses would result in a termination of the attribution of virtues to agents.

In this chapter, I argue that virtue (though not vice) attributions of the right sort are permissible even in the absence of what would ordinarily be considered sufficient evidence. Drawing on empirical studies in social psychology and behavioral economics, I show that the plausible, public attribution of virtuous traits induces in the target of the attribution both identification with those traits and a belief that others expect him to act in trait-consonant ways, which in turn leads to trait-consonant conduct. Trait attributions of the right sort function as self-fulfilling prophecies. When the trait in question is a virtue, what results is *factitious virtue*. This argument is especially attractive as a response to situationism, but it should be of interest even if you remain unconvinced of the validity of the situationist challenge.

In section 2, I discuss the phenomena of placebo effects and self-fulfilling prophecies as instructive parallels to virtue-labeling. The beliefs involved in placebo effects and the announcements involved in self-fulfilling prophecies turn out to be true (or near enough). Nevertheless, an aura of perversity surrounds these beliefs and announcements, whose contents are true because they are believed, not believed because they are true. When the placebo effect occurs, fact tracks belief, rather than belief tracking fact. When self-fulfilling prophecies occur, fact tracks announcement, rather than announcement tracking fact. By inverting the direction-of-fit characteristic of belief and assertion, these phenomena arrive at truth in a roundabout way.

Next, in section 3, I argue that judging the permissibility of an attribution solely in light of the evidence one has before the attribution is too limited. We must recognize that in some cases, the fact that a trait has been publicly attributed is causally implicated in whether that attribution turns out true. Like the beliefs involved in placebo effects and self-fulfilling prophecies, those involved in virtue attributions are true (or near enough) because believed, rather than believed because true. When factitious virtue arises, fact tracks attribution, rather than conversely. Though such attributions seem to violate the epistemic norm of saying only what one has evidence for, they may in fact be epistemically permissible. In section 4, I respond to several potential objections, and in section 5, I speculate about the psychology, semantics, pragmatics, and social ontology of factitious virtue.

2 PLACEBO EFFECTS AND SELF-FULFILLING PROPHECIES

A primary norm of both belief and assertion is sufficient evidence.[1] One should believe that *p* only if one has sufficient evidence for *p*. One should say that *p* only if one has sufficient evidence for *p*. On the face of it, there are only two ways for beliefs and assertions to relate to the evidence norm.

---

[1] The original statement of this evidentialist view is Clifford (1877/1999): "It is wrong always, everywhere, and for anyone to believe anything on insufficient evidence."

They can enjoy sufficient evidence and hence satisfy it, or they can fail to enjoy sufficient evidence and hence violate it. To go beyond one's evidence is to display a lack of intellectual sobriety or conscientiousness. This section introduces a third category: the *factitious*. When we believe that people have traits and publicly announce that belief, we sometimes cause them to acquire or simulate those very traits. Thus, even though we may not have had evidence for the belief or attribution before the announcement, the announcement itself is causally implicated in the (near enough) truth of its own content. Factitious attributions seem to violate the evidence norm, but, by causing themselves to be true, they also seem to conform to it. Despite appearances, factitious virtue attributions may in fact be epistemically permissible.

2.1   *Placebo effects*

One of the things that makes the placebo effect so intriguing is that it seems to involve a paradox of self-reference. Although the exact mechanism of the phenomenon is not well understood and is probably not univocal (Brody 2000), what seems to happen when the placebo effect occurs is that someone's beliefs or expectations about herself come true, in part because she has those beliefs and expectations. Franklin Miller (2005) argues for thinking of the placebo effect as a kind of faith healing, where 'faith' is understood secularly to refer to "belief under circumstances in which we lack adequate evidence to validate the truth of what we believe" (p. 274). Thus, the beliefs involved in the placebo effect seem to violate the evidence norm initially, yet satisfy it in the end.

I think that a majority of placebo phenomena are best characterized as a belief about oneself being a partial cause of its content's truth. In their discussion of the placebo effect Daniel Moerman, an anthropologist, and Wayne Jonas, a medical doctor, argue that because placebos are by definition causally inert, it is best to understand the placebo effect in terms of the placebo's meaning to the treated individual. "Ironically," they point out, although placebos "cannot do anything themselves, their meaning can" (2002, p. 472). For example, someone believes at t_1 that the pill she's just taken will relieve her pain, and at t_2 her pain is in fact relieved, due at least in part to her forming that very belief.

The opposite phenomenon, when someone's negative expectations lead to their own truth, is called the *nocebo* effect, and it has been implicated in a host of symptoms. David Phillips, Todd Ruth, and Lisa Wagner (1993) found, for example, that Chinese-Americans with inauspicious birth years in the Chinese astrological calendar die on average one to five years earlier than otherwise comparable individuals, and that the strength of their belief in astrology is positively correlated with morbidity. Also in this vein, simply telling men that the treatment they're undergoing may lead to adverse sexual effects has been shown to lead to a roughly 200 percent increase in erectile dysfunction (Mondaini et al. 2007). What we believe and expect of ourselves often comes true, both for good and for ill.

Such beliefs typically do not arise spontaneously; people arrive at them through reasoning. The ordinary subject of the placebo or nocebo effect doesn't arbitrarily decide that she will be cured or that that she will experience adverse side-effects. A famous surgeon slices a chunk out of her. Or a cutting-edge radiologist zaps her with gamma rays. Or a faith healer like John of God prays over her. And on the basis of this intervention, she concludes that she will recover. We can rationally reconstruct the phenomenon by supposing that she argues to herself as follows:

(P1) If John of God prays over me, I will recover.
(P2) John of God prays over me.
(C1) Hence, I will recover.

She may actually reason to herself in this way, though in all likelihood most cases of placebo effect do not involve explicit reasoning of this sort. In any event, this reconstructed argument is valid, and – if the placebo effect occurs – it has a true conclusion. Yet we are justly skeptical of (P1). Formulated as a material conditional, it might be true but uninteresting. (After all, it would then be true if he didn't pray over her.) Formulated as a subjunctive conditional (If the faith healer *were to* pray over me, I *would* recover), it suggests that the faith healer possesses causal power over her health merely in virtue of his praying – a contentious thought at best.

Nevertheless, by believing that the faith healer has such power and that he will cure her, she abets her own recovery. The beliefs involved in placebo effects seem to satisfy the evidence norm in a perverse way. They are not believed because they are true, but true because they are believed. As William James (1896/1979, p. 25) puts it in his response to Clifford, "faith in a fact can help create the fact."

2.2 *Self-fulfilling prophecies*

Self-fulfilling prophecies, like the beliefs involved in placebo effects, initially seem to violate the evidence norm, but satisfy it in the end. They introduce a further element, however: public announcement. Recent work in formal epistemology has shown just how powerful such announcements can be in creating common knowledge (Chwe 2001) and common belief (Ditmarsch, Eijck, and Verbrugge 2009), determining which of several game-theoretic equilibria is played (Aumann and Brandenburger 1995), and generating further knowledge (Plaza 2007).

Most logics of public announcement deal only with truthful, or even knowledge-grounded, announcements. A self-fulfilling prophecy, however, is neither of these. Were United States Federal Reserve Chairman Ben Bernanke to announce (arbitrarily, without any evidence) at a press conference on Sunday evening that the stock market would collapse the next day, people would react by selling their portfolios, leading indeed to a stock market crash.[2]

The explanation of a self-fulfilling prophecy of this sort resembles the explanation of the patient's mysterious recovery from illness. Bernanke appears as a harbinger of doom on Sunday night, and people reason to themselves as follows:

(P3) If Bernanke says there will be a crash tomorrow, then there will be a crash tomorrow.

(P4) If there will be a crash tomorrow, I should sell my portfolio right away.

(P5) Bernanke says there will be a crash tomorrow.

(C2) Hence, I should sell my portfolio right away.

Then, when a sufficient proportion of people act on the basis of the conclusion of this train of thought, they cause the market to crash. As before, I won't insist here that people would actually deliberate explicitly in this way; the reconstructed argument is meant to clarify what they would say their inferential process had been if they were sufficiently clear about it.

The importance of the announcement to this sequence of events is paramount: only by seeing to it that everyone had reason to think that he expected the market to crash, and everyone knew that everyone had reason to think that he expected the market to crash, and everyone knew that everyone knew that everyone had reason to think that he expected the market to crash, and so on, could Bernanke cause his announcement to turn out true in the end. Indeed, many or even all of the actors in this

---

[2] This sort of analysis of bank runs was first proposed by Robert Merton, who also coined the term 'self-fulfilling prophecy'. In his words, "The self-fulfilling prophecy is, in the beginning, a *false* definition of the situation evoking a new behavior which makes the originally false conception come *true*" (1948, p. 195).

financial drama might think that Bernanke was lying through his teeth, but if most of them expect a sufficient number of the others to believe the announcement, then it still makes sense for them to sell their portfolios. They could reason to themselves as follows:

(P6) If Bernanke says there will be a crash tomorrow, then everyone else will believe there will be a crash tomorrow.

(P7) If everyone else believes there will be a crash tomorrow, they will sell their portfolios.

(P8) If everyone else sells their portfolios, there will be a crash tomorrow.

(P9) If there will be a crash tomorrow, I should sell my portfolio right away.

(P5) Bernanke says there will be a crash tomorrow.

(C2) Hence, I should sell my portfolio right away.

If Bernanke just silently thought to himself, "The market will crash tomorrow," nothing would come of it. If he were to whisper it to just one person, nothing would come of it. Indeed, were he to whisper it to every stockholder individually (creating one level of mutual knowledge but not common knowledge), a crash would be unlikely. Only by making the announcement publicly would he generate the common expectations necessary to produce such panic.

This picture may still be overly simplified. A more nuanced reconstruction would be obtained if we assume there are four types of people: (A) those who take the Federal chairman at his word, (B) those who think there are too many people of type A, (C) those who think there are too many people of types A and B, and (D) those who do not believe him and do not think others will.[3] If there are enough people of types A, B, and C, there will be a crash. Those of type A sell because they believe Bernanke. Those of type B sell because they believe that those of type A will sell. Their belief must be general *in sensu composito* (it is believed of the class, not necessarily of any individuals in the class) as opposed to general *in sensu diviso* (believed of each individual in the class, not necessarily about the class as such). They needn't have *de re* beliefs about each of the other investors; instead, they need to have a belief about the other investors as a group. Those of type C sell because they believe (generally *in sensu composito*) that those of types A and B will sell; they do this even if there

---

[3] We could continue up the levels of pessimists indefinitely, though to posit such individuals would perhaps be too precious. The point should be clear without adding further levels.

are no people of types A or B. Those of type D are left with worthless portfolios.[4]

The differences and similarities between the beliefs involved in placebo effects and those involved in self-fulfilling prophecies bear emphasis. Placebo effects do not depend upon public announcements; self-fulfilling prophecies typically do. Placebo effects essentially involve beliefs about oneself; self-fulfilling prophecies do not. Nevertheless, the perversity of self-fulfilling prophecies parallels that of the beliefs involved in placebos: they are true because they are announced, not announced because they are true.

3 FACTITIOUS VIRTUE

It's natural to assume that if one has sufficient evidence for attributing a virtue prior to the attribution, one continues to have sufficient evidence after, and if one has insufficient evidence for attributing a virtue prior to the attribution, one continues to have insufficient evidence after. This section argues that a third possibility must be recognized: attributions that constitute evidence for themselves because they cause factitious virtue. In such cases, even if one had insufficient evidence for attributing a virtue prior to the attribution, one could end up with sufficient evidence afterwards. The expectations engendered by the attribution induce virtue-like conduct; they induce *factitious virtue*. Like placebo effects, factitious virtue depends on beliefs about oneself; like self-fulfilling prophecies, factitious attributions are causally implicated in their own (near enough) truth; like both, factitious virtue inverts the direction-of-fit characteristic of belief and assertion.

3.1 Labeling and self-concept

In a seminal study, Richard Miller, Philip Brickman, and Diana Bolen (1975) compared the effects of labeling with those of moral exhortation on the behavior of fifth graders.[5] Participants in the exhortation group

---

[4] See Keynes's famous discussion of the beauty contest in *General Theory of Employment, Interest, and Money* (2009, p. 130).

[5] For more labeling studies, see also Albarracín and McNatt (2005), Burger and Caldwell (2003), Ouellette and Wood (1998), Strenta and DeJong (1981), Tybout and Yalch (1980), and Vaidyanathan and Praveen (2005). To my knowledge, the only philosopher to cite this study in relation to the situationist challenge is Jesse Prinz (2009). His treatment is quite different from mine, as I discuss below.

were asked repeatedly by the principal, the teachers, and the janitor to keep their classroom tidy. The labeling group, by contrast, heard congratulatory (false) announcements of their above-average tidiness over the course of eight days. On Day 1, the teacher praised them for being "ecology minded" and mentioned that the janitor had commented that theirs was one of the cleanest classrooms in the school. On Day 2, the teacher noticed some litter on the floor but explained, "our class is clean and would not do that." On Day 4, the principal visited the class and commended their orderliness; after he left, the students actually complained that the *teacher's* desk was not as neat as theirs. On Day 8, the janitors washed the room and left a note thanking the students for making their job so easy.

After a brief improvement in their behavior, the exhortation group settled back into its old routine, but the labeling group exhibited higher levels of tidiness over an extended period.[6]

The experimenters' explanation of this labeling effect appeals to the notion of self-concept: the settled beliefs one has about one's own personality traits. People enjoy acting in accordance with their self-concepts, even those aspects of self-concept that are evaluatively neutral; they're averse to acting contrary to their self-concepts, especially the evaluatively positive aspects of their self-concepts. According to this explanation, the fifth graders who were labeled as tidy incorporated that claim into their self-concept, then acted accordingly. We can reconstruct their reasoning as follows:

(P10) If the teacher says I am tidy, then I am tidy.

(P11) If I am tidy, then I should act tidily.

(P12) The teacher says I am tidy.

(C3) Hence, I should act tidily.

I certainly don't want to claim that the subjects in this study always explicitly reasoned or deliberated in this way. Self-concept needn't be easily introspected, and the deliverances of introspection may diverge systematically from the actual content of self-concept. I nevertheless think that a reconstruction like this may help to clarify the phenomenon. As in the case of the self-fulfilling prophecy of financial panic, what was announced

---

[6] The failure of exhortation to produce tidy behavior may also be explained in terms of labeling. There seems to be an implicature connecting present-tense normative statements and present-tense negative statements. Uttering statements of the form "*x* should be *F*," implicates statements of the form "*x* is not *F*". Thus, when the fifth graders were told that they should be tidy, it was implicated that they were not tidy, and they may have taken the negative label to heart.

was not true until it was announced. In fact, in this case, the attribution of tidiness (where tidiness is understood as a reasons-responsive, counterfactual-supporting trait) probably doesn't quite become true, but something very closely related does: that the students reliably act tidily for an extended period. Most behavioral predictions one might make on the basis of the trait, however, would be true.

The students act tidily even though they do not possess the reasons-responsive, counterfactual-supporting trait of tidiness. Their false belief in their own traits corresponds to the placebo patient's false belief in the faith healer's otherworldly power and the shareholders' belief in Bernanke's predictive power. Their tidy behavior corresponds to the patient's recovery and the market crash. Virtue-labeling causes *factitious virtue*, in which people behave in accordance with virtue not because they possess the trait in question but because that trait has been attributed to them.

Other experiments have corroborated the tidiness study with other trait attributions. Jensen and Moore (1977), for instance, found that children labeled as charitable donated more than those who were subjected to moral suasion. Grusec, Kuczynski, Rushton, and Simutis (1978) announced to experimental participants that a questionnaire they had completed indicated either that they were competitive or that they were cooperative, inducing congruent behavior in a subsequent game. Grusec and Redler (1980; see also Mills and Grusec 1989) found that ten-year-olds who helped once and were then labeled ("You know, you certainly are a nice person. I bet you're someone who is helpful whenever possible.") contributed 350 percent more in a subsequent trial than students whose actions were praised after helping ("You know, that was certainly a nice thing to do. It was good that you helped me with my work here today."). Labeling here produced a much stronger effect than mere praise and positive reinforcement, an important point in favor of attributing virtues to people rather than simply encouraging them or praising their behavior.

The above studies were conducted on children, but similar results hold for adults. In fact, the labeling effect seems to be a function of age: older children are more susceptible to it (Grusec and Redler 1980). Allen (1982) showed that labeling a whole population in a television advertisement ("American consumers are willing participants in solving the energy problem.") increased their intention to conserve. More recently, Gert Cornelissen et al. (2006) showed that labeling adults as eco-friendly proved more successful in inducing cooperative environmental activity than providing them with information about the environmental effects of their behavior. In another study, Cornelissen et al. (2007) found that labeling even led participants to reinterpret their past behavior as springing from the trait.[7]

Labeling is a complicated phenomenon, however; calling someone virtuous by no means guarantees factitious virtue. Here it becomes necessary to refine the claim about factitious virtue, which is best induced by *plausible, public* announcements to an audience that has a *correct conception* of what is entailed by the virtue in question.

3.2   *The plausibility condition*

Labeling someone virtuous can lead her to become virtuous, but only when certain conditions are met. A doctor who predicts pain relief without making at least a sham intervention would have a hard time generating a placebo effect. Someone who publicly announced something completely implausible would find it difficult to generate a self-fulfilling prophecy. In the same way, labeling someone with a virtue when one has no evidence for the attribution is a recipe for failure. Intuitively, the announcement must be plausible for the agent to take it seriously. Telling Ebenezer Scrooge that he is generous would provoke a scoff, not a donation. Calling Shylock lenient would not compel him to forgive Antonio's debt.

Research in the social sciences bears out this intuition. Labeling has been shown to be most effective when it comes directly on the heels of trait-consonant behavior. Kraut (1973; see also Scott and Yalch 1980 and Cornelissen et al. 2007), for instance, found that individuals who were labeled generous immediately after donating to a charity were more likely to donate to another charity two weeks later. Furthermore, trait labeling is especially effective when the label is consistent with the target's initial self-concept; it seems to bolster the relevant portions of self-concept (Cornelissen et al. 2007). Tybout and Yalch (1980) showed that people who viewed themselves as political were especially responsive to labeling related to their voting habits. Also along these lines, Henderlong and Lepper (2002) found that virtue-labeling works best when it is perceived as sincere and when it attributes performance to controllable causes.

The plausibility of an attribution has several sources. The structure of such an attribution is a triadic relation among an attributor, a target, and a predicate. The attribution gains in plausibility if the target already

[7] For more corroborating studies, see Albarracín and McNatt (2005), Burger and Caldwell (2003), Ouellette and Wood (1998), Tybout and Yalch (1980), Vaidyanathan and Praveen (2005).

agrees that the predicate applies, or at least does not disagree. It gains in plausibility if the attributor can point to evidence that it applies. It gains further if the attributor is an authority of some kind, whether an epistemic authority (he tends to know about such things), a moral authority (he understands what's good, right, and virtuous), or a political or bureaucratic authority (his judgments carry consequences even when he's wrong). An ideal case of factitious virtue would presumably draw on the moral and epistemic authority of a respected attributor.

3.3   *The publicity condition*

For quite different reasons, the most effective virtue-labeling is public. Tacitly thinking of someone as courageous will have no effect on her conduct. But calling her courageous in front of a crowd could put into her the very mettle being attributed. There are several reasons for this.

First, publicly labeling someone prompts her to believe in the attribution, thus triggering a placebo-like effect through the mechanism of self-concept. When sick people are prayed for with their knowledge, they often do experience better outcomes. However, in every controlled, double-blinded study of the efficacy of prayer conducted to date, no main effect was found.[8] The same presumably applies in the case of factitious virtue. When someone is tacitly thought of as virtuous from afar, the mechanisms of self-concept and social expectation do not kick in. If, however, the target of the attribution *knows* that she's been labeled, those mechanisms may be triggered.

Second, publicly labeling someone leads the audience of the announcement to expect her to act as advertised. And, by serving as a basis for common knowledge of this expectation, it leads her to know that they expect her to behave appropriately, to know that they know that she knows that they expect her to behave appropriately, to know that they know that she knows that they know that she knows that they expect her to behave appropriately, and so on. Just as people enjoy acting in accordance with their self-concepts and are averse to violating them, so they often enjoy doing what others expect of them and are averse to letting others down. If a person is not unconditionally virtuous but prefers to act in accordance with a virtue provided others expect her to do so, then publicly labeling her with that virtue will tend to generate a self-fulfilling prophecy. Cristina Bicchieri (2006) has argued persuasively that many people fit

---

[8] Aviles et al. (2001), Benson et al. (2006), and Krucoff et al. (2005).

the description of what she calls a *conditional norm follower* – a person who prefers to comply with a norm provided a sufficient number of others comply, and that they expect him to comply in turn (even when it hurts him materially). If someone is a conditional norm follower of this sort, announcing his virtue will tend to lead him to act in accordance with it.

3.4 The correct conception condition

If you tell someone that he's *F*, but he doesn't understand what the predicate refers to, then of course it's unlikely that he'll somehow become *F*. Less abstractly, if you label someone with a virtue, but he doesn't understand what it means to possess or act in accordance with that virtue, then of course it's unlikely that you'll somehow produce factitious virtue. Less abstractly still, if you call someone honest, he will only begin to conduct himself honestly if he understands what honesty entails.

For virtue-labeling to have the desired effect, the labeled person – along with the rest of the audience – must have a roughly correct conception of the virtue. Labeling as reasonable a person with a history of unreasonable behavior who believed in his own reasonableness presumably would induce no change in his behavior. Calling a conspiracy theorist like Glenn Beck reasonable would only confirm his paranoid fantasies. It might even reinforce his unreasonable behavior. The labeled agent and the rest of the audience must understand what is being attributed to him so that he knows what will be expected of him.[9]

Since virtue concepts are quite complicated, involving sensitivity to reasons, dispositions to construe appropriately, motivations, deliberative capacities, and behavioral patterns, the target's conception of the virtue may be nil, partial, or comprehensive. The extent to which he understands the concept may in turn give shape to his manifestation of factitious virtue.[10] For simplicity's sake, let's suppose that there are three progressively more substantive levels of understanding a virtue. Someone might have a *purely behavioral* conception of virtue as a pattern of characteristic actions and avoidances. For example, someone might think of honesty as the tendency not to lie, cheat, or steal. Were this person to be labeled honest, his factitious virtue would probably be rather thin: he would act in certain ways, but his underlying motives, beliefs, and sensitivities would remain unchanged. Someone else, with a *behavioral and motivational*

---

[9] Thanks to Brian Robinson for emphasizing this point to me.
[10] Thanks to Robert Roberts for emphasizing this point to me.

conception of honesty, would be differently affected. Not only would she refrain from lying, cheating, and stealing, but she might perhaps also begin to value truth for its own sake and to want to treat others with dignity in truth-related matters. Finally, the target of the attribution could have a more or less complete understanding of honesty, thinking of it in *behavioral, motivational,* and *cognitive* terms. Were she to be successfully induced to factitious honesty, she might (in addition to behaving honestly and loving the truth for its own sake) acquire a sensitivity to honesty-relevant reasons and a disposition to construe honesty-relevant circumstances well. As I explained in Chapter 2 while rearticulating the situationist challenge, one of the chief ways in which situational factors modulate conduct and prevent virtuous behavior is by causing people to fail to attend to morally relevant cues. To the extent that labeling someone with a full-fledged conception of virtue makes her more attentive to such cues – a point about which we can speculate but about which little evidence exists – her susceptibility to such situational interferences will diminish.

If this perspective is sound, then it presumably applies not only to honesty but to all or at least most other virtues. The factitious chastity of someone who understood the virtue as a purely behavioral disposition would be merely a matter of avoiding illicit sexual encounters. The factitious chastity of someone who thought of the virtue as both motivational and behavioral would add into the bargain a desire to maintain his own body and self-respect. The factitious chastity of someone who understood the virtue in behavioral, motivational, and cognitive terms would involve a sensitivity to reasons and a disposition to construe chastity-relevant circumstances well.

This suggests that the ideal case of factitious virtue may, in the long term, bleed into outright virtue, a point about which I speculate further below. It also indicates that one of the preconditions for successful virtue-labeling is education in the conceptual analysis of moral vocabulary. The more adequate someone's conceptualization of a virtue, the more easily he will acquire the factitious counterpart of that virtue – a point that should comfort philosophers.

3.5   *The inadvisability of vice-labeling*

I've argued that virtue-labeling cultivates ethically good conduct, making it morally advisable and epistemically permissible. There's good reason to call someone virtuous, even if the evidence one has might seem inadequate. What about calling someone vicious? Would that too lead to a self-fulfilling prophecy, or might it instead lead to a self-refuting prophecy?[11]

If the foregoing arguments are on the right track, attributing vice is inadvisable. Virtue-labeling leads someone to view herself as virtuous and believe that others expect her to act virtuously, which leads her to want to act in accordance with virtue. If the same mechanism applies, then vice-labeling would lead someone to believe in her own viciousness and in others' expectation that she will act viciously, thereby leading her to want to act in accordance with vice. One might conjecture, however, that people would be less inclined to update their self-concepts in the direction of vice than in the direction of virtue. A huge majority of people think of themselves as closer to virtue than to vice (Taylor and Brown 1988). At the very least, this suggests that meeting the plausibility condition for vice attributions will be harder than meeting the plausibility condition for virtue attributions. But that would merely show that vice attributions will be less likely to lead to self-fulfilling prophecies than virtue attributions, not that vice attributions will lead to self-*refuting* prophecies.

Unfortunately, few direct studies of negative labeling have been conducted. One of the few was a field experiment by Robert Kraut (1973). Experimenters went door-to-door asking for donations. In half the cases, they applied a trait label to the potential donor ('charitable' if she gave money, 'uncharitable' if she refused); in the other half, no label was applied. Later, a second experimenter knocked on the same doors, raising money for a different cause. Labeled individuals responded in accordance with the first experimenter's attributions. Those who had been called charitable gave more than others who had previously given but went unlabeled; likewise, those who had been called uncharitable gave less than others who had previously refused but went unlabeled. This isn't a particularly strong evidential base, but it inclines me to be wary of attributing vice.

An empirical prediction of my view is that further such studies would show that plausibly and publicly calling someone (and not just someone's action) vicious would induce conduct in accordance with vice. Indirect support for this view of vice-labeling derives from two sources: the sociology of deviance, and the psychology of stereotypes.

One popular model of deviance in sociology and criminology distinguishes two stages (Lemert 1972; Dotter and Roebuck 1988). Primary deviance is commonplace; it's a matter merely of breaking social, moral, or

---

[11] Thanks to Jonathan Webber and Brian Robinson for raising this question.

legal rules. When someone is called out for primary deviance, he is labeled as a rule-breaker. This labeling can be formal (stop-and-frisk, unfriendly monitoring by social services agents, even incarceration by the police) or informal (parental or peer attribution). If the combination of formal and informal labeling succeeds in changing the target's self-concept, he progresses to the stage of secondary deviance, where the label is accepted and the labelers resented. Although the theory of primary and secondary deviance has come in for criticism, recent meta-analyses continue to support many of its main theses (Adams et al. 2003).

Secondary deviance can be seen as a kind of factitious vice which draws on institutional sanctions in addition to the more informal attributions I've described so far. Further evidence for the reality of factitious vice comes from investigations of the power of stereotypes to influence the conduct of the targets of those stereotypes. Walton and Spencer (2009), for instance, found that students belonging to groups stereotypically considered less intelligent performed worse on standardized tests when they were reminded of their group identity. Also along these lines, Hebl et al. (2002) found that job interviewers displayed more bias towards candidates they'd been led to believe were gay, which in turn caused the interviews to go less smoothly, which in turn influenced their hiring preferences.

3.6   Interpersonal forces in labeling

The explanation of the virtue-labeling effect in terms of self-concept is on the right track but incomplete because it fails to account for the interpersonal forces at work in the production of labeling effects. In the tidiness study, praise was offered publicly. Each child was told that he was tidy, but was also present while the others were told that they were tidy. Presumably this led them to acquire beliefs about one another, in addition to beliefs about themselves. If that's right, then each child was inclined to believe not only, "I am tidy," but also, "Everyone else is tidy and will act tidily." What's more, because the others were present when he was labeled, he had some evidence that they in turn expected him to be tidy. If he thought it through, he might arrive at the further belief, "Everyone else thinks I am tidy and expects me to act tidily." Indeed, continued reinforcement and sufficient reflection on the public announcement would lead the labeled students to develop common knowledge that everyone believed everyone else was tidy and would behave accordingly. The mutual nature of this social reinforcement will become important below, where I discuss the compatibility of virtue-labeling with situationism. Presently, however, there are two points to be made. The first is that self-concept alone may not be sufficient to induce factitious virtue. For a conditional norm follower, believing oneself virtuous is not as strong a spur to virtuous conduct as both believing oneself virtuous and knowing that others believe one to be virtuous.

The second, more important, point is that labeling an individual and labeling a group are crucially different. As I pointed out above, Bicchieri (2006) has argued persuasively that many people are *conditional norm followers*. The theory of conditional norm following indicates that plausibly, publicly labeling a whole group will induce more trait-consonant behavior than plausibly, publicly labeling each individual in the group. This is because simultaneous group labeling serves as a basis for common knowledge of the expectation for all to cooperate, and many people prefer to cooperate only on the condition that all (or a sufficient number) of the others cooperate and expect him to cooperate as well.

To see the difference between individual and group labeling, consider the two necessary conditions of being a conditional norm follower (expecting enough others to comply, and enough others expecting one to comply). In the individual case, plausible, public virtue-labeling tends to generate only one of these expectations. If someone is plausibly, publicly attributed the trait of charitableness, common belief may arise: everyone expects him to act accordingly, everyone knows that everyone expects him to act accordingly, everyone knows that everyone knows that everyone expects him to act accordingly, etc. However, he has no reason to expect others to act in accordance with the charity norm. In the group case, by contrast, plausible, public labeling tends to generate both of the necessary expectations: each member of the group has reason to expect the others to act charitably, and each has reason to believe that the others expect him to act charitably. If this is right, group labeling should induce more conformity to norms than individual labeling, though individual labeling in turn should induce more conformity than mere praise, exhortation, or non-intervention. Some indirect support for this hypothesis derives from the Miller, Brickman and Bolen (1975) tidiness study. During that experiment, the students were sometimes praised individually, and sometimes as a group. For instance, one of the interventions was to put up a poster of a Peanuts character that said, "We are Andersen's Litter-Conscious Class" (p. 431). Another involved the teacher commenting that "our class" was so much neater than the others (p. 431).

Even if locating the virtues internally, as counterfactual-supporting, reasons-responsive character traits, proves untenable, there are ways to salvage virtue theory. The time has come to investigate the interpersonal dynamics that enable and encourage virtuous conduct. One aspect of these dynamics is, I submit, virtue-labeling and its sustaining and bolstering effects on self-concept. Labeling shares with placebos the causal power of an agent's beliefs about herself over her fate and with self-fulfilling prophecies a reliance on public announcements.

4   REPLIES TO OBJECTIONS

"All that is well and good," responds an empirically minded critic, "but you have neglected two important things. First, research into moral credentialing shows that praising people for their morality actually leads to worse behavior, not better. Second, you claim that self-concepts have causal power, but one of the key insights of situationism is that situational variables are the primary drivers of behavior." In this section, I attempt to defuse these concerns. In addition, it might seem that even if I am right that virtue-labeling works, it should not be done. I am arguing for a sort of noble lie: people do not actually have the virtues, but we should tell them they do so that they behave themselves.

4.1   *Factitious virtue versus moral credentialing*

A recent spate of studies seems to militate against the theory of virtue-labeling. Monin and Miller (2001), for instance, found that supplying people with what they call moral credentials induced morally questionable behavior later on.[12] To understand why their results are consistent with the theory of factitious virtue, we must delve into the details of their study. In the first of two experiments, they prompted participants to agree or disagree with obviously sexist statements like "Most women are not really smart." The participants were then presented with a role-playing vignette, which asked them to decide whether a man or woman would be better suited to a sales job in the cement-manufacturing industry for which the primary task was to establish connections with foremen and building contractors. The moral credentialing effect reared its ugly head when participants who had previously disagreed with the obviously sexist statements (thereby establishing their credentials as non-sexist) said that the job would be better suited to men than women.

Monin and Miller's second experiment was similar, but involved racism rather than sexism. Each participant was given a chance to make

---

[12] Thanks to Joshua Knobe for pressing this point.

what could be construed as a non-racist choice, then was presented with a role-playing vignette. This time, the participant was to imagine that he was a police chief in a small rural area of the United States, that he knew the officers under his command were racist, and that he did not want to provoke the officers. In light of these constraints, would he hire a black officer? As in the first experiment, participants who had been given a chance to make what could be construed as an unprejudiced choice (and thus had established, at least in their own minds, their moral credentials) were less likely to say they would hire a black officer.

These results are cause for concern, but they are only indirectly relevant to factitious virtue. Although the manipulations in these experiments presumably affected self-concept, in neither was there a plausible, public attribution of virtue. Instead, participants were merely given a chance to make a choice that could be construed as moral, and it was on the basis of this choice that they acquired the 'moral credentials' that made them comfortable with their potentially prejudiced decisions. Such a choice may have had an effect on their self-concept, but it may not have influenced their beliefs about others' expectations of them. Plausible, public announcements do not merely influence self-concept; they ensure that everyone is on the same page by serving as a basis for common knowledge.

Another important difference between this study and the labeling studies I drew on earlier in this chapter is that participants in these experiments were asked to role-play; the questions were "What would you do if you were the manager of the cement manufacturing plant?" and "What would you do if you were the police chief?" Participants were asked to take on the perspective and even the motivations of another. By contrast, labeling studies measure decisions people make for themselves. Finally, given the stated goals attributed to their roles in these vignettes, participants who made the sexist or racist choice were arguably correct. After all, in the cement-manufacturing vignette, the primary hiring criterion was the ability to establish contacts with (presumably sexist) foremen and building contractors, and in the police vignette, participants were told, "you do not want to provoke any major unrest within the [explicitly racist] ranks" (Monin and Miller 2001, p. 37).[13]

Rather than showing that factitious virtue is chimerical, moral credentialing studies emphasize the boundary conditions of the power of

---

[13] Other moral credentialing studies also differ from labeling studies. In both Khan and Dhar (2006) and Sachdeva, Iliev, and Medin (2009), no plausible, public announcements were used.

self-concept and the importance of plausible, public announcements to ensuring factitious virtue. Labeling works not just through beliefs about oneself but through beliefs about what others expect from one. Self-concept is mediated by the sustaining social contribution to character.

4.2 *Self-concept and situationism: friends or foes?*

I have argued that the conjunction of self-concept and social expectation leads to cross-situationally consistent behavior. People labeled as tidy do what the tidy person does, while those labeled as charitable do what the charitable person does; labeling doesn't simply lead to all-around moral improvement, but specific moral improvement tied to the meaning of the label. In a way, then, we can predict and explain people's behavior by attributing virtues to them. This might seem to contradict my arguments in the previous chapters about the strength of the situationist challenge. Does self-concept answer the situationist challenge? Can personality traits be rehabilitated in the self-concept paradigm? I fear that the answer to both of these questions is "No."

There are three reasons for this negative response, two having to do with self-concept in general, one with the virtues in particular. First, because our self-concepts are so easily swayed by plausible, public announcements, they are personality variables only in an attenuated sense. They require frequent social reinforcement and maintenance, unlike traditional Aristotelian virtues. Someone who thinks of herself as competitive one moment or in one context may update that self-perception if a contrary trait is attributed to her. Factitious virtue may be cross-situationally consistent, but it inherits temporal instability from self-concept.

Second, understanding the difference between moral credentialing and virtue-labeling enables us to see why self-concept alone cannot simulate the virtues. Only self-concept working in tandem with the interpersonal forces that govern conditional norm following induces factitious virtuous conduct. This point is not unrelated to the Aristotelian truism that it's extremely difficult to be virtuous in a bad society.

Third, it is generally agreed that virtuous people do not tend to reason in terms of their own virtues ("Since I am honest…"), but in terms of the reasons to which virtues respond ("Since it would be a lie to say…"). To be generous is to have a complex disposition to *notice* when others are in need, to *construe* ambiguous social cues charitably, to *want* to help others whom one takes to be in need, to *deliberate* soundly about what would in fact help a given person in particular circumstances, and to *succeed* in helping when one tries. The generous person helps not because it makes her feel good (though ideally it does make her feel good as a side-effect) but because someone is in need. The deliberations of the generous person refer to need and help, not to the praise and admiration she will receive for helping the needy or to the expectations of her audience. Perhaps the most emphatic statement of this view is in Williams (1985, p. 11), which I quote at length:

> the virtue-term itself usually does not occur in the content of the [virtuous person's] deliberation. Someone who has a particular virtue does actions because they fall under certain descriptions and avoids others because they fall under other descriptions. That person is described in terms of the virtue, and so are his or her actions: thus he or she is a just or courageous person who does just or courageous things. But – and this is the point – it is rarely the case that the description that applies to the agent and to the action is the same as that in terms of which the agent chooses the action.

A pertinent illustration of this point is the joke about the rabbi who fell asleep on his deathbed. His students sat around the bed, lauding his many virtues. Eventually, he regained consciousness but pretended to sleep, listening with pleasure to their praise. During a lull in the conversation, he interjected, "And of my modesty you say nothing?"

Of course, it's consistent with most virtues to think one has them, and it may be inconsistent with most virtues (or at least a cause of cognitive dissonance) to think one does not have them. The point, though, is that, at least as I have defined it, someone with factitious virtue not only thinks that he has that virtue but is motivated in part by a desire to maintain his self-concept. In contrast with traditional virtues, self-concept-based factitious virtues essentially require appeal to one's own traits and the expectations of others. They thus simulate traditional virtues without actually being those virtues.[14]

4.3 Damning with feigned praise?

I began this chapter by saying that I would argue the virtues should be attributed to people even if one lacks what would ordinarily be considered

---

[14] It might seem that while the arguments in this section warrant the conclusion that factitious virtues are not virtues as such, they do not warrant the further conclusion that factitious virtues are global character traits of the sort Doris and Harman deny. As far as the dialectic about virtues is concerned, this concern is irrelevant. If there are non-virtue traits but no virtue traits, virtue ethics still has a problem. However, as I point out above, only self-concept working in tandem with the interpersonal forces that govern conditional norm following induces factious virtuous action, and these interpersonal forces are precisely what situationism says ordinary trait psychology ignores.

sufficient evidence for the attribution. Plausible, public virtue-labeling leads to factitious virtuous conduct even in people who do not possess the counterfactual-supporting, reasons-responsive traits presupposed by virtue ethics. If this is right, the resolution of the situationist challenge lies not in resisting it but in co-opting it. One might think, however, that my praise is so faint as to be damning. Should we, as I have argued, feign praise, intentionally lying to one another in order to trick ourselves into behaving well? Would not following this advice essentially involve the vices of dishonesty and manipulativeness?

One's answer to this question should intuitively match one's answers to parallel questions about placebo effects and self-fulfilling prophecies. There is something distinctly perverse about such phenomena. They invert the mind-to-world and word-to-world direction-of-fit characteristic of belief and assertion. Yet the beliefs involved in placebo effects and the announcements involved in self-fulfilling prophecies turn out to be true. Is this just the advantage of theft over honest toil?

In the same way, virtue-labeling inverts the word-to-world direction-of-fit characteristic of announcements, but those announcements are validated when they turn out to be true (or near enough). Is this good enough?

I would like to assuage the anxiety generated by the noble lie, and it seems to me that there are three things to be said in defense of factitious virtue in this context.

First, consider the question from the point of view of moral education and moral cultivation. From this perspective, one wants first and foremost to ensure that one's pupil becomes moral. Aristotle thought that people became courageous by acting courageously; I contend that they become courageous (or near enough) by being called courageous. Aristotle claimed that people become courteous by acting courteously; I contend that they become courteous (or near enough) by being called courteous. If this is on the right track, then to object to factitious virtue is to object to one of the most effective means of moral education and moral cultivation. Admittedly, the rider "or near enough" must be added here; as I have argued, factitious virtue isn't real virtue, at least not as traditionally conceived. But if it's the closest we can come to actual virtue, it would be strange indeed to pooh-pooh it. We may have to admit that a certain degree of (self-)deception and illusion are indispensable.

That said, over time, it might be possible to drop the "near enough" rider. It may be that, after sufficient habituation, people with merely factitious moral virtues reliant on self-concept and social expectation end up fully virtuous, unencumbered by these artificial supports. Unfortunately, social scientists have yet to investigate this question, so for now we must be content to speculate, as I do in the next section.

Second, if the noble lie is more than you can stomach, my arguments here still suggest certain reforms in how we attribute virtues and vices. I find it plausible to think that Clifford's principle never to believe except without sufficient evidence is susceptible to pragmatic intrusion: what counts as sufficient depends at least in part on the consequences likely to attend having and acting on the belief in question. If getting it wrong would lead to dire consequences, one had better acquire very good evidence indeed; if getting it wrong would lead to only trivially negative consequences, one is under less of an obligation.[15] And even if the evidence norm for *belief* doesn't allow for pragmatic intrusion, the evidence norm for *assertion* surely does. So even if it's permissible to go on believing that people aren't virtuous, it would be a mistake to say so. If attributions of virtues and vices tend to function as self-fulfilling prophecies, then the consequences of getting it wrong when it comes to virtues are much less dire than the consequences of getting it wrong when it comes to vices. Therefore, we should relax our standards of sufficient evidence for virtue but redouble our standards of sufficient evidence for vice. This, I think, is a point that even people who reject situationism should be willing to take on board. In fact, it's something that Aristotle himself seems to suggest in the *Rhetoric*, when he says,

We can always idealize any given man by drawing on the virtues akin to his actual qualities; thus we may say that the passionate and excitable man is frank; or that the arrogant man is superb or impressive. Those who run to extremes will be said to possess the corresponding good qualities: rashness will be called courage, and extravagance generosity. (1367a32–1367b7)

One rarely, if ever, has dispositive evidence of another person's trait signature. One simply has to guess. What I'm suggesting here is that the principle of charity be applied extremely aggressively to this guesswork.

Third, if the arguments I made in Chapter 2 were correct, we simply cannot help believing in traits. Factitious virtue is therefore a Strawsonian exoneration or exculpation of our inevitable practice of thinking and speaking in these terms. In "Freedom and Resentment," (1960) Peter Strawson famously argued that regardless of whether we in fact have free will, we can't help but think of ourselves and others as having it, and we

---

[15] For more on this and the related theory of epistemic contextualism, see DeRose (2005), Feltz and Zarpentine (2010), Hawthorne (2004), Montmarquet (2007), and Stanley (2005).

can't help but treating one another as if we had it. He hoped to exonerate or exculpate this practice of holding responsible. In a similar way, I would say that since we can't help believing that people have virtues, we shouldn't feel too bad about it because our thinking helps to make it so (or near enough). This is only a partial exoneration, however, because our thinking that people have vices actually leads them to act in accordance with vice.

5 SPECULATIVE CONJECTURES

In this chapter so far, I have attempted to argue that, even if the situationist challenge to virtue ethics succeeds, we have pragmatic reason to attribute virtues to people, and that these pragmatic reasons may even make the attributions epistemically permissible. In this concluding section, I turn to some speculative conjectures about the psychology, semantics, pragmatics, and social ontology of factitious virtue. So far, I have tried to argue for as little revision of neo-Aristotelian virtue ethics as possible. Now, I make arguments in a bolder, more revisionary spirit.

5.1 A developmental story

Presumably some people are more easily motivated by their self-concepts, while others are more easily motivated by social expectations. Here, I tell a developmental story that begins with lack of virtue, passes through factitious virtue, and ends in full-fledged virtue.

Suppose you take a test and, despite the fact that you could easily get away with it, it doesn't even occur to you to cheat. Along comes someone who says, "Gee, you must be really honest." You pause for a moment to consider this attribution. You don't think of yourself as dishonest, but you never really considered whether you were particularly virtuous in this way. Still, your interlocutor seems quite certain, and who are you to argue with a good thing? So you file this attribution away in your self-concept.

Weeks later, you're about to leave a restaurant when you notice that you weren't charged for dessert. Do you approach the server and let him know of his mistake, or pocket the money? Perhaps in the past, you would have felt no compunction about such a windfall, but you just so happen to be out to dinner with the very person who previously called you honest. He seems to be pretty perceptive, so he could notice that you've failed to be honest in this context. Not wanting to let him down, you flag down the server and pay your dues. While doing so, you notice his smile of approval, and you start to think that maybe there was all things considered good reason to pay for your dessert.

So far, your factitious honesty has been mostly a matter of living up to others' expectations, but in due time, you start to monitor your own behavior without so much need for social reinforcement. Perhaps you come to think of yourself as extremely honest. Your factitious virtue has transformed from being primarily sustained by social expectations to being primarily sustained by self-concept. You still don't possess the full-bore virtue of honesty, but as before, who's complaining?

As the years go by, you learn a little philosophy and come to understand the Aristotelian conception of the golden mean. You start to realize how complex a trait like honesty really is. As this happens, you update your self-concept further: now you see that in the past you weren't exactly honest because you didn't act for the right reasons. Those reasons become more and more compelling, though, and you even find yourself noticing when honesty is at stake when others fail to do so. You still are glad to have the social support of positive expectations, and you still think of yourself as on the way to honesty, but your focus has importantly shifted from what others think of you and what you think of yourself to what you take to be morally important. You perhaps never quite break free of the need for these supports, but they become less and less important.

This little story is of course just that – a story. Nevertheless, the stories we tell are important, and this one has a patina of plausibility. If something like this is possible, it suggests that different people will progress different lengths along the path to honesty. Some may stall at the social expectations stage. Others may stall at the self-concept stage. Perhaps a few will go all the way and cultivate the virtue of honesty. The idea, though, is that factitious virtue may be a developmental stage on the way to full virtue, and that even for those who never go all the way, factitious virtues are still pretty good.

5.2 *What kind of speech act is virtue-labeling?*

Another speculation has to do with the semantics and pragmatics of virtue-labeling. What kind of speech act is virtue-labeling? In particular, what is the illocutionary force of attributing a virtue to someone? On the one hand, it seems obviously to be an assertion. To say that x is F (e.g., that Jenny is generous) is just about as ordinary as assertions get. However, the way that virtue-labeling functions suggests that it's a kind of command or suggestion. When Jenny is called generous, she changes her behavior to make the content of the attribution true (or near enough). Surely it must be one or the other, not both. I want to argue otherwise, with the help of Searle's notion of an indirect speech act (1975). An indirect speech act occurs when someone uses one speech act to make another. For instance, someone might utter, "I'm tired" by way of urging her friend to drive her home. By asserting ("I'm tired"), she requests ("Please take me home").

In the same way, I want to suggest, sometimes when people make attributions they use assertions ("You're generous") to make suggestions ("You may want to help people"), issue commands ("Help people!"), or urge courses of action ("You should help people"). In the *Rhetoric* (1367–8), Aristotle says something closely related:

To praise a man is in one respect akin to urging a course of action. The suggestions which would be made in the latter case become encomiums when differently expressed. Since we know what action or character is required, then, in order to express these facts as suggestions for action, we have to change and reverse our form of words. Thus the statement "A man should be proud not of what he owes to fortune but of what he owes to himself," if put like this, amounts to a suggestion; to make it into praise we must put it thus, "Since he is proud not of what he owes to fortune but of what he owes to himself."

Of course, whether such an indirect speech act occurs is going to depend on the intentions of the utterer. I don't want to argue that making a virtue attribution always involves an indirect speech act. Nor do I want to say that when someone makes a normative suggestion by attributing a virtue, she doesn't also make an assertion. The idea is not that virtue-labeling is just a disguised form of command. Rather, the claim is that sometimes people issue imperatives by making assertions.

In a footnote earlier in this chapter (note 6), I suggested that the failure of exhortation to produce trait-consonant conduct may also be explained in terms of labeling. Uttering statements of the form "x should be F," implicates or presupposes statements of the form, "x is not F". Thus, when someone is told to be caring, the speech act suggests or presupposes that he's not already caring. By concealing the exhortation in an indirect speech act, virtue-labeling avoids this problem.

5.3   *Factitious virtue and social ontology*

It's natural to assume, as neo-Aristotelian virtue ethics does, that the bearers of virtues are individual agents. This makes virtues monadic dispositional properties. It might, however, be better to think of a virtue as a triadic relation among an agent, a social milieu, and an environment.

This relational conception of virtue folds situational features like attribution and social expectations into the very nature of virtue.

The social expectations mechanism suggests that virtues are more closely related to social categories than it might seem. Take *noble*, for example. Originally, this was clearly a social category. To be noble was to belong to a certain family, with a certain pedigree. It was a matter of being an aristocrat. Later, a more psychological conception of nobility emerged: to be noble was a disposition to act and react in certain ways. It didn't matter what social class you belonged to. What I'm suggesting is that being noble even in this latter sense may still be socially infused. Being psychologically noble depends in part on being *considered* noble. If this is on the right track, it would make virtues *looping kinds* in Ian Hacking's sense (1999, 2006). A looping kind, or a kind subject to the looping effect, is a special sort of social category. Initially, people identify the kind in the same way that they identify any kind, but because it's attributed to other people who can react to the attribution, the kind term has a moving target. Hacking thinks that *autism*, for example, is a looping kind. He seems most comfortable saying that looping kinds are essentially tied up with bureaucracy and the institutionalized classification of people; he therefore seems to think that formal labeling is the only, or at least the primary, means by which looping kinds are constituted. For that reason, it may be a bit of a stretch to think of factitious virtues as straightforward looping kinds, but the social ontology of factitious virtues and looping kinds is quite similar.

Another way of making the same point is to compare factitious virtues to Searle's *institutional facts*, for which seeming to be a certain way is logically prior to being that way. For Searle, such a fact is often created by the performative utterance of a declarative sentence. Furthermore, he contends that:

> in the very evolution of the institution the participants need not be consciously aware of the form of the collective intentionality by which they are imposing functions on objects. [...I]n extreme cases they may accept the imposition of function only because of some related theory, which may not even be true. They may believe that it is money only if it is "backed in gold" or that it is marriage only if it is sanctified by God or that so and so is the king only because he is divinely authorized. (1995, p. 47)

For some virtues (and vices) this notion is going to be more appealing than for others. For instance, it seems quite plausible that being charming depends in part on being thought charming. It's hard to charm people who sneer at you. And it seems natural to say that being leaderly (to coin a term) depends in part on being thought leaderly. Similarly for some vices: thinking that someone is antagonistic is a pretty good way to make them disposed to antagonism. Expecting unfriendliness from someone may dispose them to be unfriendly.

For other virtues and vices, this suggestion may seem more far-fetched. Is it really true that being courageous depends on being thought courageous? Is it really true that being thought unfair disposes someone to be unfair? As I mentioned earlier, this phenomenon hasn't been systematically investigated for all of the virtues and vices. It does seem to crop up at the very least, though, with charity, generosity, cooperativeness, helpfulness, and eco-friendliness, as well as with selfishness.

I'm not sure what to say about the social ontology of virtue, but it does seem attractive to build social factors into the nature of virtue. If this is right way to go, then the worry that factitious virtue involves a noble lie is misguided. It would be a mistake to worry that when a judge declares two people married, she is engaged in a noble lie. The declaration (in the right circumstances) partially constitutes the marriage. In the same way, if virtues are relations rather than monadic properties, the declaration that someone is virtuous would partially constitute her virtue.

I conclude, then, with a twist on the Parmenidean principle: it is necessary to speak and to think what *ought to be*.

PART II

Factitious intellectual virtue

Expanding the situationist challenge to responsibilist virtue epistemology

For now we see through a glass darkly.

Paul, *I Corinthians* 13:12, KJV

I INTRODUCTION

Starting with Ernest Sosa's (1980) seminal article, "The Raft and the Pyramid," the last three decades have witnessed the birth and growth of *virtue epistemology*. Following Lorraine Code's (1984) landmark article, "Toward a 'responsibilist' epistemology," virtue epistemology today is typically taken to cleave into three families of views:

- *Reliabilism*, which sees the intellectual virtues as non-motivational capacities, dispositions, or processes that tend to lead their possessors to increase the balance of truths over falsehoods in their belief sets (e.g., sound deduction, good eyesight, capacious memory).
- *Responsibilism*, which views the intellectual virtues on analogy with the neo-Aristotelian moral virtues as motivational, reasons-responsive dispositions to act and react in characteristic ways (e.g., open-mindedness, curiosity, intellectual courage).
- *Mixed virtue epistemology*, which countenances the virtues of both reliabilism and responsibilism, or hybrids of them.

Cross-cutting this classification is another tripartite distinction due to Christopher Hookway (2003a, 2003b, 2006), for whom epistemological projects can be divided into three species:

- *Classical epistemology*, which aims to answer traditional questions, such as, "Does *S* know that *p*?", "Is *S* justified in believing that *p*?"
- *Inquiry epistemology*, which aims to answer nontraditional questions, such as, "Does *S* possess understanding or wisdom?", "Is *S* a praiseworthy epistemic agent?"

- *Combined epistemology*, which aims to answer both traditional and non-traditional questions, and to explore entailments between classical and inquiry concepts.

Crossing these distinctions generates nine types of virtue epistemology. It would not be procrustean to place many prominent virtue epistemologists into one or another of these categories. Ernest Sosa is a classical reliabilist. Linda Zagzebski is a combined responsibilist. Christopher Lepock is a combined mixed theorist.

Meanwhile, the last thirteen years have seen the rise of the so-called *situationist challenge to virtue ethics*, which I rearticulated and responded to in the first half of this book. It seems only natural that eventually we would see the convergence of the twain: *the situationist challenge to virtue epistemology*. Doris (2002, pp. 69–71; 2005, p. 659; 2010, p. 142) gestures in this direction, but he has yet to publish a sustained treatment. In this chapter, I argue that all versions of responsibilist and mixed virtue epistemology must come to terms with a situationist challenge of their own.[1] I begin by spelling out in more detail the various approaches to epistemology. I then show, using evidence drawn from social and cognitive psychology, that the challenge can be expanded to both classical and inquiry variants of responsibilist virtue epistemology. This raises the specter of skepticism. In classical responsibilism, one knows that p only if one has come to believe that p through the exercise of intellectual virtue, so if the intellectual virtues are as rare as epistemic situationism suggests, then most people know very little.

2 VIRTUE EPISTEMOLOGY

As explained above, virtue epistemologists can be divided into three camps: reliabilists, responsibilists, and mixed theorists. This section sketches these approaches, after which I articulate a situationist challenge for responsibilist and mixed theories. The next chapter attempts to expand the challenge further to reliabilism about inference.

2.1 *Reliabilist virtue epistemology*

Reliabilist theories aim to resolve well-known epistemological puzzles such as Gettier cases, lottery paradoxes, and skeptical arguments.

---

[1] This chapter is based in large part on my (2012) article.

Solutions to these puzzles are framed in terms of non-motivational traits, abilities, capacities, and processes such as perception, intuition, and memory. Although such dispositions are not Aristotelian moral virtues, it is generally agreed that they are sufficiently virtue-like (because they are stable dispositions to think and reason in characteristic ways) that it is not a misnomer to class them with the virtues (Sosa 1991, p. 271). Three of the most influential virtue epistemologists are Alvin Goldman (1992), John Greco (1992, 1993, 2000, 2009), and Ernest Sosa (1980, 1991, 2001, 2007, 2011), whose views I will treat as representative.

The key to this approach to justification and knowledge is the direction of analysis. One starts with notions of the various intellectual virtues, then uses them to define more traditional epistemic concepts, such as justification and knowledge. Roughly, reliabilists define epistemic *justification* in terms of the epistemic *virtues* and define *knowledge* in terms of *truth* and epistemic *justification* (and hence indirectly in terms of the epistemic virtues).[2] Beliefs acquired through the exercise of these faculties are justified (Goldman 1992, p. 157). Or, in Sosa's words, "A belief B is justified if and only if it is the outcome of a process of belief acquisition or retention which is reliable, or leads to a sufficiently high preponderance of true beliefs over false beliefs" (1992, p. 80).[3] True beliefs so acquired count as knowledge. As Greco puts it, "S knows that p *if and only if* S believes the truth (with respect to p) because S's belief that p is produced by intellectual ability" (2009, p. 18). Or, as Sosa says, "knowledge is true belief out of intellectual virtue, belief that turns out right by reason of the virtue and not just by coincidence" (1991, p. 277).

Thus for the reliabilist, someone has a justified belief that the cat is on the mat if he comes to believe that the cat is on the mat because he *sees* the cat on the mat, whereas someone has an unjustified belief that the cat is on the mat if he comes to believe that the cat is on the mat because he *hopes* the cat is on the mat. Moreover, the belief is justified only if the agent is stably disposed to see well. If he is legally blind but occasionally identifies cats correctly after much squinting, we would be less inclined to admit that his belief is justified. If he is good at identifying tabbies as cats but only mediocre at identifying other breeds as cats, or if he only

---

[2] Note that epistemic justification and other types of justification may come apart, as Driver (2003, p. 110) and Sosa (1991, p. 165) have argued. For example, it seems that an ill person has practical but not epistemic justification for believing that he will recover. So believing would tend to trigger a placebo effect, which would in turn facilitate recovery, but that is not in itself warrant for the belief.

[3] It should be clear that I'm dealing with what Sosa refers to as "reflective knowledge," not "animal knowledge." As far as I can tell, animal knowledge is impervious to situationist critique.

identifies mats as mats when he is in a good mood, we would be reluctant to attribute justification. Reliabilists explain this reluctance in terms of the epistemic virtues: "When we categorize a belief [as justified or reasonable] we speak directly of the belief but also, indirectly, of the believer, whose intellectual reliability is also under evaluation" (Sosa 2001, p. 58; see also Sosa 2007, p. 29). If we recognize that the agent is unreliable, then – even if he gets it right this one time – we will be disinclined to say that his belief is justified.

Another example, this time having to do with knowledge: someone knows the cat is on the mat if he concludes that the cat is on the mat because he knows the cat is either on the mat or in the box, knows the cat is not in the box, and makes an inference using disjunctive syllogism. He would not know that the cat is on the mat (even if it is) if he concludes that the cat is on the mat because he knows that George Washington was the first American president, makes an inference using *tonk*-introduction to <George Washington was the first American president *tonk* the cat is on the mat>, then makes another inference using *tonk*-elimination to <the cat is on the mat>. Moreover, as before, the agent has knowledge only if he is stably disposed to use disjunctive syllogism (and other sound deductive rules) and stably disposed not to use *tonk* and its unsound ilk. If he uses the rules of classical deductive inference when it's cloudy but *tonk*y deductive inference when it's fair, we would find it difficult to attribute knowledge to him even during stormy weather. As before, reliabilists would explain this reluctance in terms of intellectual character. To say that a certain belief rises to the level of knowledge is to say something about the belief, but it's also to say something about the believer. According to Sosa (2001, p. 58), "What one cares about in oneself and in one's epistemic fellows is a relevantly stable, dependable character."

To sum up, then, reliabilist virtue epistemology starts with a subset of the stable, counterfactual-supporting traits of intellectual character – namely, the virtuous ones, which tend to increase their possessors' balance of truth over falsehood. It then defines both the epistemic justification of beliefs and the epistemic justification of agents in terms of intellectual character. An agent has justification if and only if she is exercising her intellectual virtues and not exercising any intellectual vices, and any given belief of hers is justified just in case it was acquired and retained through the exercise of her intellectual virtues (and not through the exercise of any intellectual vices). Finally, reliabilism defines knowledge as true belief acquired and retained through the exercise of intellectual virtues (and the absence of intellectual vices).

2.2   *Responsibilist virtue epistemology*

Responsibilist virtue epistemology was first so called by Code, for whom the "intellectually virtuous person" is identified not merely by his purely cognitive capacities, abilities, and dispositions but also by his conative attitudes toward truth and falsehood. He

> finds value in knowing and understanding how things really are. He resists the temptation to live with partial explanations where fuller ones are attainable, the temptation to live in a fantasy or in a world of dream or illusion, considering it better to know, despite the tempting comfort and complacency that a life of fantasy or illusion (or well-tinged with fantasy and illusion) can offer. (1984, p. 44)

Because they are motivational, reasons-responsive, and action-guiding, the responsibilist pantheon of virtues is more obviously analogous to the traditional Aristotelian moral virtues.

James Montmarquet (1987, 1993) and Linda Zagzebski (1996) have been the most articulate and prolific defenders of responsibilism, so I will treat their views as representative in this chapter. Montmarquet is an inquiry responsibilist, whereas Zagzebski is a combined responsibilist. For Montmarquet, the intellectual virtues are traits that a person who desires the truth would want to have. The sole cardinal intellectual virtue is conscientiousness, the desire to attain true belief and avoid error, but a host of lesser intellectual virtues subserve conscientiousness. They fall into three categories. First are the *virtues of impartiality*, such as openness to new ideas, willingness to exchange ideas, lack of jealousy and personal bias, and a lively sense of one's own fallibility. Next come the *virtues of sobriety*, such as the reluctance to draw outrageous conclusions based on scant evidence. Finally, there are the *virtues of intellectual courage*, such as the willingness to conceive and examine alternatives to popularly held beliefs, perseverance in one's beliefs in the face of opposition, and determination to see an intellectual project through to completion (1993, p. 23). Note that all three types of intellectual virtue involve a motivational component: unlike the reliabilist virtues, they all encompass in some way a desire to attain true beliefs and avoid error. With this theory in hand, Montmarquet defines subjective justification in terms of intellectual virtue: "A person *S* is justified in believing *p* insofar as *S* is epistemically virtuous in believing *p*" (1993, p. 99).

Zagzebski engages with both classical and inquiry epistemology, attempting to provide both a theory of justification and knowledge and a theory of intellectual credit and culpability. For Zagzebski, a virtue is

"*a deep and enduring acquired excellence of a person, involving a characteristic motivation to produce a certain desired end and reliable success in
bringing about that end*" (1996, p. 137, emphasis hers). Intellectual virtues
are a species of this general category. Zagzebski does not subdivide the
intellectual virtues into categories like Montmarquet, but her catalogue is
strikingly similar. The intellectual virtues include intellectual carefulness,
perseverance, humility, vigor, flexibility, courage, thoroughness, integrity,
as well as open-mindedness, fair-mindedness, insightfulness, originality,
and the virtues opposed to wishful thinking, obtuseness, and conformity (p. 155). The intellectual vices include intellectual pride, negligence,
idleness, cowardice, conformity, carelessness, rigidity, prejudice, wishful
thinking, close-mindedness, insensitivity to detail, obtuseness, and lack
of thoroughness (p. 152).

Like Montmarquet, then, Zagzebski sees intellectual virtues as motivational traits of character. In fact, their definitions of epistemic justification largely coincide. For Zagzebski, "A *justified belief* is what a person
who is motivated by intellectual virtue, and who has the understanding
of his cognitive situation a virtuous person would have, might believe in
like circumstances" (p. 241). Unlike Montmarquet, however, Zagzebski
goes on to define knowledge as "a state of true belief arising out of acts of
intellectual virtue" (p. 271).

In addition to analyzing justification and knowledge, responsibilists
are well-equipped to deal with the nontraditional questions of inquiry
epistemology. Code (1984, p. 46) points out that people can be legitimately praised for their possession and exercise of responsibilist intellectual
virtue but not reliabilist intellectual virtue. Similarly, they can be legitimately blamed for their possession and exercise of responsibilist intellectual
vice but not reliabilist intellectual vice. The creative person is admirable;
the person with perfect pitch is not (even though perfect pitch is desirable
as such). Dogmatism is deplorable; colorblindness is not (even though
colorblindness is undesirable as such).

Jason Baehr (2006a) emphasizes a number of further questions that
responsibilism seems especially suited to answer, including, "How are the
intellectual virtues related to one another?" "Are there any higher-order
intellectual virtues?" "How are the intellectual virtues related to the
moral virtues?" "Are intellectual virtues instrumentally or intrinsically
valuable?" and "Do intellectual virtues make their bearers' lives or the
lives of their bearers' peers better?" It is beyond the scope of this chapter
to attempt to answer these questions here; I mention them to point out
the kind of research responsibilism seems suited for.

To sum up, responsibilist virtue epistemology addresses questions of both classical and inquiry epistemology. It starts with a subset of the stable, counterfactual-supporting traits of intellectual character – namely, the virtuous ones, which are complexes consisting of a desire for truth rather than error and a capacity to satisfy that desire. It then defines epistemic justification in terms of intellectual character. An agent has justification if and only if she is exercising her intellectual virtues and not exercising any intellectual vices, and any given belief of hers is justified if it is such as the virtuous person would acquire or retain in her circumstances. Finally, responsibilism defines knowledge as true belief acquired and retained through the exercise of intellectual virtues (and the absence of intellectual vices).

2.3   Mixed virtue epistemology

More recently, epistemologists in both the reliabilist and the responsibilist camps have moved toward a consensus on mixed virtue epistemology (Baehr 2006b; Greco 1992, 2000; Lepock 2011; Sosa 2011, pp. 15–6; Zagzebski 1996, p. 149).

In the 1990s, Greco began to incorporate responsibilist insights into what he calls *agent reliabilism*, which recognizes the necessity of appropriate motivation. For instance, according to agent reliabilism, "subjective justification can be understood in terms of the dispositions a person manifests when she is thinking conscientiously – when she is *trying* to believe what is true as opposed to what is convenient, comforting, or fashionable" (1992, p. 289, emphasis mine).[4]

From the other direction, Zagzebski has not resisted saying that her responsibilist view presupposes reliabilist virtues. For one's desire to believe the truth and avoid falsehood to be satisfied, one must possess many cognitive capacities, abilities, and dispositions.

It would seem, then, that reliabilists and responsibilists have been climbing different sides of the same mountain, and that as their theories develop, they are converging. This is a welcome development. It means, however, that reliabilists who adopt mixed views make themselves susceptible to the situationist challenge to responsibilism. The attractions of mixed views notwithstanding, it might turn out that pure reliabilism should be preferred to a mixed view because it is more empirically adequate. In the balance of this chapter, I show how the situationist

---

[4] See also Greco (2003, p. 111) and Sosa (2011, pp. 15–16).

challenge to virtue *ethics* can be expanded to challenge responsibilist and mixed virtue *epistemology* as well.

3 EXPANDING THE CHALLENGE TO RESPONSIBILIST VIRTUE EPISTEMOLOGY

I want to extend the situationist challenge to responsibilist virtue epistemology, so I need to argue that its intellectual virtues are empirically inadequate: they neither explain nor predict a sufficient portion of epistemic conduct because people are inordinately susceptible to seemingly trivial and epistemically irrelevant situational influences. This section attempts to make good on that claim.

3.1 *The challenge to classical responsibilism*

At first blush, empirical evidence about what sorts of cognitive dispositions people actually possess would seem to be welcome news to responsibilists because it would help to solve the so-called *generality problem*. Recall that, on this view, knowledge is true belief acquired and retained through the exercise of intellectual virtues. However, any event of acquiring a belief could be classed under an indefinite number of headings, some of which are highly reliable, others of which are less so, still others of which are outright unreliable. Suppose that Susie comes to believe that the cat is on the mat, and that the cat really is on the mat. If we describe her belief-formation process as *seeing a cat on a mat*, then of course it is reliable. If, however, we describe it as *seeming to see a cat on a mat*, then it is less so. All seeings of cats are seemings as of cats, but not all seemings as of cats are seeings of cats. Furthermore, not all seemings as of cats are veridical, but all seeings of cats are. And if we describe her belief-formation process as *coming to believe that the cat is on the mat or that $2 + 2 = 5$*, then it is clearly unreliable.

Though the generality problem was first articulated as a hurdle for reliabilism (Pollock 1984), Zagzebski (1996, p. 300) recognizes that classical responsibilism faces its own version of the problem. Should conative virtues be coarsely individuated, so that *open-mindedness* makes the cut, or should they be finely individuated, so that *open-mindedness towards friends while in a good mood* makes the cut? She argues that this question should be answered empirically (p. 309), a point with which I wholeheartedly agree.

One thing that makes matters especially tricky here is that responsibilism imposes an additional constraint on solving the generality problem. Responsibilist virtues are meant to be not only truth-conducive but also praiseworthy. This means that the principle of individuation for intellectual traits must be such as to make the virtues thus individuated good ways to be. To that end, Zagzebski thinks that the intellectual virtues should be individuated, like the moral virtues, in part by their characteristic motivations or reasons, and thus quite coarsely. Intellectual courage involves (among other things) staying true to one's beliefs in the face of social pressure; curiosity involves wanting to learn; open-mindedness involves being willing to take seriously the opposing viewpoints of others.

Empirical evidence about what sorts of epistemically relevant motivational traits people actually possess would presumably help to solve the generality problem for responsibilism. If the solution generalizes, perhaps it could even be exported to reliabilism. Furthermore, the generality problem for virtue epistemology and the situationist challenge to virtue ethics seem to share many structural similarities. In the same way that the situationist challenge depends on whether moral virtues are coarsely individuated (e.g., honesty, courage, modesty) or finely individuated (e.g., honesty while watched by fellow parishioners, courage in the face of rifle fire, modesty before peers while in a good mood), the generality problem depends on whether intellectual virtues are coarsely individuated (e.g., curiosity, creativity, intellectual courage) or finely individuated (curiosity while in a good mood, creativity after being given candy, intellectual courage in the face of non-unanimous dissent). If this is right, then a solution to the generality problem for responsibilism might also be exported as a response to the situationist challenge to virtue ethics.

This point is not entirely novel. In a recent article, Guy Axtell (2010; see also Lepock 2009) noted a structural similarity between the generality problem for epistemology and the situationist challenge to virtue ethics. His take on the similarity is very different from mine, however. For one thing, his goal is to reconcile reliabilist virtues and responsibilist virtues by saying that reliabilist virtues should be used in evaluating the justification of doxastic states while responsibilist virtues should be used in evaluating the praiseworthiness of epistemic agents (p. 78). For another, he discusses none of the relevant psychological literature. He therefore fails to consider whether the virtues of either camp actually exist, and, if they do, how common they are.

The situationist challenge to classical responsibilism can be framed as an inconsistent triad:

(*non-skepticism*) Most people know quite a bit.

(*classical responsibilism*) Knowledge is true belief acquired and retained through responsibilist intellectual virtue.

(*epistemic situationism*) Most people's conative intellectual traits are not virtues because they are highly sensitive to seemingly trivial and epistemically irrelevant situational influences.

The thesis of *non-skepticism* is near-orthodoxy. In a recent PhilPapers survey of philosophers around the globe, 81.6 percent of philosophers and 84.3 percent of epistemologists rejected skepticism.[5] I will therefore treat *non-skepticism* as unrevisable for present purposes. At the very least, it would take impressive argumentative acrobatics to convince most epistemologists that they should abandon *non-skepticism* instead of *classical responsibilism*.

The crucial question is therefore whether to accept *epistemic situationism* and reject *classical responsibilism* or, conversely, to reject *epistemic situationism* and accept *classical responsibilism*. To motivate the thesis of *epistemic situationism*, I will describe some of the research of Alice Isen and her colleagues on the influence of positive affect on cognitive motivation and processing. It will turn out that when people behave in accordance with the intellectual virtues of *curiosity, flexibility*, and *creativity*, their conduct is often better explained in terms of situational influences like mood elevators than in terms of consistent global traits. Most people are not curious, flexible, or creative as such; instead, they are *curious-while-in-a-good-mood, flexible-while-in-a-good-mood*, and *creative-while-in-a-good-mood*. This suggests that they lack the consistent motivation required for intellectual virtue because they are susceptible to the same sorts of situational non-reasons that interfere with moral virtue.

Here's a test of your intellectual flexibility and creativity. Suppose you are given three items: a book of matches, a box of thumbtacks, and a candle. Your task is to fix the candle to a vertical cork board in such a way that, when you light it, no wax drips. What do you do? To solve this puzzle, some people try tacking the candle directly to the cork. Others try lighting the candle and using the molten wax as an adhesive. Neither method works. The only solution is to empty the box, tack it to the cork, and then place the candle on the platform thus created. This is known

---

[5] Data available at http://philpapers.org/surveys/results.pl

as the Duncker (1945) candle task. When it is presented in this way, few people are able to solve it, but when the apparatus is presented as four items (a book of matches, a box, thumbtacks, and a candle) most do solve it. When the box contains the thumbtacks, people think of it as functionally related to the tacks: it's the sort of thing to hold thumbtacks. When the box and the thumbtacks are presented separately, people think of them as functionally distinct: a box for holding things (tacks, candles, what have you) and some tacks. This allows them to see that the box could be used to support the candle. Psychologists use the candle task as a measure of flexibility and creativity. If you have the box with the tacks in it, are you intellectually limber enough to think of the box in a new way?

Another test of cognitive flexibility and creativity is the remote associates test or RAT (Mednick 1963). In this test, subjects are first presented with three words. For instance, they might see 'sore,' 'shoulder,' and 'sweat,' or 'room,' 'blood,' and 'salts'. Next, they are asked to generate a fourth word that conjoins naturally with each to generate a common phrase or compound word. The solution to the first triplet is 'cold,' which generates the phrases 'cold sore,' 'cold shoulder,' and 'cold sweat'. The solution to the second triplet is 'bath,' which generates the phrases 'bathroom,' 'blood bath,' and 'bath salts'. Creative, flexible thinkers are able to generate the fourth word for many such triplets, and able to do so more quickly and efficiently than less creative, less flexible thinkers.

In a fascinating study, Isen, Daubman, and Nowicki found that seemingly trivial and epistemically irrelevant mood elevators led to significantly increased performance on both the candle task and the RAT (Isen, Daubman, and Nowicki 1987). In the control condition, participants were simply presented with the two puzzles. In two experimental conditions, their mood was situationally elevated by showing them a short comedy film or giving them candy. Both methods of elevating mood improved participants' performance. For the candle task, being in a good mood was almost as useful as being presented with the tacks outside of the box. Only 13 percent of participants solved the candle task in the control condition, with the tacks in the box. By contrast, 83 percent solved it when the tacks were presented outside the box, compared with 75 percent in the positive affect condition. Congruent results were obtained for the RAT. Participants in a situationally-induced good mood solved almost 66 percent more of the moderately difficult triplets than those in the control condition.

It appears that many of the subjects in this study who solved the candle task and the RAT were not creative and flexible as such, but that they acted in accordance with creativity and flexibility because of the seemingly trivial and epistemically irrelevant mood elevator. Consider the participants in these experiments who arrived at the correct solution but would not have done so had they not been in a good mood. Did they know the solutions they arrived at? Responsibilist knowledge is true belief acquired through the exercise of such virtues as flexibility and creativity, yet these participants acquired their true beliefs not through flexibility and creativity but through flexibility while in a good mood and creativity while in a good mood. The responsibilist seems to be committed to saying that they did not know the solutions. If Code is right that intellectual virtue includes a disposition "not to be *unduly* swayed by affectivity" (1984, p. 42, emphasis hers), then these participants were not exercising intellectual virtue and hence did not really know the solutions they arrived at. This seems to be the wrong result. To my mind, it sounds more natural to say that they did know the solutions even though they arrived at them not through the exercise of intellectual virtue but because the funny video or the candy lifted their spirits. Thus, *non-skepticism* and *epistemic situationism* are maintained at the cost of rejecting *classical responsibilism*.

Responsibilists might be inclined to say that these studies measure only *change* in intellectually virtuous conduct. They show that people act *more* creatively when in a good mood, but that is arguably irrelevant to whether they are creative. After all, a creative person might act *even more* creatively when in a good mood, but that does not make him uncreative to begin with. Recall the saturation metaphor from Chapter 1. Basically, responsibilists might argue that you don't need to be deeply saturated with creativity through and through to count as creative. You might have a little creativity here, no creativity there, and average creativity elsewhere, and still count as creative. Such a person could become more creative even though she already is creative enough to warrant applying the predicate to her. I recognize the force of this argument, but remain unconvinced. Yes, these studies measure change, but their control conditions also measure the baseline. And the results of these control conditions suggest that people are in fact pretty bad at the candle task and other tests of creativity *unless seemingly trivial and epistemically irrelevant factors like mood enhancers come into play.*

Alternatively, the responsibilist might argue that creativity, curiosity, and flexibility are not required for justification or knowledge. Creativity especially seems to be a kind of supererogatory intellectual virtue – praiseworthy to be sure, but not necessary for ordinary doxastic justification. Perhaps conscientiousness and intellectual courage are more directly relevant to knowledge and justification (topics in classical responsibilism), while creativity and curiosity are more directly relevant to the praise-worthiness of epistemic agents (a topic in inquiry responsibilism). This argument deserves our attention, but it shifts the burden of proof to the responsibilist. If creativity, flexibility, and curiosity do not belong to classical responsibilism, which traits do? It is unfair to the situationist to force him to play whack-a-mole, claiming whenever he gives a strong argument against some intellectual virtue that he forgot to account for some other intellectual virtue that is now identified post hoc. Perhaps intellectual courage is required for justification and knowledge? I will argue in the next section that most people lack intellectual courage and are at best intellectually courageous in the face of non-unanimous dissent. Perhaps some other intellectual virtues are required, then? This is a question that classical responsibilists must answer and defend in an empirically informed way. It does not come for free. I discuss two potential answers (conscientiousness and need for cognition) in the final section of this chapter, but my conclusions there will not thrill classical responsibilists.

Isen and her colleagues have conducted dozens of further experiments in the same vein as the one described above; in the remainder of this section, I discuss just a few. In another study of the influence of positive mood on creative problem solving, Estrada, Isen, and Young (1994, 1998) presented medical internists with a task in which they had to identify the correct diagnosis of a hypothetical patient based on a description of his condition. Some of the doctors received a small gift of candy just prior to the experiment; some were asked to read aloud a humanistic statement about medical care; the remainder underwent no treatment. The experimenters observed the internists' reasoning processes for speed, accuracy, and flexibility. While most arrived at the correct diagnosis, those in the positive affect condition did so more quickly and with greater flexibility of thought than both the control group and the humanistic-reading group. One might have thought that the humanistic statement would augment the doctors' epistemic motivation more than the candy. They presumably had some degree of commitment to humanism; they had trained as doctors, after all. However, what really kicked their desire to know into gear was not a reminder of the ultimate goal of medicine but a few gobstoppers.

In a similar study, Isen, Rosenzweig, and Young (1991) measured the influence of positive affect on creativity and curiosity. They first gave third-year medical students an anagram task, then induced positive affect in some of them by reporting that they had successfully solved it. Participants were next asked to determine which of six hypothetical patients was most likely to have lung cancer. As in the previous study, positive affect did not induce higher accuracy, but it was correlated with speed, configural processing, and organization of reasoning. In addition, participants in the positive affect condition were significantly more likely to engage in supererogatory reasoning about the hypothetical cases; they expressed more interest in the five cases deemed less likely to have lung cancer, even though this was not part of the task. It would seem, then, that positive mood induced heightened efficiency, better information processing, and increased interest in the subject matter. Again, while subjects in the positive affect condition may not have been creative or curious as such, they acted in accordance with these intellectual virtues because their moods had been improved by their seemingly trivial and epistemically irrelevant success on the prior anagram task. As before, it seems more natural to say that the doctors whose performance was enhanced by their good mood knew the solutions that they arrived at, even if they did not arrive at them by exercising the intellectual virtues of creativity and curiosity. If this is so, it means that *non-skepticism* and *epistemic situationism* are accepted at the cost of rejecting *classical responsibilism*.

The results described so far accord with the view of Schaller and Cialdini (1990), who argue that positive mood induces an overall openness to new experiences and ideas. People are more curious when their mood is positive than when it is negative or neutral. Happy people are also better able to recall information (Isen 1985; Isen et al. 1978) and make connections among disparate objects (Isen and Daubman 1984).

The effects of mood elevators are quite fleeting, however. In a study of the longevity of the effects of the sorts of mood elevators discussed in this section, Isen, Clark, and Schwartz (1976) found that only twenty minutes were required for the effect to wear off completely. This is probably because mood elevators cause a temporary release of dopamine into the brain, which dissipates rather quickly (Ashby, Isen, and Turken 1999).

I could go on about the power of fleeting situational influences on epistemic conduct. I hope by now, however, to have motivated the thought that many people do not possess creativity, flexibility, and curiosity as such, but inquire and reason creatively, flexibly, and curiously when their moods have been elevated by such seemingly trivial and epistemically irrelevant situational influences as candy, success at anagrams, and comedy films. It would be tedious to document similar evidence against the other epistemic virtues. Instead, I suggest that the burden of proof is now not on the situationist but the responsibilist. If my arguments in this section are successful, three intellectual virtues have fallen prey to situationist critique (and I shall add a fourth, intellectual courage, in the next section). If some other intellectual virtue is immune to situationist critique, that needs to be established by a thorough investigation of the relevant empirical literature. It would be surprising if these were the only responsibilist traits susceptible to such criticism.

Thus, situationism offers an empirical solution to the generality problem: intellectual traits are finely individuated not only by their characteristic motivations but also by seemingly trivial and epistemically irrelevant situational influences such as mood elevators. If this is right, responsibilists face a dilemma. They can accept local traits like *curiosity-while-in-a-good-mood* as virtues, or reject them. If responsibilists say that such traits are not virtues, skepticism rears its ugly head: if most people are at best locally curious, then most people have unjustified beliefs, which do not count as knowledge. When faced with the choice between saying that the subjects in Isen's experiments did not really know the answers to the problems they solved and saying that they did know but were not intellectually virtuous, I am inclined to go with the latter option, and I suspect that most other epistemologists would be too. Results like the ones discussed here suggest that we should accept *epistemic situationism* and reject *classical responsibilism*.

On the other horn of the dilemma, if responsibilists say that such narrow traits really are intellectual virtues, then they need to explain how these dispositions are to be construed as admirable. It is hard to see why someone should be praised for being *creative-while-in-a-good-mood* or *curious-while-in-a-good-mood*. Such traits are presumably truth-conducive (that much is not at issue), but responsibilist virtues are meant to be both truth-conducive and praiseworthy. On December 9, 1906, *The New York Times* reported that ex-Senator Arthur Brown, whose mistress had fatally shot him when he refused to marry her even after she had divorced her husband to be with him, had also been assaulted by his wife for infidelity. At a loss for praise, the paper mentioned that Brown was "known to be intensely loyal to his male friends." Local moral virtues like male-friends-loyalty don't seem to pack the normative oomph of global moral virtues. Local intellectual virtues presumably face the same problem.

Perhaps local intellectual virtues really are praiseworthy, though. Perhaps they only seem not to be because of a pragmatic implicature that dogs their attribution. If someone says, "Lisa is curious while in a good mood," he might be taken to mean that Lisa is intellectually lazy otherwise. Thus, while his attribution is meant as praise, it sounds like blame.

Considerations like this might help to reconcile responsibilists to local traits. Presumably, though, full-bore global intellectual virtues are more praiseworthy than local intellectual virtues. It may be admirable to be curious while in a good mood, but presumably it is even more admirable to be curious regardless of mood. Articulating a whole theory of local intellectual virtues would take us too far afield, but such a view might plausibly serve as a fallback position for classical responsibilism.

3.2   *The challenge to inquiry responsibilism*

If the foregoing arguments are correct, classical responsibilism fails to provide an adequate account of justification and knowledge. Perhaps, though, inquiry responsibilism is unaffected by an encounter with the empirical evidence. In this section, I argue that that hope is not met. I will use the virtue of *intellectual courage* as an example of how seemingly trivial and epistemically irrelevant situational factors influence epistemic and doxastic conduct. It will turn out that most people are not intellectually courageous but at best intellectually courageous in the face of non-unanimous dissent. This fine-grained trait is only minimally admirable, like one of Doris's local virtues or Robert Merrihew Adams's "modules of virtue" (2006, p. 125). Extrapolating, I will suggest that if similar arguments apply to the other global virtues, then much of our epistemic conduct can be explained without reference to these dispositions. If this is right, inquiry responsibilism cannot claim empirical adequacy. It may stand as a purely normative theory, but as a thick, explanatory-cum-evaluative theory, it applies to few actual people.

3.2.1   *Varieties of intellectual courage*
Before proceeding with the empirical evidence, some conceptual analysis is called for. What exactly is intellectual courage? It's a specification of the generic virtue of courage, which I will gloss as a disposition to notice threats to valued or cherished ends, to construe ambiguously threatening circumstances appropriately, to desire to overcome threats when possible, and to succeed in fulfilling such desires when they arise. When a courageous person sees that some valued object or objective is threatened, she typically wants to protect it. Furthermore, she typically succeeds in fulfilling the desire to protect it.

Specifications of courage can be generated by varying the type of the threat, the type of the valued object, and the type of the means required to overcome the threat.

Threats arise from diverse corners. Some, such as tornadoes, floods, and ravenous predators, are physical. They call for physical courage. Others, such as thugs and enemy soldiers, are martial. They call for martial courage. Still others, such as ostracism and derision, are social. They call for social courage. Threats to our intellectual well-being and pursuits call for intellectual courage. There are even financial threats, which call for financial courage, and threats that tempt us to infringe on others' autonomy, which call for vicarious courage – the courage to let others fend for themselves (Adams 2006, p. 182).

These specifications of the generic trait of courage can overlap and interact in a variety of ways. Presumably physical courage is more similar to martial courage than to financial courage, while social courage is more similar to intellectual courage than physical courage. As I explained in Chapter 3, it may be futile to attempt a unique individuation of local traits. Moreover, it's sometimes hard to know whether hyper-local traits are praiseworthy enough to count as virtues. Saying that someone possesses courage in the bond market but not the stock market is at best faint praise. However, when a particular specification of courage can be shown to quite valuable, this concern may be erased. I argue below that such is the case with respect to one specification of intellectual courage.

There are two other important ways in which local specifications of courage may be picked out. Specifications of courage can be generated by varying the type of the valued end. Some threats pertain to one's family, others to oneself, still others to one's nation or culture. There are threats to nature itself, such as global warming and the dwindling of biodiversity. I here restrict my discussion to specifications of courage that protects people.

Finally, courage can be further specified by varying the means required to overcome the threat, whatever it may be. Some threats can only (or best) be overcome by direct action. Rescuing someone from a burning building cannot be accomplished except by direct action. Others require patient endurance. Sometimes the most courageous response is to bide one's time, waiting for a better tomorrow. Still other threats can only (or best) be overcome by investigation, belief, or doubt. These include threats to one's understanding of the world and how it works, to one's trust of one's peers, and even to one's trust of oneself. Yet other threats must be countered by speech or social organization.

Putting this all together, the level of specificity I countenance here derives from fixing three parameters: the threat, the end, and the means. A specification of courage is a disposition to protect an *end* from a *threat* through a *means*. Different specifications of courage are presumed to be largely independent of one another unless we have evidence to the contrary. Some specifications of courage are more valuable than others – either because they are apt for protecting more valuable ends or because they help their possessors to overcome threats that cannot be blunted or obviated in some other way.

In this section, I want to focus on the types of courage called for by intellectual threats, which challenge our beliefs, our investigations, and our collaborations. I argue that, although these threats are less dramatic than their physical and martial counterparts, overcoming them is crucial both to understanding other people and to the creation and maintenance of a just and rational society. I begin by reviewing what little has already been said about intellectual courage. Next, I develop my own account of the varieties of intellectual courage, arguing that it is a good deal more diverse than others have noted. Finally, I show how intellectual courage can overcome pluralistic ignorance, a phenomenon that tends to ensure that unpopular norms remain in force even when they are despised by a large majority. When pluralistic ignorance takes hold, everybody plays along with a system that nobody likes because everybody interprets everybody's else's conformity as sincere. Think of Hans Christian Anderson's tale of the emperor's new clothes: no one said that the emperor was naked because everyone interpreted everyone else's silence as expressing the thought that the emperor was not naked. It takes a very special person to shatter such a hypnotic norm – either, as in the story, someone ignorant of social pressure, or, as in the case of Tahrir Square during the Arab Spring, someone with the courage to announce publicly what he really thinks despite social pressure. Intellectual courage is one of the few ways to break the stranglehold of pluralistic ignorance.

There's an unfortunate paucity of responsibilist research on intellectual courage. In *Epistemic Virtue and Doxastic Responsibility*, James Montmarquet glosses it as "the willingness to conceive and examine alternatives to popularly held beliefs, perseverance in the face of opposition from others (until one is convinced one is mistaken), and the determination required to see such a project through to completion" (1993, p. 23). Elsewhere, he says that intellectual courage enables someone "to pursue his own enquiries, to learn from others, yet not to be unduly bound to their opinions regarding his enquiries" (1987, p. 487) and to avoid "forming beliefs for reasons related to their popularity with others" (p. 493). He also claims that intellectual cowardice could be manifested by shunning possible sources of contrary ideas out of fear of being misled (1987, p. 485).

Linda Zagzebski says that intellectual courage involves refraining from operating under the "assumption that the views of others are more likely to be true than her own" and that the intellectually courageous person "must be willing to withstand attack when she has good reason to think she is right" (1996, pp. 177–78; see also Baehr 2006a).

Already we can see some of the variety of the specifications of intellectual courage. Montmarquet and Zagzebski distinguish at least two: the courage to investigate and the courage to believe.

Even so, our taxonomy remains thin and under-described. Robert Roberts and Jay Wood (2007, Chapter 8) come the closest to the sort of taxonomy I develop here in their 'map' of intellectual courage, yet even they do not make some of the distinctions needed in this context. Consider for a moment just the courage to investigate. What threats might prevent one from investigating? Some are external. Recall, for instance, the tale (apocryphal, though still apt) of the bishops who refused to look through Galileo's telescope. They were afraid that the evidence of their senses might lead them to give up their faith in Ptolemaic astronomy. Since that faith was required by the church hierarchy, they did their best to avoid encountering evidence that would undermine it. Other threats to investigation are internal. A cuckold might refuse to follow the trail of evidence leading to his wife's infidelity for fear that his heart would break. Friedrich Nietzsche seems to have thought that intellectual courage of this sort was a prerequisite of fruitful moral psychology. For him, the greatest danger to the psychological investigator is not external but internal, not the minotaur but the "minotaur of conscience" (*Beyond Good and Evil*, 29). Whether we agree with Nietzsche or not, his ideas help to clarify the distinction between the intellectual courage to investigate in the face of external threats and the intellectual courage to investigate in the face of internal threats.

Congruent specifications of other varieties of intellectual courage could also be made. There is an intellectual courage to believe in the face of external threats, and a different intellectual courage to believe in the face of internal threats. As evidenced in the quotations above, Montmarquet and Zagzebski seem mostly, or perhaps entirely, concerned with the former, but the same Nietzschean point could be made with respect to the courage to believe. Some truths are hard to take; they demand a certain cruelty towards oneself. Nevertheless, someone who truly desires to believe the truth and avoid error will force herself to accept unpleasant truths.

Related to the courage to believe is the courage to trust. Modernity could be characterized by the need to trust dozens, hundreds, or even thousands of strangers on a daily basis. If one flies in a passenger jet, one trusts the pilot to guide the plane to its destination. When one eats out at a restaurant, one trusts that the cook knows how to store and prepare food hygienically. As one reads the newspaper, one trusts the reporter to get things right. Such networks of trust are astonishing both in their magnitude and in their complexity, and society would suffer without them.

The flipside of the courage to believe and trust is the courage to doubt – a topic little discussed by responsibilists. Montmarquet and Zagzebski consider only the courage to doubt popular opinion. This is one specification of the courage to doubt – the type required for external threats. But there is also the courage to doubt oneself. Sometimes the best evidence we can muster on a given question is not dispositive. Uncertainty is disquieting. It's often much easier to believe than to suspend judgment. When such a situation arises, it takes a kind of intellectual courage to remain in doubt.

Finally, consider the intellectual courage to speak and more generally to express thoughts, judgments, and opinions. It seems that this type of courage responds only or at least primarily to external threats. Saying what you really think can lead to social or legal sanction. It might therefore seem that this type of courage is actually a specification not of intellectual courage but of social courage. I claim that it's both. Consider again a more paradigmatic specification of intellectual courage: the courage to investigate. It's hard to imagine how one could investigate thoroughly without communication. The objections, suggestions, and counterarguments of other people are crucial to the pursuit of truth. While the lone genius may be able to dream up all of the potential problems with his view and respond to them, the rest of us mere mortals need to engage in dialectical scrutiny to evaluate the ultimate plausibility of our views. The entire system of peer review is based on this notion. It follows that if one wants to investigate well and believe the truth, one needs the courage to express one's own view – a point that John Stuart Mill persuasively makes in Chapter 2 of *On Liberty*.[6]

Though there may be no internal threat that the intellectual courage to speak overcomes, we should distinguish between private communication and public announcement. While both are important, it's intuitively clear that it's possible to have the courage to speak frankly with friends or family without having the courage to speak earnestly in public

---

[6] For more recent versions of the same argument, see Schulz-Hardt et al. (2000, 2002).

(and conversely). The latter specification of intellectual courage is crucial to terminating pluralistic ignorance, a phenomenon I describe in more detail in the next section.

3.2.2 Pluralistic ignorance

The phrase 'pluralistic ignorance' was coined by Daniel Katz and Floyd Allport (1931, p. 348) in their investigation of student attitudes at Syracuse University. They found that unpopular norms possessed a surprising tenacity because the students at the university all outwardly conformed to them even though most privately disapproved. While they in some sense must have realized that their behavior was indistinguishable from their peers', they interpreted others' conformity to and enforcement of these norms as sincere. Even though they knew from their own cases that someone could conform to the norm without actually approving of it, they tended not to consider such an explanation of others' behavior. Presumably this lacuna in their understanding flows from the fundamental attribution error, which I discussed in detail in Chapter 2.

The concept of pluralistic ignorance has been recruited to explain such diverse phenomena as the longevity of Soviet communism, the perseverance of the Indian caste system, and the tenacity of American racism (Kuran 1995), as well as the public behavior of hypocritical religious zealots (Schanck 1932), lack of student engagement in lecture classes (Miller and McFarland 1987, 1991), and binge-drinking by college students (Prentice and Miller 1993). The red thread running through all of these seemingly disparate social dysfunctions is that almost everyone in the relevant social group privately disapproves of the norms he conforms to outwardly and even sometimes helps to enforce, all the while interpreting others' conformity and enforcement of the very same norms as sincere.

Take, for example, the lack of student engagement in lecture classes. After the professor has tried for some time to explain difficult material, she may ask, "Does anyone have any questions?" No hands go up, not because all the students have understood the material but because they lack the intellectual courage to admit in front of their peers that they didn't understand. Simultaneously, the students quickly survey the room, noticing that no one else has raised a hand. From this they infer not that others were just as embarrassed as them but that the others in fact have no questions. This leads to further embarrassment and attempts to disguise their lack of understanding, which in turn further stifles any questions that might help to clarify the material (Miller and McFarland 1987, 1991).

Consider another case: binge-drinking by college students. Deborah Prentice and Dale Miller (1993) investigated student attitudes towards drinking as well as their thoughts about their peers' attitudes. They found that students tended to think that others' attitudes towards drinking were more positive than their own, more positive than they in fact were, and less variable than they in fact were. This misunderstanding of other students' attitudes towards drinking included not only strangers and acquaintances but also their own friends. It cropped up among freshmen, sophomores, juniors, and seniors at roughly equivalent levels. In response to the perceived discrepancy, men tended to adjust their own attitudes by becoming more comfortable with drinking (as measured by their self-reported attitudes and drinking behavior) while women tended to feel alienated from the rest of the college community (as measured by their reported intention not to attend reunions).

Both agent-based computer models (Centola, Willer, and Macy 2005) and empirical research on informational cascades (Bicchieri 2006) suggest that pluralistic ignorance is fragile: if enough people are willing to communicate their true judgments to one another, the regime of pluralistic ignorance is shattered. However, such communication requires a particular specification of intellectual courage that seems to be disappointingly rare, a problem I discuss next.

3.2.3   *Overcoming pluralistic ignorance through intellectual courage*

I claimed above that courage should be understood as a fragmented collection of local traits rather than a unified global trait. Unfortunately, even this concession to the empirical may be insufficient to allow us to make a case for the reality of the virtue most helpful in overcoming pluralistic ignorance: intellectual courage to speak publicly in the face of social pressure. For it turns out that most people lack even this local trait and are at best *intellectually-courageous-to-speak-publicly-in-the-face-of-non-unanimous-dissent*. This section reviews the evidence for this distressing claim.

In 1937, the Turkish social scientist Muzafer Sherif published a study on social power over perception. He wanted to show that many norms were upheld simply because there was apparent unanimity in support of them, and not because there was any rational reason for them. To argue for this audacious claim, he designed a clever experiment based on the so-called autokinetic effect. Imagine that you are in a room that's completely dark except for a single point of light on the wall. In such a situation, you have no absolute frame of reference for the position of the light. After you stare at it for some time, it will appear to move – not because it actually does move (in fact, it remains stationary throughout the experiment) but because your eyes wander, creating the impression of movement. How far exactly does the light appear to move? It's hard to say, especially because the correct answer (not at all) is the one thing that seems definitely wrong. Add to the situation that several experimental confederates affirm with great vigor that the light moved exactly three inches (or seven inches, or one inch, or what have you). What would you be inclined to say?

In Sherif's (1937) study, participants almost always converged on the unanimous response of the confederates – whatever it was. He took this to show that the participants' vision of reality was skewed by the announced perceptions of their peers. I and most other commentators have seen this interpretation as overblown, but at the very least the study seems to show that apparent unanimity can generate consent when the object of judgment is highly ambiguous. This is a far cry from disconfirming the existence of intellectual courage, but it suggests that unanimity might influence judgment in less uncertain cases as well.

Further studies have shown that once participants alight on an arbitrary norm, it's hard to shake them from it. Rohrer et al. (1954), for instance, showed that when participants in a Sherif-style autokinetic study were brought back to the lab months or even years later, they stuck to the norm established in their first session, even in the face of a new unanimous majority. If it were not for the arbitrary nature in which the norm was generated, this might suggest that participants had something like intellectual courage. The fact that they were so easily influenced at first, however, suggests that some other psychological mechanism is at work. In another follow-up study, Jacobs and Campbell (1961) found that norms could be passed from generation to generation, Ship of Theseus-style. Once a group had established a unanimous judgment about how far the light had moved in an autokinetic study, it was very hard to dislodge that judgment, even when the members of the group were sequentially replaced by naive participants so that, by the end of the study, all members were genuine participants rather than confederates and none had been part of the initial group.

Unsatisfied with Sherif's heroic interpretation of these studies, Solomon Asch (1951; see also Asch 1952, 1955, 1956) designed his own experiment. He wanted to show that the only reason participants' responses coalesced around an arbitrary norm in the autokinetic studies was that the stimulus was so ambiguous. After all, going along with the majority when you don't have any good independent evidence of your own isn't irrational;

it might even be wise. Surely when the correct answer was clear, he reasoned, participants would have the courage of their convictions, even in the face of unanimous dissent. To his dismay, Asch found exactly the opposite. In a now-famous experimental design eponymously titled the *Asch paradigm*, he tested the old saw, "Who are you going to believe? Me, or your own eyes?" In the experiment, seven confederates and a single participant judged serially and aloud which of two lines was longer. The correct answer was always obvious to the naked eye. Nevertheless, occasionally the confederates unanimously said that the shorter line was longer. After hearing the confederates rattle off their wrong answers, participants often went along with the majority. They did display discomfort, tension, and doubt, but all the same they announced their concurrence with the unanimous majority. Roughly a quarter of the participants refused to bend to the majority, but about a third went with the majority more often than not. Over the course of the experiment, between 50 percent and 80 percent of the participants caved at least once. I would not go so far as to conclude that the participants actually believed the statements they uttered when they concurred with the majority. It seems more likely that they were being hypocritical. Nevertheless, even if they had the intellectual courage to hold onto their beliefs privately, they lacked the intellectual courage to give voice to those beliefs publicly.

Variations on the Asch paradigm have established some boundary conditions. The effect disappeared when only one confederate was present, was quite weak when two were present, but went into full effect with just three. If just a single confederate went against the grain, conformity with the majority dropped below 10 percent. All this is comforting to a degree; the majority is not a sovereign governor of the individual. Nevertheless, the comfort is cold. If people are so easily swayed to go along with a view they realize is absurd when the potential sanction for dissent is only a rictus of scorn, how can they be counted on to display intellectual courage when the stakes are raised? How, in particular, can they be relied upon to voice their disapproval of a social norm that most of their peers conform to and enforce? Without such intellectual courage, pluralistic ignorance is likely to continue unchallenged.

In follow-ups to the initial Asch studies, other psychologists extended the domains in which the effect was found. Richard Crutchfield (1955) tested the effect of a unanimous majority on many types of judgments. In some cases, the question had to do with obvious factual, mathematical, or logical propositions, such as which of two figures had a greater area, which of two lines was longer, which of several numbers naturally followed a given sequence, and so on. In these cases, roughly a third of the participants went with the obviously wrong majority opinion. In other cases, the question had to do with more difficult matters of value, such as whether trials and tribulations made one a better person, whether the respondent would make a good leader, or whether free speech could be legitimately suspended by a threatened society. In these cases too, about a third of participants caved in the face of perceived unanimity.

Stanley Milgram – designer of the infamous studies in conformity in which participants put what they thought was 450 volts of electricity through another human being – cut his teeth on the Asch paradigm. In a cleverly designed study (1961), he had adults participate in an Asch-style experiment when they thought they were actually interviewing for a job. Subjects believed that they were testing a new signaling system for aircraft, but in fact they were part of a psychological experiment. They were asked to say which of several tones matched in pitch a given tone. As in the original Asch study, unanimity produced striking conformity. Even when they had a financial incentive to get the answer right, subjects went along with the perceived majority in a large number of cases.

Studies such as these suggest that intellectual courage – and even its specification, the intellectual courage to speak publicly in the face of unanimous dissent – are not the sorts of traits that most ordinary people possess. Rather than being *intellectually-courageous* or even *intellectually-courageous-to-speak-in-the-face-of-social-disapproval*, most people are at best *intellectually-courageous-to-speak-unless-faced-with-unanimous-dissent-of-at-least-three-other-people*.

This is a difficult conclusion to accept, for it seems to entail that once pluralistic ignorance takes hold, few people will be so bold as to challenge and overturn it. Despite the seeming fragility of pluralistic ignorance – all that's required to shatter it is a sincere expression of one's judgment – people tend to lack the requisite intellectual courage to overcome it. Now, it is of course possible to respond to this challenge as many have responded to the situationist challenge to virtue ethics by contending that, after all, virtue is quite rare, and so if most people are not intellectually courageous, that hardly counts as a bullet for virtue epistemologists to bite. On the one hand, Code seems amenable to this idea when she says, "It is important in giving an account of virtue, either moral or intellectual, to acknowledge that this is an account of an ideal, perhaps never fully realizable" (1984, p. 45). On the other hand, she quite rightly goes on to say that it is necessary "to keep its requirements nearly enough within the reach of the ordinary human being that there can be many virtuous persons, if perhaps none *perfectly* virtuous." The question is not whether the studies discussed in this section tell against ecumenical perfect virtue. The real question is whether these studies tell against "near enough" virtue for "ordinary human beings." It seems that there could not be "many virtuous persons" if the intellectual virtues are the global, coarsely individuated traits so far identified by responsibilists.

Another response available to responsibilists is to admit that many people fall short of the ideal of intellectual virtue, but to claim that it is nevertheless possible to fall short of the ideal while possessing an admirable approximation of the ideal. Someone who caves in to public opinion occasionally is more admirable than someone who caves in to public opinion often. Here it may be helpful to refer again to the distinction between high-fidelity and low-fidelity virtues, which I introduced in Chapter 1. High-fidelity virtues require near-perfect consistency; low-fidelity virtues require much better consistency than could be expected without the trait in question. For example, the high-fidelity intellectual virtues include curiosity, open-mindedness, fair-mindedness, intellectual humility, thoroughness, and intellectual carefulness. If someone acts in accordance with thoroughness in 80 percent of her inquiries, that hardly makes her thorough. By contrast, low-fidelity intellectual virtues include creativity, insightfulness, and originality. (These lists are not meant to be comprehensive or uncontroversial, but I hope they at least point in the right direction.) If someone has an original insight even once a week, that might qualify her as insightful. The evidence I have brought to bear in this chapter is more damning to high-fidelity intellectual virtues than to low-fidelity intellectual virtues. However, the low-fidelity intellectual virtues of creativity, insightfulness, and originality are also the least truth-conducive. At most this distinction will salvage the low-fidelity inquiry virtues, at best a partial victory for responsibilism.

4 CONCLUSION

I have argued that several of the intellectual virtues traditionally countenanced by classical responsibilism and inquiry responsibilism are empirically inadequate. They fail to explain a sufficient portion of conduct when compared with the explanatory power of seemingly trivial and epistemically irrelevant situational factors such as mood elevators. While it may be possible to retreat by claiming that virtue is rare, such a retreat threatens to make justification and knowledge rare as well. One could opt instead for a theory of local intellectual virtues, which are empirically supportable and even truth-conducive. They are only minimally admirable, however, so retrenching into a theory of local intellectual virtues would make it difficult for responsibilism to address questions of epistemic value.

My arguments thus far have critiqued only some of the intellectual virtues. Others remain unexplored. Perhaps they resist the situationist challenge better than curiosity, creativity, intellectual flexibility, and intellectual courage. In this concluding section, I consider two candidates for overcoming the situationist challenge to responsibilism: conscientiousness and the need for cognition. Echoing Jesse Prinz's (2009) normativity challenge to virtue ethics, I argue that neither is admirable in the way that responsibilists require.

One prominent model in personality psychology is the so-called 'Big Five' – openness, conscientiousness, extraversion, agreeableness, and neuroticism – which was discussed above in Chapter 2. Someone's personality can be sketched in broad outline by assigning him an ordered quintuple on these dimensions. For instance, someone might be highly conscientious, slightly introverted, rather disagreeable, and quite neurotic. Responsibilists consider conscientiousness an intellectual virtue; Montmarquet even considers it the sole cardinal intellectual virtue. It is therefore tempting to look to the Big Five for empirical credentials. Unfortunately, the conscientiousness of personality psychology has little to do with the conscientiousness of responsibilism. Recall that, according to Montmarquet, conscientiousness is the desire to attain truth and avoid error. When personality psychologists use the term, however, they have something much broader and less intellectually focused in mind. Conscientiousness for them includes personal austerity, the ability to delay gratification, productivity, the need for control, and compulsivity (McCrae and John 1996). While some of these dispositions may be both epistemically relevant and admirable, others are not. In addition, conscientiousness is correlated with unhappiness in the face of difficulty, which makes it hard to reconcile with any view that treats the intellectual virtues as components of eudaimonia (Boyce, Wood, and Brown 2010). This trait, whatever its empirical credentials, hardly seems like an intellectual virtue.

Need for cognition seems to suffer from the same problem. This personality trait was initially studied by Cohen, Stotland, and Wolfe (1955, p. 291), who glossed it as "a need to structure relevant situations in meaningful, integrated ways [...] to understand and make reasonable the experiential world." However, the methods they used to test for expressions of the need for cognition reveal that it was far from an intellectual virtue. People score high in need for cognition if they find it hard to tolerate ambiguity and rely on heuristics and experts rather than investigating for themselves (Adams 1959).

More recent studies of need for cognition have revised the meaning of the term to avoid this unwanted association. Cacioppo et al. (1996), for instance, characterizes it as a "tendency to engage in and enjoy effortful cognitive activity." This is more promising, but it seems that need for cognition so construed accounts for 4 percent to 16 percent of the variance in relevant behavior (pp. 199–203) – a figure that puts it right up against the Mischellian ceiling but would at best qualify it as a low-fidelity virtue. Furthermore, in the only philosophical investigation of need for cognition currently in the literature Reza Lahroodi (2007) concludes that the drawbacks of need for cognition may outweigh its benefits because its bearers allocate their intellectual resources inefficiently (p. 232) and are especially prone to the sorts of mood effects discussed above (p. 237). In addition, the need for cognition as studied by psychologists so far is just a general tendency to engage in effortful thinking and to enjoy such activity, regardless of topic (p. 235). Just as giving money to others thoughtlessly is not the same thing as generosity, so enjoying thinking about any topic whatsoever should not be considered an intellectual virtue.

Although need for cognition and the conscientiousness of personality psychology may not provide the succor responsibilists seek in response to the situationist challenge, other intellectual virtues may yet withstand critique. Showing that they do is a task responsibilists will presumably clamor to accomplish. If they fail, though, reliabilists would do well to steer clear of mixed theories as much as they can – assuming, of course, that reliabilism itself is immune to situationist critique, a point I dispute in the next chapter.

CHAPTER 6

Expanding the situationist challenge to reliabilist virtue epistemology

What a strange simplification and falsification people live in! The wonders never cease, for those who devote their eyes to such wondering. How we have made everything around us so bright and easy and free and simple! How we have given our senses a *carte blanche* for everything superficial, given our thoughts a divine craving for high-spirited leaps and false inferences! – How we have known from the start to hold on to our ignorance in order to enjoy a barely comprehensible freedom, thoughtlessness, recklessness, bravery, and joy in life; to delight in life itself! And, until now, science could arise only on this solidified, granite foundation of ignorance, the will to know rising up on the foundation of a much more powerful will, the will to not know, to uncertainty, to untruth! Not as its opposite, but rather – as its refinement!

Friedrich Nietzsche, *Beyond Good and Evil*, 24

I INTRODUCTION

In the previous chapter, I argued that the situationist challenge extends to responsibilist and mixed virtue epistemology. The sorts of seemingly trivial and normatively irrelevant situational factors that plague traditional moral virtues (mood elevators, mood depressors, situational demand characteristics) also wreak havoc in our epistemic lives, at least when it comes to our motivation to believe the truth and avoid error. In this chapter, I attempt to expand the situationist challenge further, to reliabilist virtue epistemology.[1] My arguments here are more narrowly targeted than in the previous chapter; rather than arguing that all cognitive dispositions are subject to situational intrusion, I argue that our *inferential* dispositions are especially suspect. If this is right, reliabilists must either retract the

---

[1] This article is based in large part on my (forthcoming a) article.

claim that a reliable disposition is necessary for inferential knowledge or fall into skepticism about inference.

As before, at first blush, empirical evidence about what sorts of cognitive dispositions people actually *possess* would seem to be welcome news to reliabilists because it would help to solve the generality problem. Recall that, on this view, knowledge is true belief acquired and retained through the exercise of reliable intellectual virtues. In other words, someone knows that *p* just in case her belief that *p* was acquired and retained through a reliable process or disposition. However, any event of acquiring a belief could be classed under indefinitely many headings, some of which are reliable, others of which are not. Suppose that Susie comes to believe that the cat is on the mat, and that the cat really is on the mat. If we describe her belief-formation process as *seeing a cat on a mat*, then of course it is reliable. If, however, we describe it as *seeming to see a cat on a mat*, then it's not so obvious. All seeings of cats are seemings as of cats, but not all seemings as of cats are seeings of cats. Furthermore, not all seemings as of cats are veridical, but all seeings of cats are. And if we describe her belief-formation process as *seeing or hoping that the cat is on the mat*, then it's downright unreliable.

The problem is one of picking out the right principle of individuation for belief-formation processes. Should cognitive virtues be coarsely individuated, so that *inference* makes the cut, or should they be finely individuated, so that *disjunctive syllogism* makes the cut? Various answers have been proposed to the individuation question. Alvin Goldman (1986, p. 50) conjectures that "the critical type is the *narrowest* type that is *causally operative* in producing the belief token in question." James Beebe (2004) argues that cognitive processes should be individuated by the problems they solve, the algorithms they instantiate, and the cognitive architecture backing them. I've argued (2009) that they should be individuated more finely than the sense modalities (where two tokens fall under the same heading if and only if they are both cases of vision, or both cases of hearing, etc.) but less finely than doxastic equivalence (where two tokens fall under the same heading if and only if they would lead to all and only the same beliefs). Empirical evidence about what cognitive processes people actually use would help in sorting out such proposals. Instead of sitting in our armchairs wondering how to individuate cognitive dispositions, we could consult the psychological literature to find out what kinds of cognitive dispositions people actually have.

2 EXTENDING THE CHALLENGE TO RELIABILISM ABOUT INFERENCE

However, my interpretation of the empirical literature bodes ill for relia-bilism, for it's hard to construe the cognitive dispositions we do in fact possess as intellectual virtues. A first-pass elaboration of the situationist challenge to reliabilism can be framed as an inconsistent triad that resem-bles the inconsistent triad discussed in the previous chapter:

(*inferential non-skepticism*) Most people know quite a bit inferentially.

(*inferential reliabilism*) Inferential knowledge is true belief acquired and retained through inferential reliabilist intellectual virtue.

(*inferential cognitive situationism*) People acquire and retain most of their inferential beliefs through heuristics rather than intellectual virtues.

As I mentioned in the previous chapter, the thesis of *non-skepticism* is near-orthodoxy. Inferential non-skepticism is a specification of non-skepticism, so I will treat it as unrevisable for now, though I will return to it near the end of the chapter. At the very least, it would take impressive argumentative acrobatics to convince most epistemologists that they should abandon *inferential non-skepticism* instead of *inferential reliabilism*; if one of the three propositions must go, it's unlikely to be *inferential non-skepticism*.

The crucial question is therefore whether to accept *inferential cognitive situationism* and reject *inferential reliabilism* or, conversely, to reject *infer-ential cognitive situationism* and accept *inferential reliabilism*. Though I could not hope to summarize even a substantial plurality of the relevant research, my interpretation of the cognitive psychology literature is that both ordinary people and experts utilize a motley of fine-grained heuris-tics to arrive at their inferential beliefs. These heuristics are surprisingly accurate in some ordinary circumstances, but they can easily lead to gross error. In other words, they're unreliable. In this section, I will describe in some detail just a few illustrative studies of the *availability* and *represen-tativeness heuristics*.

2.1 The availability heuristic

In Chapter 2, I introduced the availability bias, which leads people to overestimate the probability of events and properties they're familiar with. For instance, if someone has always been nice to you, it's natural to infer that she's nice in general, but such an inference is generally not warranted; she may be nice to you but a hellion to her family. Biases of this sort, provided they are systematic, are useful to researchers because they reveal the processes that people use to arrive at their beliefs. Thus, the availability bias indicates that people tend to infer based on availability: they use what's come to be known as the availability heuristic.

Ask yourself the following question: "In four pages of a novel (about 2,000 words), how many words would you expect to find that have the form _ _ _ _ *ing* (seven-letter words that end with 'ing')?" If you're like the subjects in Amos Tversky and Daniel Kahneman's (1973) study, you probably guessed 13 or 14. Now ask yourself a slightly different question: "In four pages of a novel (about 2,000 words), how many would you expect to find that have the form _ _ _ _ _ *n* _ (seven-letter words whose second-to-last letter is 'n')?" If you're like those subjects, then you probably guessed 4 or 5. Note, however, that any word of the form _ _ _ _ *ing* is necessarily of the form _ _ _ _ _ *n* _. Hence, to be consistent, your answer to the second question must be at least as high as your answer to the first.

The availability heuristic leads people to expect that the probability of an event or the proportion of a property in a population is directly correlated to the ease with which examples can be brought to mind. It's easy enough to think of an example of a seven-letter word ending in 'ing': just start with a four-letter verb, then form a participle. It's not so easy to think of a seven-letter word whose penultimate letter is 'n'. Thus, our use of the availability heuristic leads us to estimate inconsistently in this case. One might respond that of course most people don't know how many words of a given lexicographical type occur on average in a given stretch of prose. Why should they? This in no way impugns the inferential knowledge that we are inclined to attribute to ordinary people. The point here, though, is not just about typography: the availability heuristic is used in a wide variety of contexts. Furthermore, the narrower point here is not about estimating *correctly* but about the *internal consistency* of one's estimates. Because people use the availability heuristic, they don't just end up with false beliefs. They end up with inconsistent beliefs, from which any further inferences are pretty much guaranteed to be unreliable.

The same phenomenon occurs when subjects are asked to guess the number of words of the form _ _ _ _ _ *ly* and the number of words of the form _ _ _ _ _ *l* _ in a stretch of 2,000 words of prose. Average estimates in Tversky and Kahneman's study were 8.8 and 4.4, respectively.

As in the previous example, every seven-letter word ending in 'ly' is also a seven-letter word whose penultimate letter is 'l', but because it's easier to think of an example of the former than the latter, people inconsistently estimate that the latter is less common than the former.

2.2 *The representativeness heuristic*

The availability heuristic uses availability or ease of recall as an index of probability or frequency. Because words ending in 'ing' are easier to conjure up than words whose penultimate letter is 'n', people take them to be more common. Another, closely related, cognitive process is the representativeness heuristic, in which the representativeness of a token is treated as an index of probability or frequency. For Tversky and Kahneman, "*Representativeness* is an assessment of the degree of correspondence between a sample and a population, an instance and a category, an act and an actor, or more generally, between an outcome and a model." They elaborate further, saying that representativeness "can be investigated empirically by asking people, for example, which of two sequences of heads and tails is more representative of a fair coin or which of two professions is more representative of a given personality" (2002, p. 22). If x is more representative of F than of G, then people typically say that it's more likely that x is F than that x is G, even when that's logically impossible because F is the property of being G and H. The upshot is that the representativeness heuristic leads to the conjunction fallacy.

Consider the now-infamous case of Linda: "Linda is 31 years old, single, outspoken and very bright. She majored in philosophy. As a student, she was deeply concerned with issues of discrimination and social justice, and also participated in anti-nuclear demonstrations." In a preliminary survey, Kahneman and Tversky had participants rate the degree to which Linda was representative of the following classes: elementary school teachers, bookstore employees who take yoga classes, feminists, psychiatric social workers, members of the League of Women Voters, bank tellers, insurance salespeople, and feminist bank tellers. 85 percent said that Linda was more representative of feminists than feminist bank tellers. This is unobjectionable. The representativeness heuristic means, however, that people will therefore say that it's also *more likely* that Linda is a feminist bank teller than a bank teller. This is objectionable.

Tversky and Kahneman (2002) went on to investigate the effects of the representativeness heuristic using the case of Linda with a series of increasingly direct studies. In the least direct study, participants read the description of Linda, then ranked for probability (1 = most probable, 2 = second most probable, etc.) the following statements:

(T) Linda is a teacher in elementary school.
(S&Y) Linda works in a bookstore and takes yoga classes.
(F) Linda is active in the feminist movement.
(P) Linda is a psychiatric worker.
(L) Linda is a member of the League of Women Voters.
(B) Linda is a bank teller.
(I) Linda is an insurance salesperson.
(B&F) Linda is a bank teller and is active in the feminist movement.

In this study, either B and F were dropped from the list or B&F was dropped from the list. Therefore, no participants were afforded the opportunity to rank the conjunction as more probable than one of its conjuncts. Pooling the results, however, showed that statistically naive subjects on average ranked B&F at 3.3 and B at 4.4. That is, they considered it more likely that Linda was a feminist bank teller than that she was a bank teller. Statistically sophisticated subjects fared no better: they ranked B&F at 3.1 and B at 4.3. This is troubling, but only minimally so. After all, we don't expect people to be infallible in their inferences. Perhaps when given the opportunity to stare the conjunction fallacy in the eye, people would not make a mistake.

In a more direct test, all eight items were included in the list for subjects to rank. The results were even more troubling. 89 percent of naive subjects and 85 percent of sophisticated subjects committed the conjunction fallacy by ranking B&F higher than B. Worse still, the directness of the test had no measurable effect in helping participants to avoid the conjunction fallacy. The average rank of B&F was 3.3 for naive and 3.2 for sophisticated subjects, while the average rank of B was 4.4 and 4.3, respectively. Even when they had the chance to compare B with B&F directly, a huge majority of participants ranked the conjunction as more probable than its conjunct. Bovens and Hartmann (2003) attempt to explain this and related results away by saying that people quite reasonably trust a source more when it tells them things they expected or already knew. Hence, when one source says that Linda is a feminist and the other doesn't, they are inclined to trust the former source more than the latter, which in turn means that they are rational in placing more confidence in that source when it also tells them that Linda is a bank teller than the other source which tells them that Linda is a bank teller out of the blue. This is a clever work-around, but I fear it doesn't work. For one thing, in this study the propositions B, F, and B&F are all simply listed; they aren't presented as if they came from different sources. For another, subjects explicitly put their trust in representativeness, not the reliability of the source, as the studies I cite below demonstrate.

Even so, the reliabilist might push back by saying that it's unsurprising that people have trouble keeping track of eight propositions simultaneously. Most people rarely undertake such a task, so their inability to do so without committing the conjunction fallacy is consistent with modest reliabilism about simpler inferential knowledge. The implicit assumption here is that when the task is simplified in the appropriate way, the conjunction fallacy will go away. Kahneman and Tversky set out to test this assumption, embarking upon what they describe as "a series of increasingly desperate manipulations designed to induce subjects to obey the conjunction rule" (2002, p. 26). The filler items were deleted, and a new batch of subjects was asked to rank just B and B&F. Even with the distractions removed, 85 percent of respondents committed the conjunction fallacy. Defenders of inferential reliability cannot shrug this result off as easily. Deciding which of two similar propositions is more probable is actually something that people do on a regular basis, and the propositions being compared related to personal and vocational characteristics, properties that we often attribute and reason about. The familiarity defense has no purchase here.

Still, one could respond that Kahneman and Tversky were merely exploiting a trick. Surely, one might think, participants would realize their mistake and make the correct judgment if the reason for choosing B over B&F were made clear. Were this so, it would show that the representativeness heuristic is easily triggered but corrigible. To test this hypothesis, Kahneman and Tversky designed another study in which participants read the description of Linda, then were asked to indicate which of the following arguments they found more persuasive:

(A1) Linda is more likely to be a bank teller than she is to be a feminist bank teller, because every feminist bank teller is a bank teller, but some women bank tellers are not feminists, and Linda could be one of them.
(A2) Linda is more likely to be a feminist bank teller than she is likely to be a bank teller, because she resembles an active feminist more than she resembles a bank teller.

A solid majority of 65 percent chose A2. This is an improvement, but it provides only cold comfort. The representativeness heuristic overpowered the natural light of reason in a large majority of participants.

Furthermore, this study indicates an important difference between cognitive situationism and moral situationism. Subjects in this study actually reasoned in terms of the situational factor of representativeness.[2] In the moral studies, subjects typically do not reason in terms of their moods or the level of ambient noise. They don't reason in terms of situational non-reasons. They also don't tend to reason explicitly in terms of situational demand characteristics. Subjects in the Milgram experiment presumably didn't think to themselves, "The experimenter is wearing a lab coat, so I should obey him." Subjects in the Good Samaritan experiment presumably didn't think, "I'm in a hurry to lecture about the Good Samaritan, so that justifies not acting like a Good Samaritan." This feature of cognitive situationism suggests that, even if the challenge is fended off, higher-order knowledge on the reliabilist model faces a distinct challenge. Ordinary people not only deploy the heuristic but also reflectively endorse it over the sound rule of inference. If that's right, then even if it could be shown that heuristics are reliable, we should conclude that most people don't have second-order knowledge of their heuristically derived knowledge. Suppose I arrive at knowledge of p based on a heuristic inference: Kp. Do I know that I know that p? That is to say, is KKp true? Probably not, because I have a false belief about the reliability of my way of arriving at Kp: I think that it's more reliable than it really is, and I think that it's more reliable than a relevant alternative rule of inference.

Proponents of ecological validity might retrench further, claiming that when we make comparative judgments of likelihood, it's usually with an eye to the potential payoffs for being right (or wrong). Moreover, one might worry that the thorny semantics and pragmatics of terms such as 'probability' and 'likelihood' make the results cited so far difficult to interpret. What would really show that people employ the representativeness heuristic is the introduction of stakes for being right or wrong, as well as the elimination of troublesome vocabulary. To ensure that their results could not be explained away in this fashion, Kahneman and Tversky conducted a study in which participants read the description of Linda, then answered the following question: "If you could win $10 by betting on an event, which of the following would you choose? [B or B&F]" This time, 56 percent of respondents committed the conjunction fallacy – a lower proportion than in the other studies but still more than half.

The question now arises whether the representativeness heuristic is used only in making person-level judgments. If its use is highly circumscribed,

---

[2] Thanks to Jonathan Adler for emphasizing this point to me.

the argument for epistemic situationism would also be highly circum-scribed. Epistemic situationism would entail at worst skepticism about inference about people, not skepticism about inference in general. In a series of follow-up studies, Kahneman and Tversky (2002) investigated whether the representativeness heuristic would induce the conjunction fallacy in other content areas (medicine, sports, and betting) and whether it would be undercut by expertise and monetary incentives. The results are a source of genuine consternation.

In the medical study, internists enrolled in Harvard postgraduate courses or with admitting privileges at the New England Medical Center responded to surveys like the following:

A 55-year-old woman had pulmonary embolism documented angiographically 10 days after a cholecystectomy. Please rank order the following in terms of the probability that they will be among the conditions experienced by the patient (use 1 for the most likely and 6 for the least likely). Naturally, a patient could experience more than one of these conditions.

Dyspnea and hemiparesis	Syncope and tachycardia
Calf pain	Hemiparesis
Pleuritic chest pain	Hemoptysis

Consulting physicians had determined that hemiparesis (partial paraly-sis) was highly unrepresentative of pulmonary embolism (blood clots in the lungs) while dyspnea (shortness of breath) was highly representative. The question, then, was whether statistically sophisticated physicians would commit the conjunction fallacy even in a content area where they were experts. In all five versions of the case, the conjunction was ranked more probable (2.7) than its conjunct (4.6). In the best case, 73 percent of the physicians committed the conjunction fallacy; in the worst, 100 percent did. Unlike ordinary participants, the doctors were quick to revise their judgments when the fallacy was pointed out. This suggests that statistical expertise does make people's use of heuristics corrigible. However, it's unclear how comforting this should be. It seems to indi-cate that experts are just as likely as ordinary people to have unreliably formed beliefs but that they will be quick to revise those beliefs in the rare circumstances where their errors are pointed out to them. Such an outcome would still lead to a kind of skepticism, along with a slew of misdiagnoses.

In other studies, the pattern of responses was just as dismaying. Adult Oregonians said it was more likely that Bjorn Borg would win the finals at Wimbledon after losing the first set than that he would lose the first set.³ In another study, undergraduates at the University of British Columbia and Stanford responded to the following prompt:

Consider a regular six-sided die with four green faces and two red faces. The die will be rolled 20 times and the sequence of greens (G) and reds (R) will be recorded. You are asked to select one sequence, from a set of three, and you will win $25 if the sequence you chose appears on successive rolls of the die. Please check the sequence of greens and reds on which you prefer to bet.

1. RGRRR
2. GRGRRR
3. GRRRRR

In this study, the words 'probability' and 'likelihood' made no appearance. In addition, subjects had monetary skin in the game: they would be rewarded with a non-trivial sum if they predicted correctly. Although sequence 2 is more representative of the die (2 greens, 4 reds), sequence 1 is necessarily more likely than sequence 2. In the language of decision theory, choosing 1 weakly dominates choosing 2. Nevertheless, 65 percent of participants chose sequence 2. Even when sequence 2 was replaced with 'RGRRRG' in a follow-up study to make it clearer that it contained sequence 1, 63 percent of respondents chose it.

3   THE PHILOSOPHICAL UPSHOT: UNRELIABLE HEURISTICS

It should be clear that I could go on about the availability heuristic, the representativeness heuristic, and the conjunction fallacy, but I want to step back now to draw a tentative philosophical conclusion. The robustness of these heuristics throws a pall of doubt over the notion that most people possess the intellectual virtues related to even rudimentary inferential reasoning. The processes used to arrive at beliefs about likelihood in no way resemble sound inferential practice; rather, people follow heuristics that treat availability and representativeness as indices of probability. My claim is that the same holds true for other heuristics, and that this creates trouble not only for the cognitive virtues related to deductive and inductive reasoning, but for many of the

---

³ Michael Levin has emphasized to me that this result could be explained by assuming not that participants used the representativeness heuristic but that they compared the unconditional probability P(Borg loses the opening set) to the conditional probability P(Borg wins the match | Borg loses the opening set). I agree, but it seems to me that the more parsimonious explanation appeals to the representativeness heuristic, since that seems to figure in many other judgments as well. In any event, conditionalizing explanations of this sort will not salvage most of the other violations of the conjunction fallacy canvassed in this chapter.

other cognitive virtues related to inference, such as abduction. If this is right, reliabilists face a dilemma. If they say that such heuristics are not intellectual virtues, skepticism looms: if most people use non-virtuous heuristics to arrive at their inferential beliefs, then most people have unjustified beliefs, which do not count as knowledge even when true. If, however, reliabilists say that these heuristics are intellectual virtues, then they need to explain how these dispositions are to be construed as reliable.

3.1   Partial defeat

The first horn of the dilemma faced by reliabilists is to admit partial defeat in the sphere of inference. This admission could take three forms. First, one could adopt a mixed theory of knowledge, according to which a non-inferential belief counts as knowledge only if it was formed by a reliable process, while an inferential belief counts as knowledge only if it satisfies some to-be-specified criterion. Reliabilists could even say that reliability is still sufficient for inferential knowledge, but that it's not necessary. This would save inferential non-skepticism at the cost of circumscribing the applicable domain of the reliability criterion of knowledge. I am unfamiliar with any extant mixed theories of knowledge, so I'm not sure how appealing this option might be. Hybrid theories do have their appeal in ethics. Perhaps epistemologists should try them on for size.

Alternatively, reliabilists could maintain their theory even in the realm of inference. This leads to the second way of admitting partial defeat, which is to give up on egalitarianism about intellectual virtue and knowledge. As I explained in Chapter 3, many virtue ethicists have made this move in responding to the situationist challenge to virtue ethics, claiming that virtue is rare, so empirical studies of groups should not be expected to turn up a great deal of virtuous conduct. I don't find this response appealing in the case of virtue ethics, and it seems even less appealing for virtue epistemology, for it would entail a great deal of skepticism. Yes, some people have knowledge, but they're an elite epistemic minority. This flies in the face of the Moorean platitude of *non-skepticism.*

The third way of admitting partial defeat attempts to partition off a class of knowledge claims rather than a class of knowers. In the face of the evidence for inferential situationism, reliabilists might want to conclude that people who use these heuristics really *don't* have inferential knowledge but that they could still have knowledge derived from many other sources, such as perception, memory, testimony, etc. The Moorean platitude of non-skepticism may not extend to the far reaches of inference. Perhaps it really only includes more mundane things like knowledge that the external world exists, that I have a hand, and so on.

To bolster this reply, reliabilists might try to argue that really, when you think about it, most human beliefs are not arrived at through inference. So even if we are forced to concede skepticism about inference, that would not impugn a critical mass of our beliefs. And when people do use sound inferential practices, such as Bayes' Law or *modus tollens*, their beliefs can still count as knowledge. This would rescue scientific inference, which is typically much more careful than everyday inference because scientists presumably avoid using heuristics when they can.

There is some precedent for localized skepticism of this sort. The reply in some ways resembles Nozick's (1981) admission that the negations of skeptical hypotheses are not known, even when truly believed. Of course, extending ignorance from the negations of skeptical hypotheses to most inferential beliefs is a step, but it may not be so a big step as to be unacceptable.

3.2   *The reliabilists strike back*

If the first horn of the dilemma doesn't tempt you, perhaps you'd prefer to argue that, despite what I've said so far, heuristics such as availability and representativeness really *are* reliable. After all, I did mention above that heuristics can be surprisingly accurate. Perhaps the cases where they break down – the cases that I harped on above – are quite rare. They can be constructed *ad infinitum* in laboratory contexts, but in the real world perhaps they don't crop up too often. If they are sufficiently rare, then heuristics may not be so bad after all.

A related argument holds that heuristics are reliable in the appropriate domain; it's only when they're used outside that domain that they lead to systematic error. In a slogan, "heuristics are reliable except when they aren't."[4] Well, bully for them. So is flipping a coin to decide whether it's raining: if you only flip the coin, or only infer based on the result of the flip, when it's right, then of course it's reliable. Heuristics, along with every other decision procedure one can imagine, satisfy that condition of reliability. The idea must be something more like this: heuristics are

---

[4] Thanks to Guy Axtell for emphasizing this argument to me.

reliable *when we're disposed to use them*, and when they're unreliable *we stop using them*.

This suggests an interesting difference between heuristics and sound inference rules. If you input truths to *modus ponens*, it outputs truths. If you input truths to disjunctive inference, it outputs truths. If you input good evidence to Bayes' Law, it outputs rational probabilities. If you input triggering conditions into a heuristic – well, it depends. Sound inference rules are context neutral. Heuristics aren't. So, instead of talking about whether heuristics are categorically reliable, perhaps it would be better to talk about the contexts in which heuristics are reliable or unreliable. To do so sensibly, it would be useful to distinguish two kinds of reliability: trigger reliability and output reliability. Belief-formation processes are like tools in a certain way. Just as you wouldn't want to say that a hacksaw is unreliable because it's no good at driving nails, you wouldn't want to say that vision is unreliable because it's no good at determining how something smells. Match the tool to its function, and it turns out to be reliable. Match the belief-formation process to the context it's appropriate for, and it turns out to be reliable. Let the *trigger reliability* of a process be the ratio of the times it's used in appropriate circumstances to the total times it's used. We can then distinguish two kinds of output reliability. The *ideal output reliability* of a process is the ratio of the true to total beliefs it produces when used in appropriate circumstances. The *actual output reliability* of a process is the ratio of true to total beliefs it produces when used. When we talk about whether a process is reliable, sometimes we have in mind its ideal output reliability, but I would argue that it's better to use its actual output reliability, which takes into account trigger (un)reliability. By way of analogy, the ideal effectiveness of the male condom is 98 percent, but its actual effectiveness, as used by ordinary people, is 85 percent (Hatcher et al. 2008, p. 210). When thinking about unwanted pregnancy, it's clearly important to take into account the fact that people don't tend to use condoms exactly as they should. In the same way, a process may be reliable when used only in appropriate circumstances, but if the trigger reliability of the process is low, its actual output reliability will be low as well.

Consider the availability heuristic, for example: it's pretty good when you've had a large, unbiased sample of the domain, but not otherwise. So instead of talking about whether the availability heuristic is reliable, we should talk about whether large-unbiased-sample-availability is reliable (maybe), whether small-unbiased-sample-availability is reliable (no), whether small-biased-sample-availability is reliable (no), and so on. The question then is whether people tend to use the availability heuristic only in appropriate circumstances, or whether they use it willy-nilly. In other words, what is the trigger reliability of the availability heuristic?

This move parallels Doris's theory of local moral virtues. Instead of asking whether someone is generous, he thinks it's more fruitful to ask whether she's good-mood-generous, bad-mood-generous, etc. If you relativize to context, you can start to make supportable attributions. There's an important difference, though. On the moral side, global dispositions are normatively adequate but empirically inadequate: they're what you'd want, but most people don't have them. On the epistemic side, global heuristics are normatively inadequate but empirically adequate: they're unreliable, and most people use them. Relativizing moral virtues to contexts makes them empirically adequate but threatens to leave them normatively uninspiring. It might be seen as damning with faint praise to say that someone is loyal to his male friends, as I argued in the previous chapter. Relativizing heuristics to contexts could make them reliable, but at the cost empirical adequacy. Why? Because, if the data cited above on the representativeness heuristic is any guide, that's not how most people deploy them. Heuristics may have ideal output reliability, but poor trigger reliability and hence poor actual output reliability.

One might retreat even further and say that, while people *don't* curb their use of heuristics in the right way, they *could learn to.* The example of the corrigible doctors who revised their judgments when it was pointed out that they'd committed the conjunction fallacy supports this move. My initial response, however, is to shrug. Here's how I see the dialectic: the defender of reliabilism wants to fend off the skeptical challenge, according to which the processes people actually use to arrive at their inferential beliefs are unreliable. It doesn't help to say that, though the processes people actually use to arrive at their inferential beliefs are unreliable, *people could use reliable processes.* That wouldn't show that people have knowledge; what it would show is that they *could* have knowledge. I haven't been arguing here that inferential knowledge is impossible, just that most people don't have it if it's defined in reliabilist terms. Furthermore, it remains to be shown that people can actually use heuristics responsibly. The place to look would be the Kahneman–Gigerenzer controversy, but my own reading of that controversy is that Kahneman's side prevails.[5]

---

[5] The crux of this controversy is the question of human rationality, with Kahneman and his allies arguing that the research on heuristics and biases has bleak implications, while Gigerenzer and his allies argue that suitably contextualized heuristics are not only rational but extremely efficient. See Samuels, Stich, and Bishop (2002) for an even-handed discussion.

Consider instead the following claim in favor of the reliability of heuristics, which has the flavor of a transcendental argument:

Let's grant that people often arrive at their inferential beliefs via heuristics. It follows that heuristics *must* be reliable. Furthermore, there's good evolutionary reason for this supposition. People who routinely make unreliable inferences are less fit than people who routinely make reliable inferences, so the fact that most people are strongly disposed to use heuristics means that heuristics must be adaptive and, hence, reliable.[6]

I say the argument has a transcendental flavor because it takes for granted some empirical claim (widespread use of heuristics), then articulates what would have to be the case for that empirical claim to be possible. Let's first consider the argument without the evolutionary backstory. The granted claim is that heuristic use is widespread. The conclusion is that heuristics must be reliable. There's a missing premise here: *inferential non-skepticism*. If we add that in, the granted claim is that, although heuristic use is widespread, most people know quite a bit on the basis of inference. And the conclusion of the argument remains that heuristics must be reliable. Even as amended, the transcendental argument is clearly invalid. What needs to be added is that knowledge is arrived at by reliable processes. Otherwise, it remains open to say that people acquire inferential knowledge on the basis of *un*reliable processes, such as the availability and representativeness heuristics.[7] While it is of course possible to add this further premise to the argument, to do so would beg the question. Reliabilism is precisely what is at stake in this debate. The defender of reliabilism is not entitled to use it as a premise.

Though the purely transcendental form of the argument is invalid, perhaps the evolutionary backstory will help. I take it that a fleshed-out version of the argument would go like this:

Suppose that some of our ancestors tended to make inferences using processes p, q, and r, and that other of our ancestors tended to make inferences using processes s, t, and u. Suppose further that p, q, and r are more reliable than s, t, and u. Then the pqr-ancestors would have ended up with more reliable beliefs than the stu-ancestors, which in turn means that they would outcompete the stus. We are the offspring of the pqrs, so they must have used reliable decision processes, which were passed on to us. Hence, the heuristics we use must be reliable.

---

[6] Guy Axtell, Abrol Fairweather, Jennifer Lackey, and Carlos Montemayor have all made versions of this argument in conversation.

[7] John Turri (*Unreliable Knowledge*, unpublished manuscript) holds that knowledge can sometimes be acquired through unreliable processes.

Consider again the availability heuristic, which treats ease of recall as an index of frequency and probability. Certainly, one might argue, it's got to be better to use the availability heuristic than many other rules of inference. For example, it's clearly better to use the availability heuristic than the *unavailability* heuristic, an artificial monstrosity that treats difficulty of recall as an index of frequency and probability. People wander around the world, encountering objects of various sorts. If their encounters are sufficiently like a random sample, and if accessibility depends largely on the number of encounters with things of a given type, then the easier it is to recall something, the more frequently one encountered it in the past and, hence, the more common it is (or at least was). Yes, the heuristic can go haywire sometimes, but it does a solid job in most ordinary circumstances. Presumably a similar argument could be made in defense of the recognition heuristic. And then, the reliabilist might point out, heuristics may often be the only or the best thing we have to go on. People lack the time, processing power, memory, and skill to apply sound deductive and inductive rules in all cases. Sometimes they have to slum it by using heuristics. But when they do, they tend to use heuristics that work well enough to be adaptive.

There are several problems with this argument. First, at best it shows that we are descendants of our most epistemically reliable ancestors, and hence that we tend to use the most epistemically reliable heuristics available to the species tens of thousands of years ago. But that is plainly irrelevant to whether the heuristics we use are reliable *enough* to lead to knowledge. Maybe the available decision rules were all pretty bad; then the ones that survived would merely be the best of a bad lot: more reliable than some, but not reliable enough to yield knowledge.

Second, even assuming that the *pqr*s used outright reliable heuristics, and not just the best of a bad lot, the argument assumes that the contemporary inferential setting is relevantly similar to that of our ancestors. Since it's best to talk about the reliability of heuristics relative to some context, it's quite possible that using p, q, and r was reliable relative to the context of hunter-gatherer nomads in the African savannah, but that using p, q, and r is unreliable relative to the context of modern humans navigating highways, cities, and online media. Since we've changed our environment so much in the last ten millennia, the fact that something used to work is moot on the question of whether it still works.

Third, the argument crucially assumes that reliability is adaptive. This is not obvious. In recent years, the so-called *value problem* for epistemology has loomed large: why is knowledge better than mere true belief? The answer, as Plato already understood in the *Meno*, is not that knowledge is more practically useful: someone who has a true belief about how to get from point A to point B will arrive there just as surely as someone who knows the way from A to B. What I take to be the best proposed solution to the value problem is that knowledge is an achievement (Greco 2010), and achievements are intrinsically valuable. But are achievements intrinsically adaptive? I see little reason to think so.

But, one might argue, if the *pqr*s use more reliable decision rules than the *stu*s, surely they will end up with more true beliefs (or a higher proportion of true to false beliefs), so even if their having more knowledge isn't adaptive, their having more verisimilar beliefs is. At this point I think it is essential to distinguish reliability, which is a purely epistemic notion, from adaptiveness, which is both epistemic and practical. The adaptiveness of a decision rule isn't identical to its reliability. It is, roughly speaking, the product of reliability and average payoff. An example illustrates this point. Compare two decision procedures, P1 and P2, used over ten cases. P1 leads to eight true beliefs, while P2 leads to six. So P1 is 80 percent reliable, while P2 is only 60 percent reliable. Surely, one might think, P1 is more adaptive than P2. On the contrary, it depends on what happens when the agent gets things right and what happens when he gets them wrong. For if P1 goes astray when it would be disastrous to be wrong, while P2 goes astray when it doesn't hurt too much to be wrong, then it may well be the case that P2 is more adaptive than P1. So the adaptiveness of a belief-formation process isn't just its reliability; it's reliability *when it matters*.

This just shows that it's possible for reliability and adaptiveness to come apart, which casts doubt on the evolutionary argument, but perhaps not too much. It would be more persuasive to show that, for the heuristics we actually use, reliability and adaptiveness diverge. There's reason to think that, for many of them, this is the case. Consider the disgust reaction. Much recent research in moral and social psychology (e.g., Kelly 2011) suggests that the human disgust reaction originally evolved to detect potentially poisonous and infectious objects. However, it very easily associates new triggers with the disgust script, so that one becomes disgusted by, for instance, the food and cultural practices of outgroup members. Ex-senator and then-presidential candidate Rick Santorum claimed in early 2012 that John F. Kennedy's speech in favor of the separation of church and state made him want to vomit. In our evolutionary history, it probably was adaptive to have an oversensitive disgust reaction because the payoff of a false negative (being poisoned) was so much worse than the payoff of a false positive (failing to eat something benign). If this is right, the disgust heuristic is adaptive but unreliable.

Or consider again the fundamental attribution error: the tendency to attribute others' behavior to dispositional factors rather than situational ones, even when it should be clear that situation is importantly operative. Presumably the pattern of judgments identified by this error stems from the use of a heuristic. Call it the *disposition heuristic*: when someone does something of type *t*, infer that she is a *t*er. For example, if someone lies, infer she's a liar. If someone cheats, infer she's a cheater. If someone helps, infer she's a helper. This isn't a particularly reliable heuristic, but when it goes wrong (i.e., when it leads to the fundamental attribution error), it's often self-confirming. If you think that someone is a helper, you tend to signal that expectation to her, which in turn will make her more inclined to help. If a waiter thinks that someone is a low tipper, he'll tend to give them bad service, which in turn will lead to a low tip. This is of course what I called factitious virtue and vice in the first half of the book. It would appear, then, that the disposition heuristic, like the disgust heuristic, is adaptive but unreliable.

4 CONCLUSION

In this chapter, I've attempted to argue that the situationist challenges to virtue ethics and virtue responsibilism have a reliabilist cousin. I documented evidence that people are disposed to use a variety of heuristics, such as availability and representativeness, to arrive at their inferential beliefs, and argued that these heuristics are not reliable enough to lead to knowledge – at least not as they are ordinarily deployed. A number of potential counterarguments were canvassed, but it was unclear whether any of them succeed. If the arguments developed in this chapter are on the right track, reliabilists need to come to grips with a situationist challenge of their own. Furthermore, mixed views now need to grapple with both the challenge to responsibilism developed in the previous chapter and the challenge to reliabilism developed here. In the next chapter, I ask whether the factitious virtue response to the situationist challenge to virtue ethics can be modified to defend virtue epistemology as well.

CHAPTER 7

Factitious intellectual virtue

Whatever they may think and say about their "egoism," the great majority nonetheless do nothing for their ego their whole life long: what they do is done for the phantom of their ego which has formed itself in the heads of those around them and has been communicated to them; – as a consequence they all of them dwell in a fog of impersonal, semi-personal opinions, and arbitrary, as it were poetical evaluations, the one for ever in the head of someone else, and the head of this someone else again in the heads of others: a strange world of phantasms.

Friedrich Nietzsche, *Daybreak*, 105

I   INTRODUCTION

In the first half of this book, I argued that moral virtues should often be attributed even in the absence of what would ordinarily be considered sufficient evidence because such attributions tend to function as self-fulfilling prophecies. When someone is told that she's honest, she becomes honest (or near enough). When someone is told that he's considerate, he becomes considerate (or near enough). When someone is told that she's just, she becomes just (or near enough).

In the two preceding chapters, I advanced the situationist challenge to virtue epistemology. If my arguments there were correct, most people do not possess the intellectual virtues countenanced by responsibilism or inferential reliabilism. This would be a damning result for both classical virtue epistemology, which would then be committed to skepticism, and inquiry virtue epistemology, which would then be committed to negative evaluative judgments about most epistemic agents. Perhaps the factitious virtue response works for virtue epistemology as well, though. Perhaps we should attribute intellectual virtues even in the absence of what would ordinarily be considered sufficient evidence because such attributions tend to function as self-fulfilling prophecies. Perhaps when someone is told she's intelligent, she becomes intelligent (or near enough). Perhaps when someone is told he's open-minded, he becomes open-minded (or near enough).

This would be welcome news, as the rejoinders from virtue epistemologists to the situationist challenge to virtue ethics have so far have been scant and inadequate.[1] James Montmarquet's response has been to abandon the explanatory power and counterfactual validity of the virtues. He claims that "how virtuously one has acted in a given situation depends only on one's act and motivation *in that situation* and not, as such, on how one would have acted in other situations" (2003, p. 360). To opt for this standard of evaluation would be to give up the idea that if someone has a virtue responsive to reasons of type r, then, whenever (or at least most of the times when) r is decisive, he would act from that virtue. It is pretty much an endorsement of Thomas Hurka's (2001, 2006) act-based approach to the virtues, which puts little emphasis on the consistency and stability of agents' traits.

From a different point of view, Ernest Sosa (2008) has recognized that virtue theorists' responses to situationism have been insufficient thus far. His main positive suggestion is that we should aim to better learn what situational influences there are, and then pare down the more audacious commitments of virtue theory to stay within empirically established boundaries. This is a version of the *retreat* discussed in Chapter 3. It attempts merely to weaken virtue theory in such a way as to make it empirically adequate – a not unreasonable position. I am proposing a more adventuresome response, which is to co-opt the power of the situation to encourage thought, feeling, and action in accordance with the intellectual virtues.

Here, as in the previous chapters, we must distinguish the cognitive intellectual virtues of reliabilism from the conative intellectual virtues of responsibilism. This point is crucial because I will argue that factitious reliabilist virtue does not exist while factitious responsibilist virtue does. This is not too disappointing a result, as reliabilism turned out to be less susceptible to situationist critique than responsibilism.

For there to be factitious reliabilist virtue, attributions of intellectual capacities and dispositions would have to function as self-fulfilling

---

[1] Note that until now the challenge to virtue *epistemology* has been but a gleam in the situationist's eye. Responses by virtue *epistemologists* have all been to the challenge to virtue *ethics*. Perhaps they would respond differently to the arguments presented in Chapter 5 and Chapter 6.

prophecies. Does telling someone that she is intelligent make her intelligent? Does telling someone that he has good eyesight improve his vision? In the latter case, this seems quite dubious, but researchers in educational psychology such as Robert Rosenthal and Lenore Jacobson (1968) have argued that intelligence attributions do function as self-fulfilling prophecies, raising schoolchildren's IQ scores by a full standard deviation over the course of a few years. Their research is much cited but extremely controversial. Carol Dweck and her colleagues (e.g., Mueller and Dweck 1998) have gone so far as to say that attributions of intelligence often *backfire* because (among other things) they put too much pressure on students to perform.

For there to be factitious responsibilist virtue, attributions of intellectual motivations would have to function as self-fulfilling prophecies. Does telling someone that she's conscientious make her conscientious (or near enough)? Does telling someone that he's academically sedulous make him a hard worker (or near enough)? Rosenthal and Jacobson make arguments about responsibilist traits similar to the ones they make about intelligence; however, they often conflate cognitive and conative intellectual virtues, so it's hard to know what exactly to make of their claims. In the same vein, Ray Rist (1970, 1972, 1973, 1977) argues that attributions of motivational intellectual virtues and of motivational intellectual vices function as self-fulfilling prophecies in schools. Positively labeled students receive more time and praise from their teachers, along with indications of high expectations; negatively labeled students receive less time and more discipline, along with indications of low expectations. Over time, such differential treatment influences students' motivation to learn, squeezing them into preexisting molds.

In this chapter, I take up the question whether factitious intellectual virtue is a real phenomenon. I will argue that the answer for reliabilist intellectual virtues is, "Typically not," but that the answer for responsibilist intellectual virtues is, "Yes, with some caveats." This should be unsurprising to some extent, as the motivational responsibilist virtues are clearly more analogous to the traditional moral virtues (which I've already argued are susceptible to factitious attributions) than the non-motivational reliabilist virtues. Thus, I will suggest that instead of resisting the situationist challenge to virtue epistemology, we should aim to co-opt it. If seemingly trivial and normatively irrelevant situational factors influence the degree to which people are honest, intellectually courageous, conscientious, careful, flexible, curious, and creative, then we should seek out and deploy just those situational factors that will make us and our peers act more intellectually virtuous than we would otherwise. In particular, I shall marshal evidence from educational and social psychology to show that the act of *publicly attributing responsibilist but not reliabilist intellectual virtues* tends to function as a self-fulfilling prophecy. People who are not yet curious start to act curiously when they are called curious. People who are not yet academically sedulous begin to work hard in school when they are labeled as hard-working. People who are not yet conscientious become so by being called conscientious. Even if we do not as a matter of fact possess the responsibilist intellectual virtues, the tactical use of certain fictions leads to *factitious intellectual virtue.*

As before, this startling phenomenon appears to derive from two distinct but related psychological mechanisms: self-concept and social expectations. People are averse to cognitive dissonance – acting contrary to their images of themselves – so if someone begins to think of himself as open-minded because he has been labeled thus, he will act open-mindedly to maintain his self-concept.[2] In addition, people are typically averse to disappointing others' expectations, so when someone is publicly labeled conscientious, she will be more inclined to act the part. Furthermore, students who have been labeled as intellectually virtuous are treated differently from those who have not been thus labeled; this differential treatment encourages the cultivation of the intellectual virtues, even if they were not there to begin with.

It may be that we have to remain content with merely factitious intellectual virtue, without ever advancing to full virtue; few studies are directly relevant to this question. However, as in the case of the moral virtues, I will speculate that, after sufficient habituation, people with merely factitious intellectual virtues reliant on self-concept and social expectation may end up fully virtuous, unencumbered by these artificial supports. It is not clear from the research that this is so, but it's also not clear that it's not so.

A further question concerns the status of the beliefs involved in factitious intellectual virtue. When I successfully label someone curious, do I thereby come to know that she is curious (or near enough)? Does she? When someone labels me open-minded, does he thereby come to know that I'm open-minded (or near enough)? Do I? I will argue that knowledge is only generated by factitious attributions when the attributor intends to make a factitious attribution. If someone mistakenly believes another person is intellectually virtuous, and says so, he might end up

---

[2] Cognitive dissonance theory was first promulgated in Festinger et al. (1956). For a contemporary treatment, see Cooper (2007).

making a self-fulfilling prophecy, but he does not know that the target of the attribution is virtuous (at least, not until much later). However, when someone intends to make a self-fulfilling prophecy, and does so successfully, she does know that the target of the attribution will turn out to be intellectually virtuous (or near enough). This is because in the latter but not the former case, the attributor has a correct understanding of the mechanism at work.

After discussing the co-opting response to the situationist challenge to virtue epistemology and the question of knowledge of the content of factitious attributions, I conclude by responding to a number of potential criticisms and pointing toward directions for future research. One potential worry about factitious intellectual virtue is that it seems to involve the intellectual vice of dishonesty; telling people they have traits that they do not possess is morally and epistemically troubling. While I recognize the discomfort this proposal may engender, it seems to me that, as with factitious moral virtue, it can be massaged away. Another potential worry is that factitious intellectual virtue essentially involves the intellectual vice of overconfidence. These and other concerns are addressed in the final section of the chapter.

2   FACTITIOUS INTELLECTUAL VIRTUE

The 1960s and 1970s were a heyday for liberal-minded social engineering in the United States. Drawing on research and theories developed by sociologists, criminologists, and others, the social scientists of this period seemed to think almost anything could be accomplished (or prevented) through well-intentioned interventions. One of the guiding lights of this era was the sociologist William Isaac Thomas, who had epigrammatically stated, "If men define their situations as real, they are real in their consequences" (1929, p. 572). Guided by this and related principles, they set to work to establish that many seemingly intrinsic qualities – from delinquency to accomplishment, from retardation to genius – were the product of social influences. If such influences could be strategically harnessed, perhaps society could be changed for the better. Chief among these researchers was Robert Rosenthal, a luminary in social psychology for over three decades. Rosenthal was committed to the idea that both intelligence and academic motivation were largely a matter of the expectations levied on students by their teachers, their principals, their parents, and others. The controversy surrounding his research serves as a narrative background for this chapter.

2.1   Factitious reliabilist virtue

In 1968, Robert Rosenthal and Lenore Jacobson published *Pygmalion in the Classroom: Teacher Expectations and Pupils' Intellectual Development*, in which they described a longitudinal study of the effects of labeling on students and teachers. Based on the research of Rosenthal and Lawson (1964), they had come to think that if teachers expected great things from their students, they would act in such a way as to generate great things from them. Rosenthal and Lawson had discovered that when experimenters believed a lab rat to be intelligent, they handled it differently, which led it to perform better in Skinner boxes and mazes. Conversely, if they thought they had a particularly stupid rat on their hands, they handled it in such a way that it performed worse in the Skinner boxes and mazes. If experimenters' expectations influenced rat intelligence, they reasoned, perhaps teachers' expectations would influence student intelligence.

The design of Rosenthal and Jacobson's study was straightforward. Elementary school students, along with their teachers, in a primarily Mexican-American neighborhood of San Francisco were the subjects. At the beginning of the school year, the students were given the Test of General Ability (TOGA), which measures IQ. Teachers were deceived into thinking that the test was actually a new assessment tool called the "Harvard Test of Inflected Acquisition," which measured not IQ but the potential for academic improvement. They were also deceived with respect to how students did on the test: a few of the students were randomly selected as "high potential gainers," and this label was conveyed to their teachers. Over the course of the following months, Rosenthal and Jacobson observed how these students were treated, how they performed in their classes, and how their IQ scores changed on follow-up tests. The effect was impressive, especially for the younger students. After one year, the average IQ increase for students in the experimental condition was over 12 points, roughly a full standard deviation. Students in the first and second grades gained 27 and 17 points, respectively, while their peers in the control group gained only 12 and 7 points, respectively (p. 75). Among the first- and second-graders, 79 percent increased their IQ scores at least 10 points. One boy raised his IQ score 69 points (over four standard deviations!) to 202, well above the threshold of genius (p. 85). Another went from a 'moron' score of 61 to a respectable 106 (p. 86).[3]

---

[3] For a discussion of the converse phenomenon – negative effects of labeling children as intellectually retarded – see Guskin (1978).

Rosenthal and Jacobson's results floored many in the fields of education and psychology, and received rhapsodic treatment in the popular media. *The New York Times* ran a front-page headline declaring, "Study Indicates Pupils Do Well When Teacher Is Told They Will." *Pygmalion* was positively reviewed in the *New York Review of Books*. It even made its way into courtrooms. In *Hobson v. Hansen*, the plaintiffs drew on *Pygmalion* in convincing the jury to restrict the use of tests for placing students in ability tracks. In *Bradley v. Milliken*, *Pygmalion* was cited by both plaintiffs and defendants.

Other researchers attempted to replicate and extend Rosenthal and Jacobson's results. Lieutenant Colonel Wilburn Schrank conducted a pair of studies at the US Air Force Academy preparatory school. At this institution, students were typically divided into five groups based on their (perceived) mathematical ability: the high-level students in one class, the mid-level students in another, and so on. In his initial study, Schrank (1968a) instead divided them randomly, but didn't tell the teachers or students that the method of division had changed. Consistent with Rosenthal and Jacobson's theory, those in the highest ability group outperformed those in the other groups, those in the second-highest ability group outperformed those in the next three groups, and so on. In a follow-up study (1968b), the teachers but not the students were informed that the division into groups was random, which presumably negated their usual expectations. This time, all groups performed about the same. Schrank plausibly interprets these results as showing that for the division into high- and low-ability groups to function as a self-fulfilling prophecy, the teachers must believe in the labels, which would lead them to treat the classes differently, thereby generating the self-fulfilling prophecy. This is further evidence for the plausibility condition on factitious virtue attributions discussed in Chapter 4.

In another replication, Meichenbaum, Bowers, and Ross (1969) identified a randomly selected subset of the students at an all-girls school as 'late bloomers,' a label which they explained to the teachers as indicating a combination of intelligence, interest, and motivation. Some of the 'late bloomers' had already been picked out by the teachers as having high potential; others had been relegated to the ranks of low-potential students. When teachers first heard which students could be expected to show substantial improvements, they were surprised about the latter students, but they quickly confabulated corroborating evidence and eventually concluded that the researchers had "hit the nail on the head" (p. 309) – an instance of confirmation bias. Over the course of the academic year, these 'late bloomers' were treated with more positive affect and less negative affect than their peers (e.g., more praise and less discipline); they also outperformed their peers, both academically and behaviorally. This study again suggests that labeling students with intellectual virtues functions as a self-fulfilling prophecy, with teacher expectations mediating the effect.

In a follow-up to their experiment on tidiness discussed in Chapter 4, Miller, Brickman, and Bolen (1975) conducted an experiment on the effects of teacher expectations on second-graders' performance in mathematics. They randomly divided the students into several groups. The *attribution-ability* students were repeatedly told that they were intelligent. The teachers said things like, "You are a very good arithmetic student," and "You seem to know your arithmetic assignments well." Notes were sent home to these students' parents saying they had "excellent arithmetic ability." Those in the *attribution-motivation* condition were told that they were hard workers. Teachers said things like, "You really work hard in arithmetic," and sent home notes that included phrases like, "working hard," "trying," and "applying himself." In two further conditions, *persuasion-ability* and *persuasion-motivation*, students were told not that they already had desirable intellectual traits, but that they *should* have them. Thus, this study attempted to generate both factitious reliabilist virtue and factitious responsibilist virtue, and to compare those attempts with more traditional persuasive techniques. The results were promising. Students in both of the attribution conditions increased their measured math self-esteem and performed better in their math classes; the effect occurred immediately and lasted the whole academic year. Those in the persuasion conditions underwent no change in self-esteem, did increase their performance initially, but showed no solid gains later in the semester.

Along the same lines, Zanna, Sheras, Cooper, and Shaw (1975) found that manipulating either student or teacher expectations of intellectual potential induced congruent behavior. Their subjects were sixth- to eighth-grade students and teachers in a summer enrichment program in mathematics and English. The instructors at this summer school were given reason to expect intelligent behavior from some of the students, who subsequently outperformed the others. At the same time, some of the students were told that they "would probably perform well in the program." These students also outperformed the controls. These results further corroborate the mediating effects of self-concept and social expectations. Being thought and treated smart makes people act smart. Thinking one-self smart makes one act smart.

Literally hundreds of further studies that support this basic line of thought have been conducted and published.[4] Rosenthal (1974) found that teachers give 'bright' students more differentiated performance feedback, more material to learn, more difficult material to learn, and more opportunities to respond in class. Rosenthal and Rubin (1978) showed that teachers pay more attention to, give different verbal and non-verbal feedback to, and make extra efforts for students they perceive to be intelligent. In a meta-analysis of 464 studies, Rosenthal (1994) found the average Cohen's *d* value of *Pygmalion*-style studies to be 0.63, which indicates a medium-to-large effect size.

As you will probably have noticed, however, in most of the studies discussed so far, intelligence and epistemic motivation were conflated. Expecting a student to do well in a mathematics class assumes that she possesses at least a modicum of intelligence, but it also assumes an adequate degree of motivation to succeed at mathematics. Unfortunately, Rosenthal and other researchers in this field have often conflated the cognitive and conative intellectual virtues, so it's difficult to say whether attributions of *intelligence* as such function as self-fulfilling prophecies, or only attributions of *expected achievement*. And despite the astonishing IQ increases reported in *Pygmalion in the Classroom*, there are weighty reasons to fear that intelligence is not all that susceptible to factitious attributions, or at the very least that intelligence labeling undermines the motivational intellectual virtues.

In one important study, Claudia Mueller and Carol Dweck (1998) found that when sixth-graders were labeled as intelligent, they ended up much worse off academically. Their motivation became largely extrinsic (keyed to rewards and teacher feedback). They gave up in the face of initial failure.[5] They enjoyed intellectual work less than before the intervention and less than matched controls, and their overall performance suffered. In a synthesis of much of the recent research on this issue, Jennifer Henderlong and Mark Lepper (2002) explain this backfiring effect as the result of several interrelated processes. First, they point out that, especially for students with sufficient meta-cognitive resources, praise for ability implies teacher expectations. If someone congratulates you for doing something that would ordinarily be considered easy, then you'll be inclined to think that he has a low estimation of your ability. Praising

---

[4] See, among many others, Rosenthal (1974, 1985, 1987, 1994, 2002), Rosenthal and Rubin (1978), and Harris and Rosenthal (1985).
[5] See also Cimpian et al. (2007).

a first-grader for successfully multiplying two numbers constitutes real praise; praising a high-schooler for successfully multiplying two numbers would often be taken as a thinly disguised insult. Telling an education major that he'd make a great high-school teacher counts as praise; telling a Ph.D. candidate that she'd make a great high-school teacher suggests that nothing more could be expected of her.[6] On the other side of the spectrum, offering praise only for extremely difficult accomplishments conveys such high standards that students may suffer from performance anxiety (Henderlong and Lepper 2002, p. 786). Congruent with Mueller and Dweck's research, Henderlong and Lepper also argue that praising someone for intellectual work that she was intrinsically motivated to do can lead her to want to engage in it only for extrinsic reasons in the future (2002, p. 777). Failure to find the sweet spot between the soft bigotry of low expectations and the apprehension-inducing demand of too-high expectations can transform attempts at intelligence labeling into stumbling blocks for the target.

These and other disappointing investigations of the effects of labeling with purely cognitive traits suggest that reliabilist factitious virtue is a mirage. Herman Spitz (1999), in an important meta-analysis, shows that the self-fulfilling prophecy effects documented by Rosenthal and his colleagues provide little evidence that *intelligence* can be influenced by labeling but plenty of support for the idea that *performance* can. The massive IQ gains documented in studies like *Pygmalion* are better explained as artifacts of the experimental design than as actual gains in intelligence. Thus, we have a mixed result for factitious reliabilist virtue. It seems that purely cognitive traits such as intelligence cannot be instilled through labeling, but achievement can be brought about through self-fulfilling prophecy. It seems to me that the best way to explain this is through factitious responsibilist virtue: something is happening, but it's not purely cognitive; perhaps it's conative. In the next section, I will argue that responsibilist factitious virtue is quite real and a welcome addition to the factitious virtue fold.

Before turning to factitious responsibilist virtue, I should point out that I am by no means arguing that it's advisable to tell people that they're stupid or unintelligent. The fact that attributions of intelligence backfire does not mean that attributions of unintelligence will result in a self-refuting prophecy. For obvious reasons, there have been no studies (at least that I've been able to find) of labeling people stupid, but presumably

---

[6] See also Graham (1990) and Meyer et al. (1979).

such attributions would not tend to induce intelligence, enhanced motivation, or higher achievement.

2.2 *Factitious responsibilist virtue*

Even if attributing intelligence often backfires, perhaps attributing conscientiousness and related motivational intellectual virtues does not. The light shed by the studies discussed in the previous section – especially Miller, Brickman, and Bolen (1975), Mueller and Dweck (1998), and Spitz (1999) – on the difference between attributions of intelligence, which often backfire, and attributions of motivation, which don't, suggests that unlike factitious reliabilist virtue, factitious responsibilist virtue is no chimera.

I will use Ray Rist's (1973; see also 1970, 1972, 1977) three-year longitudinal study of a de facto segregated school in urban St. Louis to illustrate how calling someone intellectually virtuous or vicious can function as a self-fulfilling prophecy. Rist begins his study with a class of kindergarteners and systematically records their progress (or lack of progress) through to the end of second grade. He notes that by the end of the second week, the kindergarteners' teacher assigned them permanent seating arrangements based on what she called their 'qualities,' and what we might think of as intellectual virtues. These qualities had to do with motivation to learn, inclination to pay attention in class, and so on – precisely the sorts of intellectual virtues that responsibilists emphasize. However, the teacher used no formal test to make this assessment; she made her determination based only on their behavior in the first few days of class, dividing the students into 'fast learners' and 'failures.' As it turned out, her impressions were heavily biased by the socioeconomic status of the students. Those from more affluent families were seated at Table 1; those from working-class families were seated at Table 2; those from families on welfare were seated at Table 3.

After these seating assignments were put in place, the teacher devoted most of her time and effort to Table 1, which unsurprisingly led to their learning more and faster, as well as developing intellectual motivations. She scolded the students at Tables 2 and 3 more than those at Table 1, and she disciplined those at Table 3 even more than those at Table 2. Many students from Tables 2 and 3 failed to advance to the next grade. When those who did advance entered first grade, the Table 1 students now had an objective record of superior performance and better attitudes, so the teacher assigned them all to sit at her best table: Table A (nine students in total). Most of the students from kindergarten Tables 2 and 3 were condensed into Table B (ten students in total), and nine students who had failed first grade were seated together at Table C, along with a few stragglers from the old Table 3 (fourteen students in total). Table C was placed off to the side, away from Tables A and B, to reduce the potential for interaction between the failures and the non-failures. As before, more teaching time, more praise, less discipline, and greater autonomy were afforded the students at Table A, who unsurprisingly benefited from this differential treatment, thereby 'justifying' the kindergarten teacher's beliefs about their 'qualities.'

In second grade, the same caste structure prevailed: the teacher divided the students into three groups, following the tradition handed down to her from the two previous teachers. The top group she labeled the "Tigers." The middle group she called the "Cardinals." The bottom group were "Clowns." Sure enough, the Tigers became tigers and the Clowns became clowns. While the Tigers learned grade-level math and reading skills, the Clowns pasted flowers on construction paper. While the Tigers were allowed to bully the other children, the Clowns were scolded whenever they spoke up. The initial assignment of students to tables in kindergarten had become a self-fulfilling prophecy: those from whom scholastic effort was expected lived up to expectations, while those from whom only trouble was expected became trouble-makers.

This formula appears to be repeated in other schools and at higher grade levels. Lee Jussim (1986) describes how teachers develop expectations based on students' early behavior in the classroom, past grades, disciplinary reports, race, gender, socioeconomic status, and other factors; these expectations then lead teachers to treat the students differently, which in turn prompts a reaction on the part of the students that often confirms the original (often unwarranted) expectations. Unlike most of the virtue- and vice-labeling discussed in Chapter 4, which was highly informal, these labels were institutionalized and bureaucratized in exactly the way that Hacking's (1999) looping kinds are.

The point here is not that intellectual motivation is solely determined by expectations, or that it's impossible to form correct or at least reasonable judgments about pupils' intellectual motivation. Rather, the point is that expectations often have an unnoticed but important effect, and that while they often lead to negative consequences, it is possible to "harness" them (Jussim 1990, p. 31) by making factitious attributions. Alvin So (1987) found, for instance, that once teachers had applied the "is going to college" label to students, they treated them in ways that encouraged critical thinking and intellectual ambition. Unfortunately, Anglo teachers were less inclined than Hispanic teachers to apply the label to Hispanic students, but once they did, the effects of ethnicity on scholastic conduct disappeared.

2.3   More on the mechanism of factitious virtue

In Chapter 4, I argued that attributions of moral virtues are most likely to function as self-fulfilling prophecies if they are *publicly* and *plausibly* attributed to someone with a *correct conception* of what the virtue entails. The same seems to hold for the responsibilist intellectual virtues. Brian McNatt and Timothy Judge (2004) found that interns training to be accountants responded as desired to attributions of motivation when the attributions seemed to be based on sufficient evidence, but not otherwise. People often engage in meta-cognitive analysis of what others really think about them. If someone tells you that you're diligent from out of a blue sky, you'll be less inclined to take him seriously than if he tells you that you're diligent right after you succeed at a difficult task. As McNatt and Judge put it, the attribution must be "credible" (p. 551).

For the same reasons discussed in Chapter 4, public attributions can be expected to be more effective than non-public attributions. Rist's "Clowns" behaved clownishly in part because they knew everyone else expected them to do so, while the "Tigers" studied hard because the other students, as well as the teacher, expected them to do so. As I explained in Chapter 4, public announcements serve as a basis for common knowledge, which enables thoughts of the form, "He expects me to be conscientious, and he knows that I know he expects me to be conscientious, and he knows that I know that he knows that I know he expects me to be conscientious." Such thoughts can play an integral role in conscientious conduct.

Also as before, self-concept is importantly implicated in factitious intellectual virtue. Robert Hoge and Joseph Renzulli (1993) found that so-called gifted children – many of whom are placed into special tracks at school – had higher reported levels of intellectual self-esteem than their unlabeled peers. Thinking of oneself as especially creative or curious or conscientious is one way to become creative, curious, or conscientious. One wants to avoid cognitive dissonance and to live up to one's aspirational self-image, so one keeps trying even in the face of difficulties and setbacks. This seems to work fairly well for the motivational intellectual virtues but not for the purely cognitive ones because of the different reactions people are likely to have to failure if they think of themselves as diligent or intelligent, respectively. If, on the one hand, I consider myself diligent, then initial failure is just another reason to try again and to try harder. "I am a hard worker" is one of the twelve items in the Duckworth grit scale discussed in Chapter 3. "I finish whatever I begin" and "I am diligent" are two others. If, on the other hand, I consider myself intelligent, then initial failure signals the impossibility of the task. I might reason to myself like this: "Well, if I'm smart, and even I can't figure it out, maybe it just can't be done."

Also as before, social expectations play a key role in generating factitious intellectual virtue. Part of the reason for this is that people are often averse to failing to fulfill others' expectations, whatever they might be. We don't like to let people down.

But when there is a possibility of interaction, social expectations also lead to congruent treatment, which can contribute to the self-fulfilling prophecy. As Edward Jones puts it, "We act while we see, and what we see is in part affected by our actions" (1990, p. 237). Chaikin, Sigler, and Derlega (1974), for instance, found that teachers gave more eye contact and smiles to students who were labeled bright. The best worked-out theory of how this dialectic proceeds is in an article by John Darley and Russell Fazio, which I quote at length:

(1) Either because of past observations of the other or because of the categories into which he or she has encoded the other, a perceiver develops a set of expectancies about a target person. (2) The perceiver then acts toward the target person in a way that is in accord with his or her expectations of the target person. (3) Next, the target interprets the meaning of the perceiver's action. (4) Based on the interpretation, the target responds to the perceiver's action, and (5) the perceiver interprets the target's action. At this point, the perceiver again acts toward the target person and so can be regarded as reentering the interaction sequence loop at Step 2. [...] (6) After acting toward the perceiver, the target person interprets the meaning of his or her own action. Ordinarily, of course, the interpretation will be that the action was the appropriate one and was "caused" by the perceiver's action to which it was the response. However, other possibilities do exist. From his or her action, the individual may infer something new about himself or herself. As a result, the individual's self-concept may be modified. (1980, p. 868)[7]

This account is pretty well confirmed, though it is perhaps a bit too overtly conscious. Mark Chen and John Bargh point out that much of the interaction between expectations, behaviors, reactions, and belief-updating could occur below the level of conscious reasoning and explicit inference. As they put it, "the direct behavioral consequences of social perception

---

[7] See also Chen and Bargh (1997), Good and Brophy (1973), Hamilton, Sherman, and Ruvolo (1990), Snyder (1984, 1992), and Snyder and Swann (1978).

can produce behavioral confirmation effects automatically, without any mediation by conscious perceptual interpretation" (1997, p. 545). To summarize, factitious responsibilist virtue is aided and abetted by self-concept, credible public attributions, and the differential treatment and changes in self-concept that follow.

3   KNOWLEDGE AND FACTITIOUS VIRTUE

I've argued that responsibilist but not reliabilist intellectual virtues are susceptible to factitious attribution. Though telling someone that she's intelligent is unlikely to make her intelligent, telling someone that he's diligent – especially when the attribution is plausible and public, and when the attributor continues to act in ways that encourage conduct in accordance with attribution – will tend to make him diligent (or near enough). What are we to think of the beliefs involved in factitious attributions?

Suppose Abigail tells Boris that he's open-minded right after he changes his mind in light of arguments she's given him. She continues to think of him and treat him as an open-minded person, and he often acts the part, in part because he now thinks of himself as open-minded and knows that Abigail thinks he's open-minded. Does Abigail know that Boris is open-minded? If she does, when does she acquire the knowledge? Before the attribution, when he changes his mind? At the moment of the attribution? Only after he acts open-mindedly later on? What about Boris? Does he know that he's open-minded? If he does, when?

The same questions apply to factitious attributions of moral virtues. Suppose Candice tells Dario that he's generous after seeing him donate to Oxfam. She continues to think of him and treat him as a generous person, and he acts the part. He gives 10 percent of his income to worthy charities every year, and he is also open-handed with his time and attention, in part because he now thinks of himself as generous and knows that Candice thinks he's generous. Does Candice know that Dario is generous? If she does, when? What about Dario? Does he know that he's generous? If he does, when?

These are tricky questions, which I will try to answer in this section. My proposal is that people do not typically know the contents of factitious virtue attributions initially, that they may acquire this knowledge after a long period during which the target of the attribution acts from factitious virtue, but that when the attributor intends to make a self-fulfilling prophecy, she (but not the target) may know the content of the attribution both initially and later on.

Before rushing to judgment on these questions, however, consider the following two transcripts from Paul Haggis's 2004 film, *Crash*, which dramatize the quandary posed by the question of knowledge of the content of factitious attributions. In the first transcript, two black men, Anthony (played by Christopher "Ludacris" Bridges) and Peter (played by Larenz Tate), are walking out of an LA restaurant. Anthony turns to Peter, and the following conversation ensues:

> ANTHONY: You see any white people in there waitin' a hour and thirty-two minutes for a plate of spaghetti? Huh? And how many cups of coffee did we get?
>
> PETER: You don't drink coffee, and I didn't want any.
>
> ANTHONY: Man, that woman in there poured cup after cup to every single white person around us, but did she even ask you if you wanted any?
>
> PETER: We didn't get any coffee that you didn't want and I didn't order. And that's evidence of racial discrimination? Did you notice that our waitress was black?
>
> ANTHONY: And black women don't think in stereotypes? You tell me somethin' man. When was the last time you met one who didn't think she knew everything about your little lazy ass before you even opened your mouth? Huh? That waitress sized us up in two seconds. We're black, and black people don't tip. So she wasn't gonna waste her time. Now somebody like that – nothing you can do to change their mind.
>
> PETER: Yeah, well, how much did you leave?
>
> ANTHONY: You expect me to pay for that kind of service?

Let's assume for the sake of argument that Anthony's interpretation is correct, that their waitress gave bad service because she assumed that since they were black they wouldn't tip well. Did she know that she was going to receive a bad tip from Anthony and Peter? It might seem that the answer is obviously negative: she had no justification for her paltry expectations when they first sat down. It might also seem, however, that the answer is obviously positive: she surely knew that almost any customer would tip poorly for terrible service (e.g., having to wait 92 minutes for a plate of spaghetti), so if she intended to give bad service, she should have been unsurprised to receive a bad tip. She saw to it that she got a bad tip, but only because she expected a bad tip regardless of what she did. At what point did she know that Anthony would tip poorly? As soon as he walked in? When she decided to provide bad service? After providing bad service? Or only when she saw the actual tip on the table? These are vexing questions.

In the second transcript, from just a moment later, Anthony and Peter have just seen a white woman draw close to her partner as she walks down the street:

> ANTHONY: Wait wait wait. See what that woman just did? You see that?
>
> PETER: What, she's cold?
>
> ANTHONY: She got colder as soon as she saw us, dog.
>
> PETER: Oh, no, come on man, don't start.
>
> ANTHONY: Man, look around you, man. You couldn't find a whiter, safer, or better lit part of this city right now, but yet this white woman sees two black guys, who look like UCLA students, strollin' down the sidewalk and her reaction is blind fear? I mean, look at us, dog. Are we dressed like gang-bangers? Huh? No. Do we look threatening? No. Fact: if anybody should be scared around here, it's us. We're the only two black faces surrounded by a sea of over-caffeineated white people patrolled by the trigger-happy LAPD. So you tell me: why aren't we scared?
>
> PETER: Cuz we got guns?
>
> ANTHONY: You could be right.

In an act of poetic justice, they carjack the woman on the spot, confirming her expectation that they were criminals with evil intentions towards her. At what point did she know that they were criminals, or that they harbored criminal intentions towards her? As soon as she saw them? After they interpreted her reaction? Only after they stuck a gun in her face? Again, these are vexing questions precisely because they involve the sorts of self-fulfilling prophecies at work in factitious trait attributions. Ideally, we could find a solution that covers all of these cases.

My proposed solution to the conundrum is to focus on the mechanisms by which the relevant belief is acquired and retained.[8] Consider again the case of Abigail and Boris. Abigail forms her belief that Boris is open-minded by seeing him act in accordance with the trait once. From an evidential point of view, this is small beer, as I discussed at length in the first half of the book. Later, though, once Boris has acquired the factitious virtue, if not the full virtue, she has a great deal more evidence. Perhaps at this point, though only at this point, she may come to know something of the following form: "Boris reliably acts open-mindedly," or perhaps even, "Boris is open-minded." Although her belief was acquired

---

[8] This might seem to be inconsistent with my argument against reliabilism about inference in the previous chapter. However, as I pointed out there, there's no reason to think that reliability isn't sufficient for knowledge. What I aimed to show is that reliability isn't necessary for knowledge.

through an unreliable process, it was retained by something like enumerative induction, which is fairly reliable.

Now look at the same case from Boris's point of view. Suppose that he takes on the belief that he's open-minded when Abigail first attributes the trait to him. How is his belief formed? It seems most natural to say that he's agreeing with an attribution based on a single piece of evidence. He might also introspect, asking himself whether he feels like an open-minded person, but introspection is notoriously unreliable, especially when self-serving biases are prone to lead someone towards a particular conclusion. Later, though, after he has been acting in accordance with open-mindedness, doing and saying what an open-minded person would do and say, he acquires a great deal more evidence. Now it might just work to say that Boris knows that he reliably acts open-mindedly, or perhaps even that he knows that he's open-minded. Again, while his belief was acquired through an unreliable process, it was retained through a more reliable one.

This seems to be the best we can say. Although the relevant beliefs are typically acquired in unreliable ways, they may be retained through reliable processes. If this is right, then neither the attributor nor the attributee typically knows anything like the content of the attribution initially, though they may come to have knowledge of a weakened version of that content over time.

There is a special case, though: intentionally using factitious attributions, as when someone uses an indirect speech act as discussed in Chapter 4. If Candice calls Dario generous, aiming to generate a self-fulfilling prophecy, perhaps she does know. In this case, her belief would be acquired not through an inference based on a single piece of evidence but through using a method she knows to be reliable: factitious virtue attribution. If she is under no illusion that Dario already is generous, but she treats him as if he is generous, calls him generous, and thereby leads him to become generous, then she may know at the moment of the attribution. What exactly she knows is a bit tricky. Presumably she doesn't know that he is generous, but she could know that he's factitiously generous or that he's about to become factitiously generous. In the same way, if United States Federal Reserve Chairman Ben Bernanke intentionally causes a stock market crash by publicly and plausibly predicting one, he could know that the market is about to take a tumble.

One concern about this way of looking at things is that factitious virtue is generated in part by the actions and expectations of the attributor.

Recall that when Schrank told the teachers at the US Air Force Academy that their students had been divided not by their tested ability but by a random process, they no longer taught in such a way as to generate a self-fulfilling prophecy. More generally, if a factitious virtue attribution is perceived as insincere by the target, the plausibility condition will not be met. This suggests that one can only know the content of a factitious virtue attribution in advance if one is a very good actor – an odd condition to put on knowledge. I'm not sure whether this constitutes an objection or just an unexpected caveat, but it does indicate a kind of tension between the theory and the practice of factitious virtue. It might be that in this sphere, we are like Wile E. Coyote, the Looney Toons character who can walk off a cliff and not fall, but only if he refuses to look down and recognize that he's walking on air.

4   OBJECTIONS AND REPLIES

As in Chapter 4, I hope to have convinced you here that some of the intellectual virtues are susceptible to factitious attribution. When someone publicly and plausibly calls a person a good student, a hard-working scholar, or the like, the attribution tends to function as a self-fulfilling prophecy. After making the attribution, one typically treats its target as if she had the trait in question, and she may begin to incorporate that trait into her self-concept. Together, these factors conspire to induce her to act as if she were intellectually virtuous, even if she isn't. This is a rather audacious claim, but I've marshaled what I consider to be suggestive though not dispositive evidence for it. Still, there are bound to be objections. In this section, I attempt to respond to a few of them.

4.1   *Factitious intellectual virtue essentially involves dishonesty*

Like factitious moral virtue, factitious intellectual virtue might seem to involve the vices of dishonesty and manipulativeness. It might seem that factitious virtue is belied by its reliance on lies. This is worrisome, but I would again like to assuage that worry.

First, virtue ethicists, unlike Kantians, typically do not espouse an exceptionless condemnation of lying. Philippa Foot (2001, p. 77) even says that it's "ludicrous" to think that it's always wrong to lie. Perhaps the cultivation of factitious virtue is one of those cases where a quantum of dishonesty is justified. If the only or best way to help people become honest (or near enough) is to lie to them, perhaps that's just what virtue requires. If the only, or best, way to help people become academically sedulous (or near enough) is to lie to them, perhaps that's just what virtue requires. This would give new impetus to Nietzsche's pronouncement that morality is built on a lie (*The Gay Science*, 344; *On the Genealogy of Morality*, III:27).

Second, as in the case of factitious moral virtues, if the noble lie makes you squeamish, my arguments here still suggest certain reforms in how we attribute intellectual virtues and vices. If what counts as sufficient evidence depends at least in part on the consequences likely to attend having and acting on the belief in question, then believing someone to be virtuous should have a much lower evidential bar to clear than believing someone to be vicious. If, as I have argued, attributions of intellectual virtues and vices tend to function as self-fulfilling prophecies, then the consequences of getting it wrong when it comes to virtues are much less dire than the consequences of getting it wrong when it comes to vices. Therefore, we should relax our standards of sufficient evidence for virtue but redouble them for vice. Again, this is a point that even people who reject the arguments I've made so far should be willing to take on board.

Third, and also for the faint of heart, if the arguments I made in Chapter 2 were correct, we simply cannot help believing in intellectual virtues, just like moral virtues. Factitious intellectual virtue is therefore a Strawsonian exoneration or exculpation of our inevitable practice of thinking in these terms. I claim that since we can't help believing that people have intellectual virtues, we shouldn't feel too bad about it because our thinking it makes it so (or near enough). This is only a partial exoneration, though, because our thinking that people have intellectual vices actually leads them to act in accordance with those vices.

4.2 *Factitious intellectual virtue leads to overconfidence, an intellectual vice*

In *Lack of Character*, John Doris asks his reader to imagine how she might respond to an invitation to dinner from a colleague with whom she'd "had a long flirtation" (2002, p. 147). He points out that if she thinks of herself as "an upright person," then she might conclude that there is "little cause for concern." Overconfidence in the robustness of her fidelity is likely to lead her to accept the invitation, "secure," as Doris puts it, in the knowledge of her "righteousness." As Doris insinuates, this overconfidence is likely to lead to disaster. According to a 2009 Gallup poll, 92 percent of

Americans believe extramarital affairs are "morally wrong."[9] According to a 2008 poll, 64 percent said they would not forgive and 62 percent said they would divorce a spouse who engaged in an affair.[10] Those aren't very good odds, even leaving aside the sting of conscience that's likely to result from falling into temptation.

It might seem that factitious virtue, both moral and intellectual, involves precisely the sort of overconfidence that Doris decries. Since factitious virtue depends on self-concept – on thinking oneself virtuous – then someone with factitious virtue would be likely to feel secure in her own righteousness. This is a cause for concern, but I think the objection can be blunted somewhat because factitious virtue depends not only on self-concept but also on social expectations. My reply to the charge of moral credentialing in Chapter 4 was similar. Self-concept alone may not do the job, but self-concept in tandem with knowledge that others (including, in Doris's vignette, the flirtatious colleague) expect her to act in accordance with virtue and (as I argued in this chapter) treat her thusly, may serve as an adequate buffer to overconfidence.

4.3 *What about social ontology?*

In Chapter 4, I speculated that it might make sense to think of virtue not as a monadic property of an agent but as a triadic relation among an agent, a social milieu, and an environment. Each of these factors contributes something to virtue, as do the interactions among them. I then compared the relational conception of virtue with Ian Hacking's (1999, 2006) notion of a looping kind and John Searle's (1995) conception of an institutional fact. I pointed out that factitious moral virtue differs from looping kinds because virtue-labeling tends to be informal whereas looping kinds tend to involve formal labels. Because contemporary society spends the first eighteen to twenty-five years of people's lives institutionally labeling them with intellectual virtues and vices, the disanalogy does not crop up for intellectual virtues.

Treating intellectual virtues as relations rather than properties would shift virtue epistemology from traditional epistemology into the realm of social epistemology.[11] Curiosity would inhere not (solely) in individual investigators, but in investigators-in-social-and-material-contexts.

---

[9] Source: www.gallup.com/poll/121253/extramarital-affairs-sanford-morally-taboo.aspx.
[10] Source: www.gallup.com/poll/105682/most-americans-willing-forgive-unfaithful-spouse.aspx.
[11] For a magisterial introduction, see Goldman (1999).

Open-mindedness would inhere not (solely) in individual investigators, but in investigators-in-social-and-material contexts. The cultivation of intellectual virtue would then be properly pursued not only by habituating and instructing individuals, but also by designing material environments (e.g., with mood elevators and depressors) and social contexts.

For an example of how this might work, I will return to the virtue of intellectual courage, which I discussed in detail in Chapter 5. Recall that pluralistic ignorance is a social disorder of our own creation, yet most of us lack the intellectual courage required to overcome it. Faced with this problem, what are we to do? It seems to me that three other, mutually compatible responses are more advisable: call them the *agential strategy*, the *social strategy*, and the *environmental strategy*.

First the agential strategy: virtue ethicists from Aristotle to the present have emphasized the crucial role that habituation plays in the inculcation of virtue. Most of us are not so lucky as to be born with (only) good dispositions. They must be acquired, and one way to acquire them is through training and habituation. This raises the question of what sorts of behaviors might be best suited to training people to overcome intellectual cowardice, especially the cowardice that prevents people from voicing their own opinions in the face of a unanimous dissent. Would it be best to teach children *directly* to say what they really think? This method has the advantage of being straightforward, but it also suffers from an internal tension. What if the moral acolyte doesn't want to be instructed? If he says so, he's resisting training by exercising the very intellectual courage that the teacher is trying to inculcate. If he doesn't object, then in fact he's being trained to keep his real opinions to himself. Neither outcome is desirable.

One way around this difficulty would be to try to help moral acolytes to become habituated through less direct routes. Literature and other types of fiction seem to be an ideal medium in this regard. Instead of telling the moral pupil, "Say what you really think," the instructor could make available novels, films, and other media in which the consequences of speaking up (and of not speaking up) are dramatized. The moral pupil could then be left to draw her own conclusions, without the internal tension of the direct method of instruction getting in the way.

It looks like the agential strategy might not be well suited to the development of intellectual courage, so let's look instead at the social strategy. The idea here would be to inculcate the intellectual courage to express thoughts and preferences by shaping the social context appropriately. This could take a wide variety of forms, so I will explore several of them.

Consider again the problem of lack of student engagement in lecture classes. After the professor tries to explain difficult material, she may ask whether there are any questions. Hands do not immediately fly up, which the students notice and interpret as a sign that their classmates in fact do not have any questions. Here the default was crucial: inaction was to be interpreted as understanding, while action was to be interpreted as lack of understanding. What if the professor instead had said, "Raise your hand if you *do* understand"? Then the default would be reversed: inaction would represent lack of understanding while action represented understanding. Having tried this in my own classroom, I can say that merely switching the default like this can have dramatic consequences, with students admitting their unclarity, asking more questions, and even helping each other to grasp difficult concepts.

Alternatively, the professor could use 'clickers' – electronic devices that anonymously transmit answers to multiple-choice questions to the instructor's computer. In a classroom equipped for clickers, the professor could say, "Answer A if you feel comfortable with the material, B if you don't." This solution offers two advantages. First, as with the previous suggestion, this changes the default. Students are faced with a forced choice; inaction is not an option. Second, without having to worry about what their peers thought of them, students would presumably feel more comfortable admitting ignorance to the instructor.

It looks like the social strategy may be a better fit for inculcating intellectual courage, at least when the virtue is conceived as a triadic relation rather than a monadic property. The third available strategy is the environmental strategy, which would somehow involve altering the non-social environment in such a way as to make people more disposed to say what they really think and want. As I explained in Chapter 2, the influence of non-social environmental factors has not been systematically explored by psychologists yet: we know about the influence of mood elevators and depressors on generosity and aggressiveness, but not on courage and honesty. It wouldn't be surprising, though, to find that situational non-reasons could be harnessed to encourage intellectual courage, or at least not to dampen it.

5   CONCLUSION

In this chapter, I explored whether the factitious virtue response to moral situationism could be translated into a response to the situationist challenges to reliabilist and responsibilist virtue epistemology. Although attributing intelligence seems to be counter-productive, attributing motivational intellectual virtues like academic diligence does seem to produce factitious intellectual virtue. I also addressed the questions of whether and when the content of factitious virtue attributions are known. In most cases, neither the attributor nor the attributee has knowledge of the content of the attribution, at least at the time of the labeling, but they may eventually acquire such knowledge. Finally, I responded to several objections and further explored the social ontology of factitious virtue. In the remainder of this book, I introduce an entirely new form of moral technology and continue the exploration of the triadic relational conception of virtue.

PART III

Programmatic conclusion

To see as we are seen: an investigation of social distance heuristics

We are all in the gutter, but some of us are looking at the stars.
Oscar Wilde, *Lady Windermere's Fan*, act 3, line 340.
Published 1893.

I   INTRODUCTION

I began this book by distinguishing normative theory, moral psychology, and moral technology. I further claimed that all three must be developed in parallel, so that they can be holistically calibrated with one another. The bulk of the book has been an attempt to do exactly that. In the first half, I started with normative theory, identifying the hard core of virtue ethics. I then turned to moral psychology, rearticulating the situationist challenge. Next, I explained why most attempts to fend off situationism have failed, which set the stage for the moral technology that I call factitious virtue: because virtue attributions tend to function as self-fulfilling prophecies, we have reason to attribute them even when it's unclear whether the target of the attribution really is virtuous. If the argument developed in Chapters 1 through 4 is on the right track, the problem posed for normative theory by moral psychology can be resolved through moral technology. This in turn suggests a number of potential ways to revise the normative theory. We could continue to use the traditional conception of virtue, in which case factitious virtue would involve a sort of noble lie, or at least asymmetric standards of evidence for virtue and vice attributions. Alternatively, we could think of factitious virtue as a developmental stage on the way to traditional virtue. More radically, we could reconceptualize virtue as a triadic relation among an agent, a social milieu, and an environment, which would then make the social expectations (and the potential for common knowledge of those expectations) that underlie factitious virtue part of the metaphysics of virtue, rather than a situational influence that induces virtue.

In the second half of the book, I followed the same recipe. I began by introducing the normative theory of virtue epistemology in both its reliabilist and responsibilist forms. I then turned to moral psychology, articulating situationist challenges to both forms of virtue epistemology. The challenge to responsibilism closely paralleled the challenge to virtue ethics, drawing on evidence of the power of situational demand characteristics and situational non-reasons such as mood elevators. The challenge to reliabilism strayed further from the model. The challenge to virtue ethics contends that global dispositions are normatively adequate but empirically inadequate, and that local dispositions are normatively inadequate but empirically adequate. The challenge to reliabilism inverts that argument: global inferential dispositions are normatively inadequate but empirically adequate, and local inferential dispositions are normatively adequate but empirically inadequate. These arguments opened a wedge for moral technology, so I then explored the extent to which the factitious virtue response might also apply to epistemic situationism. The answer was mixed: while it appears that attributing cognitive intellectual virtues tends to backfire, the attribution of motivational intellectual virtues appears to function as a self-fulfilling prophecy in precisely the same way that the attribution of moral virtues does. If the argument developed in Chapters 5 through 7 is on the right track, then, as before, the problem posed for normative theory by moral psychology can be resolved through moral technology. And, as before, this suggests a number of potential ways to revise the normative theory. We could continue to use the traditional conception of intellectual virtue, in which case factitious virtue would involve a sort of noble lie, or at least asymmetric standards of evidence for virtue and vice attributions. Alternatively, we could think of factitious intellectual virtue as a developmental stage on the way to traditional intellectual virtue. More radically, we could reconceptualize virtue as a triadic relation among an agent, a social milieu, and an environment, which would then make the social expectations (and the potential for common knowledge of those expectations) that underlie factitious intellectual virtue part of the metaphysics of virtue, rather than a situational influence that induces virtue.

Whether you're inclined to take the more conservative route, according to which social expectations (and the signaling thereof) are non-moral situational influences that induce conduct in accordance with virtue, or the more expansive route, according to which social expectations (and the signaling thereof) partially constitute virtue, I hope that it's now plausible to assert that virtue (or at least virtuous conduct) can be fostered by working on any of the relata in the triadic account. For instance, one way to cultivate someone's generosity (or at least reliably generous conduct) is to habituate her to giving. One way to cultivate someone's honesty (or at least reliably honest conduct) is to label her honest. One way to cultivate someone's creativity (or at least reliably creative conduct) is to see to it that she's in a good mood. On the conservative view, virtue inheres in the person, and is artificially supported by the labeling or the mood elevator. On the expansive view, virtue inheres in the interstices between the person, the labeler, and the mood elevator – in the relation, that is, among the agent, the social milieu, and the environment.

So far, when discussing social expectations I have tended to focus on expectations generated by explicit attributions and announcements: "You're courageous," "You're industrious." In the previous chapter, I pointed out that expectations needn't be signaled so directly. Indeed, they needn't be signaled verbally at all to do their work. I (forthcoming c) argue, for instance, that the phenomena of stereotype threat and stereotype boost can be understood in terms of the implicit, automatic signaling of expectations. When someone is reminded, even in a subtle, unconscious way, that he belongs to a stereotyped group, he tends to behave in accordance with the stereotype. For instance, African-Americans tend to perform worse on standardized tests when they are asked to record their race before taking the test than when they do so after taking the test. Women tend to perform worse on mathematics tests when they are asked to record their gender before taking the test than when they do so afterwards. And the effect works in both directions: Asian-Americans tend to perform better on mathematics tests when they are reminded of their ethnicity. I argue that this phenomenon depends in large part on the expectations generated when stereotypes are raised to salience.

If this is on the right track, still further ways of signaling expectations should produce similar effects. In this chapter, I investigate one: *social distance cues*.

We help our friends pack up their belongings and relocate, but do nothing for victims of famine in the antipodes. We would give anything for our family and lovers, but we ignore the pleas of charity organizations. From one point of view, this is unremarkable, bordering on analytic: we care for those we care about and show no concern for those who do not concern us. From another point of view, however, it's striking: do we really think that people deserve help only if they're friends or family? Was Christ wrong in thinking that everyone is everyone else's neighbor?

Was the Roman poet Terence mistaken to think that nothing human was alien to him? In human evolutionary prehistory, physical distance and social distance largely coincided. Had our ancestors desired to help people in distant climes, they would have been stymied. From a practical perspective, then, caring only for those in one's physical and social sphere had the same effect as caring for everyone. The rise of telecommunication and cheap, high-speed transportation, however, moots physical distance, laying bare the power of social distance and forcing us to question the legitimacy of that power.

But what exactly is this thing called social distance? How robust is the metaphor with physical distance? Can I take a social trip to reduce the distance between you and me? What sense can be given to the notions of social area, social velocity, and social momentum?

To give you a rough sense of what social distance is, this chapter begins with a discussion of three historical models. Plato addressed social distance in the myth of the ring of Gyges; Epicurus emphasized it in both his writings and the moral technology he deployed in the Garden; Jeremy Bentham's Panopticon relied on asymmetries of social distance to control the conduct of prison inmates. Next, I offer a definition of social distance as a measure of one's willingness to treat the preferences, needs, and well-being of another person as one's own. The closer a is to b, the more a countenances b's preferences. The further a is from b, the less a cares what b wants or needs. Drawing on recent work in behavioral economics, I argue that social distance is a function of three dimensions: *interaction*, *group identity*, and *information*. The greater the potential for punishment or reward, the closer people are. The more group identities people share, the closer they are. The more people can or do find out about one another, the closer they are. I also argue that we use automatic heuristics to gauge all three dimensions of social distance. This means that we are liable to systematically over- and underestimate our social distance from other people, and this enables a kind of moral technology: the tactical use of social distance cues to reduce perceived social distance and thereby induce other-regarding conduct. We can make ourselves feel closer to one another than we otherwise would, which in turn leads us to take each other's preferences into account in our thought, feeling, deliberation, and behavior. Just as social expectations are a key determinant in the effect of virtue-labeling, so unconsciously processed social distance cues raise to salience the wants and needs of others. For this reason, the moral technology discussed in this chapter fits neatly together with the themes developed throughout the book.

2 THREE HISTORICAL MODELS

Social distance, though new to many contemporary philosophers, was historically an important aspect of moral thought. In this section, I address a three noteworthy historical models.

2.1 Social distance in the Republic

An early example of theorizing about social distance occurs in Plato's *Republic* (359c–360d), where Glaucon recounts the myth of the ring of Gyges, an artifact with the power to make its bearer invisible. After finding the ring, Gyges contrived to visit the royal palace. "When he arrived, he committed adultery with the king's wife and, along with her, set upon the king and killed him. And so he took over the rule." Glaucon proposes that everyone is like Gyges, and hence that inferences based on attributions of virtues like honesty, justice, and fealty are unsound. What really predicts someone's behavior is his social distance from others:

> Now if there were two such rings, and the just man would put one on, and the unjust man the other, no one, as it would seem, would be so adamant as to stick by justice and bring himself to keep away from what belongs to others and not lay hold of it, although he had license to take what he wanted from the market without fear, and to go into houses and have intercourse with whomever he wanted, and to slay or release from bonds whomever he wanted, and to do other things as an equal to a god among humans. And in so doing, one would act no differently from the other, but both would go the same way. (360a–c)

According to the Gyges conjecture, immunity from the monitoring gaze of others (and the potential for sanction that such monitoring entails) overpowers whatever virtues someone might have, leading him to behave abominably. This is just another example of the intrusion of situational influences into moral psychology, a theme developed at length in Chapters 2 and 5.

If this is right, it suggests that from a third-person perspective, civil society should be guaranteed not only by giving the population reasons to act but also by manipulating social distance cues. In late 2009, the New York City Metropolitan Transit Authority began running audio announcements in the subway that said, "If you see an elderly, pregnant, or handicapped person near you, offer your seat. You'll be standing up for what's right. Courtesy is contagious and it starts with you." Such an intervention epitomizes the reason-giving paradigm. If the moral of the myth of Gyges is correct, however, a more effective intervention might involve somehow decreasing the social distance (or the perceived social distance) between subway riders, thereby leading the young and healthy to make room for those who most needed a seat.

From a first-person perspective, if the Gyges conjecture is right, it suggests that a project of self-improvement should focus more on avoiding anonymity than on cultivating virtuous thoughts and motives. If one were able to engineer situations such that one's social distance from other people never grew too great, one would reliably behave in accordance with the other-regarding virtues.

2.2   Social distance in Epicurean theory and practice

Epicurus seems to have taken this message to heart when he developed a splendid piece of moral technology. The theoretical basis of this moral technology is nicely summarized in Seneca's letters to Lucilius, where he reports Epicurus as having said, "We need to set our affections on some good man and keep him constantly before our eyes, so that we may live as if he were watching us and do everything as if he saw what we were doing" (11.8). By voluntarily decreasing their social distance from a revered symbol of authority, Epicurean acolytes did not give themselves reasons to act; they followed Epicurus' advice to artificially decrease their social distance from the watcher, thereby inducing themselves to behave as their better angels would have them behave.

Interestingly, the moral technology behind this social distance intervention did not require that a real individual actually watch the Epicurean novices. Instead, they were to vividly imagine him as watching, which presumably would trigger the heuristics associated with real surveillance.

This theoretical basis became the groundwork for Epicurean moral technology. In light of the facts that a real watcher was unnecessary and that trainees needed to *feel* that they were watched, Epicurus used a surrogate watcher to guide his disciples on the path to virtue. Diogenes Laertius says in the *Lives of Eminent Philosophers* that many bronze statues of Epicurus were erected in Greece (1965, p. 537). The location and number of these bronzes is still a matter of contention, but almost certainly there was at least one in Athens. Furthermore, historians suspect that a statue of Epicurus stood in the Garden itself. It's likely that this statue was commissioned by Epicurus, but at the very least it was commissioned by someone of his generation (Frischer 1982, p. 182). A statue, like a painting, tends to be experienced by those in its vicinity as a vigilant agency. And as we have already seen, the presence (real or fictive) of a monitor figured importantly in Epicurean moral training. It therefore seems plausible to speculate that the statue of Epicurus in the Garden was set up for the express purpose of reminding his disciples of the sage's monitoring gaze. What better way could there be to ensure that his followers at all times kept in mind the maxim, "Do everything as if Epicurus were watching you" (25.5)? Constantly reminded of their master's fictive presence, the converts of Epicurus would consistently curb their conduct as if he were watching.

At the end of this process of internalizing a revered monitoring authority, Epicureans needed no external props at all. In fragment 83, Epicurus is recorded as saying: "The man who has attained the natural end of the human race will be equally good, even though no one is present" (p. 51) and – presumably, watching. In psychoanalytic argot, we might say that, having introjected the revered watcher, they needed neither a real monitor nor the fiction of an *other* who watches. This is akin to my speculation that people may become so habituated to factitious virtue that they eventually acquire full virtue.

2.3   Social distance in Bentham's Panopticon

My final historical model is Bentham's Panopticon, an architectural-geometric innovation. A building of this type consists of a hub of cells around an imposing guard tower. The cells have exactly two windows: one opening onto the outside of the ring, the other providing a vantage on the inside. In this way, the inmates are rendered incapable of communicating with their neighbors while the warden in the central tower is able to inspect many of them at once. What is more, the windows of the guard tower are shielded by Venetian blinds so that the prisoners cannot determine whether they are under the warden's critical gaze. It's a simple idea, but a brilliant one. By a few tricks of geometry and architecture, three asymmetries of social distance are guaranteed. First, the warden can see without being seen. Second, inmates are prevented from communicating with one another because radially the whole building lies open to view, but laterally the perspective is constricted. Third, the warden has full freedom of movement, while the prisoners' freedom of movement is severely hampered.[1] In short: ignorance and impotence from one point of view is paired with omniscience and omnipotence on the other. Bentham

---

[1] See Chwe (2001) for a discussion of the common knowledge-generating aspects of the Panopticon's design.

believed that situating the inmates of the Panopticon appropriately in the world of social distance would ensure desirable conduct. He insisted not that their characters be reformed but that they be isolated and watched.

> [T]he more constantly the persons to be inspected are under the eyes of the persons who should inspect them, the more perfectly will the purpose of the establishment have been attained. Ideal perfection, if that were the object, would require that each person should actually be in that predicament, during every instant of time. This being impossible, the next thing to be wished for is, that, at every instant, seeing reason to believe as such, and not being able to satisfy himself to the contrary, he should *conceive* himself to be so. (1995, p. 34)

Just as Epicurean acolytes internalized Epicurus as a monitoring agency with the help of the statue in the Garden, so the inmates of Bentham's Panopticon would internalize the disciplinarian warden in the watch-tower. As Michel Foucault in his study of the Panopticon puts it, "He who is subjected to a field of visibility, and who knows it, assumes responsibility for the constraints of power; he makes them play spontaneously upon himself" (1997, pp. 202–3).

While Plato emphasized the importance of social distance as such, Epicurus and Bentham invented moral technologies that used the power of social distance to regulate behavior. Epicurus' revered, symbolic watcher (the statue) and Bentham's anonymous, unblinking watcher (the guard tower) stand at opposite poles of the surveillance spectrum, but their similarities are perhaps more important than their differences.[2] By ensuring that their targets felt watched at all times, these interventions used social distance cues to shape conduct.

3   SOCIAL DISTANCE TODAY

Behavioral economists have recently begun struggling towards a definition of social distance. For instance, Elizabeth Hoffman, Kevin McCabe, and Vernon Smith define it as "the degree of reciprocity that people believe is inherent within a social interaction" (1996, p. 429), and provide some evidence that social distance so construed is correlated with giving behavior. This definition is clearly flawed, however. First of all, it builds a sort of infallibility into the definition of social distance. If the social distance between *a* and *b* is what *a* and *b* *believe to be* the distance between them,

---

[2] The political scientist Fonna Forman-Barzilai (2010) independently hit upon the similarity of the ring of Gyges and the Panopticon. She does not seem to have noticed the further similarity with the statue of Epicurus.

then of course they are right. One reason to quibble with this definition is that even when people agree in their assessments of social distance, they may both be wrong. Consider two sworn enemies, both of whom have adopted clever disguises. They meet, fall in together, and think themselves good friends. Then each discovers the other's identity. "I was wrong about him all along!" each declares. They both perceived the social distance between them to be small, yet it was great. Or consider the fact that *a* may believe there is a high degree of reciprocity inherent in his relation to *b*, whereas *b* believes there is a low degree of reciprocity inherent in their relation. They disagree. According to the Hoffman, McCabe, and Smith definition, the social distance between them is undefined, since there is no one thing that is *the* unique degree of reciprocity they believe to be inherent within their interaction.

Iris Bohnet and Bruno Frey have proposed a revised definition, according to which "social distance is a much broader phenomenon that is not only relevant for social exchange-type relations but applies to all human interactions where some kind of other-regarding behavior is involved" (1999b, p. 44). This is an improvement but leaves much to be desired. Presumably social distance is a relation that holds all the time, not just when people are interacting in a potentially other-regarding situation. Just as there is a physical distance from Marathon to Athens regardless of whether someone is planning to run between them, so there is a social distance between people regardless of whether they are about to interact. In addition, Bohnet and Frey's definition provides no criteria for measuring social distance. For the metaphor of social distance to bear any weight, there must be criteria that enable us to answer questions of the form: is *a* socially further from *b* than from *c*?

In this chapter, I shall use the following definition of social distance:

(*social distance*) The social distance from *a* to *b* is a measure of the degree to which *a* is disposed to treat *b*'s preferences, needs, or well-being as her own. The greater the distance, the less *a* identifies with *b*'s preferences.

In addition, I shall argue that we often use automatic heuristics to gauge social distance. For my purposes, a *social distance heuristic* is an automatic mechanism or process used to track social distance. Such a heuristic treats some other, contingently related property (a *social distance cue*) as an index of social distance, which means that even though it may be accurate much of the time, it's prone to systematic mistakes of over- and underestimation. This means that the strategic deployment of social distance cues can increase (or decrease) the likelihood of other-regarding conduct.

In this section, I articulate a theory of social distance in terms of *inter-action*, *group identity*, and *information*. At first, I just dogmatically present the theory. Then I go into the details of each aspect of it, simultaneously explaining what they mean and what reason we have to include them in the definition.

Ordinarily, distance is a gradable, symmetric relation. The distance from x to y can be the same as, greater than, or less than the distance from x to z. And the distance from x to y is the same as the distance from y to x. Furthermore, the minimum distance of 0 is reserved for identity: everything is at a distance of 0 from itself, and everything at 0 distance from a given object is identical to that object. Social distance, being a metaphor, doesn't preserve all of these properties. For one thing, it should be obvious that social distance is not symmetric. The degree to which a is disposed to treat b's preferences as her own needn't be identical to the degree to which b is disposed to treat a's preferences as his own. In addition, minimum social distance may differ from minimal physical distance in at least two ways. First, if someone is alienated from himself, he may be disposed to act against his own interests. In other words, the distance from someone to himself needn't be 0, though Harry Frankfurt (2001) eloquently argues that love of self is an ideal model for love of others.[3] Second, pure love or friendship may lead someone to treat another's preferences as entirely her own, which would make the social distance between them 0 even though they are not the same person. This point is clearly related to Aristotle's claim in the *Nicomachean Ethics* that a friend is a second self (1166a30).

With these clarifications out of the way, we can say that the social distance relation has three dimensions: interaction, information, and group identity. The more easily a and b can interact, the closer they are. The better a and b (can) know each other, the closer they are. The more group identities, especially important group identities, a and b share, the closer they are. One of the reasons that social distance itself is not symmetric is that these dimensions are not symmetric. In many situations, one person can choose to initiate an interaction with another, but not conversely. Similarly, in many situations, one person knows about another (or can know about the other), but not conversely. What follows is a discussion of the evidence for these conditions and for the idea that we use heuristics to track them.

---

[3] Woody Allen apparently once quipped, "Don't knock masturbation. It's sex with someone I love."

3.1   The interaction dimension

The ability to interact affords the application of sanctions, which may be rewarding or punitive, material or social. Reputation management becomes a pressing issue when others are able to retaliate against or shun one for behavior they consider inappropriate, or reward one for behavior they consider appropriate. Indeed, egoistic but rational utility-maximizers can be brought to see cooperation and following social norms as their best option, provided they put some utility on the sanction they might receive for (not) cooperating or (not) following norms.

To investigate this idea, Robert Kurzban, Peter DeScioli, and Erin O'Brien (2007) conducted a study in which participants played a prisoner's dilemma game[4] in which, after each round, players were able to allocate some of their funds to a 'punishment' account which would reduce the funds of the player with whom they had just interacted. Note that from a purely material point of view, using the punishment account is irrational. Since players interacted only once, they could not intimidate their partners into cooperating with them in the future. Despite this fact, participants did in fact use their punishment accounts. Even more interesting, however, is the fact that fewer people defected when punishment was a live option than when it was not. The mere possibility of punishment made it unnecessary to punish. Perhaps most surprising, however, is the fact that players even engaged in third-party punishment. When given the opportunity to expend some of their own funds to decrease the funds of a player who had failed to cooperate with *someone else*, they often chose to do so (though not as much as when they were given the chance to punish someone who had defected against them). Since players cooperated more when punishment was possible and even more when the punishment was coming from someone who might have a personal reason to punish them, we have a prima facie case for *interaction* as a dimension of social distance.

Monetary punishment is not the only type of sanction; social sanction may also be leveraged to transform prima facie prisoner's dilemma games into coordination games.[5] Social sanctions are cheers and jeers, that is, any form of non-material approval or disapproval. In addition, social sanctions are unlike market exchanges of other forms of utility in that they do not require two willing counterparties (the person being abused cannot

---

[4] See Table 8.1 below for typical payouts of a prisoner's dilemma game.
[5] See Bicchieri (2006), Gächter and Fehr (1999), and Rege and Telle (2004).

Table 8.1 *Material prisoner's dilemma game*

	Cooperate	Defect
Cooperate	$10, $10	$0, $20
Defect	$20, $0	$1, $1

Table 8.2 *Material prisoner's dilemma game + social sanctions*

	Cooperate	Defect
Cooperate	$10, $10 cheer, cheer	$0, $20 cheer, jeer
Defect	$20, $0 jeer, cheer	$1, $1 jeer, jeer

simply decline it), are not fungible (you cannot buy and sell praise, at least not sincere praise), and cost very little to give. If social norms forbid defecting in a situation that looks from the material point of view like a prisoner's dilemma game, the introduction of social sanctions may transform it into a coordination game.

In a game like the one illustrated in Table 8.1, the dominant strategy for both players is to defect, despite the fact that when they employ this strategy they walk away with just $1 each. If we introduce the social sanctions of jeering and cheering, however, things change, as is shown in Table 8.2.

Provided the marginal utility of a cheer over a jeer is greater than the utility of $1, defecting ceases to be the dominant strategy in this game.

In a recent study, Masclet, Noussair, Tucker, and Villeval (2001; see also Rege and Telle 2004) conducted a prisoner's dilemma experiment to test the power of both monetary and social sanctions. In the *no sanction (control)* condition participants could not sanction one another in any way. In the *monetary sanction* condition, participants could sanction one another by paying to decrease the other's payoff; this condition therefore replicated the Kurzban, De Scioli, and O'Brien (2007) study. Finally, in the *social sanction* condition, participants could sanction one another by assigning non-monetary punishment points. These punishment points did not affect players' material payoffs but did register disapproval. The question was whether simply knowing that they could be tagged with disapproval in this way would motivate participants to behave more cooperatively. In line with their predictions and with the theory of social sanction, Masclet and colleagues found higher cooperation rates in both experimental conditions. In the monetary sanction condition, cooperation increased 85 percent compared to the control condition, whereas in the social sanction condition, cooperation increased 37 percent compared to the control. Though social sanction did not induce as large an effect as monetary sanction, a 37 percent increase is far from negligible.

Interaction affects moral behavior beyond the wallet. The proximity series in Milgram's (1974) studies in obedience also provides interesting evidence for the power of interaction. This experimental paradigm involves an experimenter, a confederate, and a subject. The experimenter tells the confederate and subject that they are participating in a study of the effects of punishment on learning. Through a rigged randomization mechanism, the confederate is assigned the role of *learner*, while the subject is assigned the role of *teacher*. The learner is strapped into a chair and fitted with electrodes, which are first tested on both the teacher and the learner to show that they give painful shocks. The teacher then quizzes the learner, whom he is prompted to shock after each wrong answer. Shocks start at 15 volts and increase by 15-volt increments.

At 75 volts, the "learner" grunts. At 120 volts he complains verbally; at 150 volts he demands to be released from the experiment. His protests continue as the shocks escalate, growing increasingly vehement and emotional. At 285 volts his response can only be described as an agonized scream. [...] At 300 volts the victim shouted in desperation that he would no longer provide answers to the memory test. [...] At 315 volts, after a violent scream, the victim reaffirmed vehemently that he was no longer a participant. He provided no answers, but shrieked in agony whenever a shock was administered. After 330 volts he was not heard from, nor did his answers reappear on the four-way signal box. (pp. 22–23)

If the teacher dissents, the experimenter replies politely but confidently, with an escalating sequence of prods. He first says, "Please continue," or, "Please go on." If the teacher dissents again, he is told, "The experiment requires that you continue." If he dissents a third time, the experimenter says, "It is absolutely essential that you continue." And if he dissents a fourth time, the reply is, "You have no other choice, you *must* go on." If the teacher refuses once more after the fourth prod, the experiment ends. Otherwise, the experiment ends after the seemingly incapacitated learner is shocked three times at the maximum voltage of 450, which is labeled on the teacher's dial merely as XXX.

The most astonishing result of the study is that a large majority of sub-jects were maximally obedient; that is, they failed to disobey five times consecutively and thereby end the study early. For our purposes, however, a secondary phenomenon proves quite interesting. Social distance was manipulated both between teacher and learner and between experimenter and teacher. Social distance between the teacher and learner was varied in the four treatments of the proximity series, during which social distance between experimenter and teacher was kept constant (and small, since the teacher was in the same room as the experimenter):

> *Remote.* The learner is in a separate room and indicates his answers to the quiz questions by sending a signal of A, B, C, or D.
> *Voice-feedback.* The learner is in a separate room connected by an intercom.
> *Proximity.* The learner is in the same room as the teacher.
> *Touch proximity.* The learner is in the same room as the teacher; as the study progresses, the teacher must manually force the learner's arm onto the electrode in order to shock him. (p. 34)

As Milgram points out, the ability to interact increases from the remote condition through the touch proximity condition. Predictably, as social distance increased, mean maximum shock level increased from 270 volts to 405 volts, a jump of 50 percent. The smaller the social distance between the teacher and the learner, the less willing the teacher was to shock the learner. While one may feel that even 270 volts is an appallingly large amount of electricity to put through another human being, it is much better than 405 volts.

Social distance between experimenter and teacher was varied in one further condition, where the experimenter left the room immediately after the experiment began and communicated only by phone. This served to increase social distance between experimenter and teacher, and it had pro-found effects: subjects reached a mean maximum shock level of 270 volts (the same as the touch proximity condition) and were fully obedient just 20 percent of the time (significantly lower than in the touch proximity condition, where full obedience was 30 percent). Note, by the way, that increasing social distance here resulted in morally *better* behavior. Social distance is a measure of the inclination to treat another's desires and pref-erences as one's own. If the other person has evil desires, then decreasing one's social distance from him means that one will be more inclined to evil. This means that arbitrarily decreasing (perceived) social distance is not the right strategy: what we should aim to do is to decrease (perceived) social distance from people *unless they have sufficiently bad preferences*, in which case we should actually aim to *increase* (perceived) social distance.

3.2   The information dimension

Knowing about people and being able to find out more about them tends to decrease social distance, and, if others do or can know about one, social distance decreases as well. The limit case is one of free communication, where each person may learn anything she wants about the other and convey any information she wants to the other. In such situations, people may communicate social sanctions (jeers and cheers), strategy-relevant information, and personal information, each of which influences moral behavior (Frey and Bohnet 1995). As mentioned above, Bentham's Panopticon paradigm institutes a fantasy of asymmetric omniscience where every twitch of a prisoner is observable by the guard. In the Milgram (1974) proximity series, when teachers were able to find out more information about learners (and, since this paradigm was symmetric, when learners were able to find out more information about teachers), destructive obedience decreased, and when experimenters could not find out whether teachers were following orders, destructive obedience also decreased.

Along the same lines, James Andreoni and Ragan Petrie (2004) found that providing participants in a public-good game with information about the strategies of other players and photos of other players resulted in 59 percent higher contributions to the public good. Iris Bohnet and Bruno Frey (1999a) used the dictator game paradigm to study giving behavior under four conditions: total anonymity, one-way identification (dictator knows who recipient is), one-way identification with information (dictator knows who recipient is, as well as some information about her), and two-way identification (both dictator and recipient know who the other is). They found a strong correlation between giving behavior and the informational aspect of social distance: even though dictators in the one-way identification conditions were unidentifiable by recipients, in both of these conditions giving increased. Merely knowing something about one's beneficiary (or victim) decreases social distance and encourages acts of generosity.

This phenomenon – when merely knowing the identity of one's potential victim or beneficiary increases pro-social behavior – was first discussed by Thomas Schelling (1968; see Eckel and Grossman 1996), who dubbed it the *identifiable victim effect*. Bohnet and Frey (1999b) conducted studies using both the prisoner's dilemma game and the dictator game, and found that mere silent identification of the beneficiary (but not the benefactor) was sufficient to induce fewer defections in prisoner's dilemma games and more altruism in dictator games. Here's how they explain this surprising result, "One-way identification where potential benefactors receive some information on who their counterpart is induces solidarity by transforming an abstract, anonymous stranger into a visible, specified individual" (1999b, p. 53). When Gary Charness and Uri Gneezy (2007) had participants play variants of the dictator and ultimatum games, they found that merely providing the surname of the receiver or responder increased the allocation made by the dictator or offerer.

These are just a few of the relevant studies. Others have shown that personal information decreases social distance more than impersonal information (Fox and Guyer 1978; Rege and Telle 2004) and that strategy-relevant information decreases social distance more than strategy-irrelevant information (Hoffman, McCabe, Shachat, and Smith 1994; Rege and Telle 2004). In the Kurzban, De Scioli, and O'Brien (2007) experiment discussed above, it turned out that knowledge "that the experimenter, or the experimenter and other participants were going to know how much an individual punished increased this amount – more than tripling it in the latter case." All of these studies support Barclay's (2004, p. 209) contention that "competition for scarce reputational benefits can help maintain cooperative behaviour because of competitive altruism" and thereby "solve" the tragedy of the commons, essentially transforming a mixed-motive prisoner's dilemma game into a coordination game.

Just as our assessment of shared group identities may be biased by recently acquired identities (as in the minimal group paradigm, which I discuss below), so may our assessment of levels of privacy be influenced by unconscious indices of privacy. In particular, we systematically underestimate social distance when faces and face-like objects are in our field of vision (as Epicurus seems to have understood), leading us to act as if someone were watching us even when we are alone. Evolutionary arguments have been made to explain why humans are so keenly aware of faces and face-like objects in their environments (Barclay 2004); indeed, the fusiform face area of the brain seems to be a devoted module for facial recognition. Burnham and Hare (2007, p. 90) argue that:

some of the anonymity effect in existing public goods experiments may be caused by activation of the dedicated neural architecture to detect faces. In other words, individuals may alter their level of prosocial behavior in the form of public goods contributions, in part, because of involuntary neural activation caused by the presence of human eyes and faces.

Burnham (2003, p. 141) points out that one-way identification is evolutionarily anomalous, so it would have made sense for our ancestors to infer from "I see him" to "He sees me." In an experiment associated with this argument, he varied the perception of privacy in a dictator game with three conditions: anonymity (neither participant knows about or sees the other), recipient photo (the dictator privately sees a photo of the recipient), and dictator photo (the recipient privately sees a photo of the dictator). In the dictator photo condition, the interaction and information dimensions of social distance confound the perception of privacy: dissatisfied recipients know their dictators by sight, and may be able to find and sanction them outside the lab. In the recipient photo condition, however, neither of these confounds exists. Giving was enhanced in both experimental conditions, supporting the idea that mere information is a dimension of social distance.

Burnham's results have been corroborated by a string of subsequent studies. Burnham and Hare (2007) had participants play a dictator game on a computer, guided by an image of a robot named KISMET. Even though it was clear that they were not actually being watched, participants *felt* they were being watched by KISMET. And KISMET had the intended effect, inducing an increase in dictators' allocations of about one-third. Haley and Fessler (2005) replicated this experiment with a computerized dictator game in which the presence of 'eye spots' on the computer's background induced extra giving. Bateson, Nettle, and Roberts (2006) replicated these results with a real-world experiment: they set up an honesty box in an academic tearoom to test whether perceived level of privacy would influence whether people paid in full for their beverages. On alternate weeks the experimenters put up either an unobtrusive photograph of flowers or a small photograph of human eyes. "On average, people paid 2.76 times as much [per cup] in the weeks with eyes" (p. 1). Presence of eyes explained 63.8 percent of the variance. In another ecologically valid experiment, Ernest-Jones, Nettle, and Bateson (2011) showed that people littered a university cafeteria roughly half as much when there were posters that featured eyes on the walls than when there were posters with flowers. Perhaps the most astonishing evidence in this paradigm comes from Rigdon, Ishii, Watabe, and Kitayama's (2009) study, which used a minimal stimulus known to activate the fusiform face area of the brain (three dots arranged to resemble a nose and two eyes). Merely presenting dictators with this arrangement of dots induced more giving, but when the figure was inverted (so that the 'face' was upside down and unrecognizable as a face) the effect disappeared. An exit interview with the dictators in this experiment found that they did not realize that they felt watched, even though their behavior showed clear signs of it. It seems that people can be brought to behave more generously through unobtrusive, unconsciously processed stimuli.

The eye-dot experiment demonstrates how subtle the influence of social distance cues can be. At the other end of the spectrum, one may wonder whether what matters in these experiments is the mere presence of a face or the precise features of that face. For instance, would people be even more pro-social if they were watched by an image of a respected authority (as in Epicurus' Garden), or is the effect more of a binary phenomenon? One would expect that the features of the face would make a difference, a conjecture that gains indirect support from the work of Oosterhof and Todorov (2008), who found that people automatically evaluate faces on the social dimensions of dominance/submissiveness and trustworthiness/untrustworthiness, and proceed to make decisions in a variety of domains, such as voting and trust behavior, based on these evaluations.

3.3   The group identity dimension

Group identity is a matter of belonging to the same social group. Every person belongs to myriad such groups, which include old warhorses such as socioeconomic status, gender, and race, as well as everything from alma mater to family to location. Thus, every pair of people shares many group identities and fails to share many others. The group identity dimension of social distance is therefore not a measure of whether there's some group that two people both belong to (there always is) or whether there's some group only one of them belongs to (there always is). It's a matter of the number and importance of shared group identities. And, since we often use heuristics to track this dimension of social distance, we commonly over- and underestimate our social distance from other people by focusing too heavily on one group identity or another.

The infamous Haney, Banks, and Zimbardo (1973) prison simulation supports the view that social distance as measured by group identity influences moral conduct. In this study, participants were randomly assigned the role of either guard or prisoner. To heighten the sense that there was a difference between the guard identity and the prisoner identity, Zimbardo ordered different uniforms for each group. He reinforced the distinction between guards and prisoners by forbidding the use of prisoners' names; instead, each was addressed by the number sewn onto his uniform. By the end of the study, the prisoners had so internalized their new group identities that when they were offered 'parole' (i.e., the chance to exit the experiment early) in exchange for forfeiture of their stipend, most accepted; then, when their parole application was 'rejected,' none left the experiment. They could, of course, have simply walked out, but they identified so strongly as prisoners that leaving without the consent of the experimenter was not a live option for them.

Zimbardo's experiment artificially increased social distance. He made salient to the guards and prisoners that they did not share what they perceived to be an important group identity. By contrast, Epicurus' statue illustrates the use of perceptual cues to decrease social distance. Since everyone in the Garden was surveyed by the same statue, and the statue represented a figure they all knew and respected, group identity was affirmed and strengthened.

Evidence from social psychology and behavioral economics also supports the hypothesis that *group identity* is a dimension of social distance. People are more generous with members of their in-group, even when it is common knowledge that the group was established by an arbitrary procedure immediately prior to the economic decision-making. Tajfel (1970; see also Tajfel 1973, 1981, 1982), for example, established group identity by asking participants to estimate the number of dots on a page. This is known as the *minimal group paradigm*. Those who overestimated were classed into one group, those who underestimated another. Members of the same group were significantly more generous towards and trusting of each other than were members of different groups. By focusing only on their most recently acquired group identity, they underestimated social distance from members of their own group and overestimated social distance from members of the other group.

Hoffman, McCabe, Shachat, and Smith (1994) varied Tajfel's paradigm in studies using the ultimatum and dictator games. They divided participants into groups based on their scores on a trivia quiz. High-scoring dictators showed less generosity. In the ultimatum game, high-scoring offerers offered less to low-scoring responders, who accepted these atypically low offers. Along these lines, Charness, Haruvy, and Sonsino (2007) tested the group identity hypothesis by having participants play economic games over the internet. They found that participants were less generous with one another when they did not share national identities. Interestingly, Mifune, Hashimoto, and Yamagishi (2010) found that the eye-spot effect on beneficence disappeared when the recipient was not perceived as a member of the in-group.

4 CONCLUSION, WITH A MEDITATION ON THE ART OF J.R.

In the previous section, I aimed to show that social distance is a function of three dimensions: interaction, information, and group identity. I furthermore endeavored to show that we use heuristics, such as the presence of faces or recently acquired group identities, to track social distance, which in turn means that we are prone to systematically under- and overestimate it. If these arguments are on the right track, then the strategic deployment of social distance cues can be used to modulate perceived social distance and thereby to guide moral conduct. Such interventions would constitute a kind of moral technology different from the factitious virtue discussed hitherto, but also similar in that it relies on social expectations and (in ideal cases) the internalization of appropriate contextual features. In this concluding section, I want to take up the question again whether the moral technology I'm commending is a potentially objectionable situational influence. The argument I want to develop is that characterizing moral technology in this way involves an erroneous conception of a situational influence.

The notion of a situational influence is essentially indexed to a conception of the normal. To say, for instance, that mood elevators induce creativity assumes that the normal state of affairs is one in which mood is not elevated. To say that calling someone honest induces honest conduct assumes that the normal state of affairs is one in which the agent has not been called honest. To say that feeling watched induces other-regarding preferences assumes that the normal state of affairs is one in which the agent is not watched. To see why, consider the fact that each of these statements could be turned around. Instead of saying that mood elevators induce creativity, we could say that mood neutralizers dampen creativity. Instead of saying that calling someone honest induces honest conduct, we could say that not calling someone honest dampens honesty. Instead of saying that feeling watched induces other-regarding preferences, we could say that anonymity destroys other-regarding preferences. What counts as a situational influence depends on what you think the starting point or norm is.

If this is right, it further supports the triadic relational conception of virtue, for that conception allows us to build in the right social and contextual norms. The question then arises what the right norms are. We could define them purely descriptively, as whatever happens most often. Thus, if people tend to be unhappy, then negative mood is the norm and mood neutralizers count as situational influences, as do mood elevators.

And if people tend to think highly (or ill) of each other's character, then perceived virtue (vice) is the norm and calling someone vicious (virtuous) counts as situational influences. And if people tend to be locked away in their private rooms, then anonymity is the norm and visibility is a situational influence.

It seems to me plainly mistaken to define norms in this way. Instead, I contend that norms should be defined with one eye on the flourishing of people and societies and the other eye on empirical reality. This suggestion is another instance of the holistic calibration of normative theory, moral psychology, and moral technology. If this is the right way to go, then we need to think very carefully about what's possible and desirable for both individuals and societies. For instance, it seems biologically unlikely, if not impossible, for people always to be in bad (or good) moods. Neutral mood with some room for variance is probably the right norm. If this is the right norm, then both mood elevators and mood depressors are situational influences.

What about self-concept and social expectations? Is it both possible and desirable for people to think one another virtuous, and to be right (or near enough) in part because they think so? In other words, is factitious virtue both possible and desirable? I would urge that it is, or at least that it's more desirable than the state of affairs where people are stingy with their praise and are therefore less (factitiously) virtuous. If this is the right norm, then virtue-labeling (up to a point) is not a situational influence; instead, the failure to praise the (nascent, developing, partial) virtue of other people is a situational influence, and one that induces lack of virtue.

And what about anonymity and social distance? Is it both possible and desirable for people to engage with each other face-to-face, and to express other-regarding preferences in part because they are face-to-face? Again, I would urge that it is. Consider the alternative, in which people are mostly anonymous, and tend to express less other-regarding preferences in part because they do not engage with each other face-to-face. Such a society is possible. Indeed, I'm tempted to say that contemporary society has moved too far in this direction. In support of this claim, consider again the myth of Gyges, the statue of Epicurus, and the Panopticon. It seems clear that the absolute anonymity of a Gyges is bad for both society and, in many ways, Gyges himself. For he ends up unable to enjoy friendship, love, and a host of other values. At the other end of the anonymity spectrum we have absolute panopticism, which also seems quite undesirable. Somewhere in between, I want to suggest, is the sweet spot, both empirically and normatively. In fact, the statue of Epicurus seems to me to be awfully close to the sweet spot.

To see why, I want to conclude with a meditation on the work of J.R., a contemporary French artist. J.R.'s career began in 2002, when he pasted several large photographs of local residents on walls in the projects of Les Bosquets, a run-down suburb of Paris. In 2003, when riots boiled over in Les Bosquets, some of these photos were captured on news footage, illuminated by burning cars. J.R. later said, "It was kind of weird to see those images, and those eyes staring back" (Khatchadourian 2011, p. 61). He returned to the slum to take portraits of the rioters, using a wide-angle lens so that he would have to stand just inches away from them while taking the photographs. "They were making scary faces to play the caricature of themselves. [...] I pasted huge posters of them everywhere in the bourgeois part of Paris, with their name, age, and even building number" (p. 61). These faces stared out at the middle-class Parisians, demanding recognition as individuals, as humans, as worthy of respect.

After the success of his project in Paris, J.R. began to travel the world, pasting huge close-up photos of faces in public places. He went to the border of Israel and Palestine to work on a project titled Face2Face.[6] In a short film associated with this project, he explains his motives:

For an Israeli, a Palestinian is a terrorist who commits suicide attacks on a marketplace, killing women and children. For a Palestinian, an Israeli is an occupation soldier who humiliates him at the checkpoint and shoots civilians and ambulances. The reality is infinitely more complex. The idea is to post their portraits face to face in huge formats, in unavoidable places on the Israeli and Palestinian sides [of the security wall]. We took people who had the same job on both sides: hairdressers, actors, musicians, teachers, etc. We chose them for their faces. Basically, we go to a Palestinian hairdresser. We tell him that we are French. We tell him that we are neither anti-Israeli nor anti-Palestinian, but in favor of a realistic peace. We want to put you against a wall and shoot you with a 28 millimeter [camera]. Then, we take your picture in huge format and we post it everywhere – in Israel, in Palestine, in this town, on the wall, everywhere. The crazy thing is that the guys accepted.

Members of the local community not only agreed to pose for the photos, they also helped to paste them up. Of course, this art project did not suffice to end the conflict between Israel and Palestine, but it did to some extent humanize many people on both sides of the divide. They

---

[6] The website for this project is www.face2faceproject.com. Many of the images associated with this project, along with several interesting videos, are available there.

were forced to recognize one another, to see the humanity in each other's faces. And that alone is worth something.

After his trip to Israel and Palestine, J.R. worked on similar projects around the world. His most recent project, titled *Women Are Heroes* (2012), involved the pasting of gigantic close-ups of women's faces in Sierra Leone, Liberia, Sudan, Kenya, Brazil, India, and Cambodia. Many of the women pictured in these monumental photographs were (or were related to) victims of violence or sexual assault. By pasting their own faces on the walls of their neighborhoods, they set up Epicurus-like symbolic watchers. Their faces simultaneously demanded recognition and held accountable. Of the installation in Morro da Providência, the oldest favela in Rio de Janeiro, J.R. said, "That favela is in the center of town, but when you look at a map it is like it is not there. [...] So the people were saying, 'Hey, we are there, we are right there in front of you, and you pretend that we don't exist'" (Khatchadourian 2011, p. 58).

So here's the question: is anonymity normal and face-to-face engagement a situational influence, or is face-to-face engagement normal and anonymity a situational influence?

References

Adams, J. (1959). Advice seeking of mothers as a function of need for cognition. *Child Development*, 30, 171–76.

Adams, M., Robertson, C., Gray-Ray, P., and Ray, M. (2003). Labeling and delinquency. *Adolescence*, 38, 171–86.

Adams, R. (2006). *A Theory of Virtue*. Oxford University Press.

Albarracín, D., and McNatt, P. (2005). Maintenance and decay of past behavior influences: anchoring attitudes on beliefs following inconsistent actions. *Personality and Social Psychology Bulletin*, 31:6, 719–33.

Alfano, M. (2009). Sensitivity theory and the individuation of belief-formation methods. *Erkenntnis*, 70:2, 271–81.

(2011). Explaining away intuitions about traits: why virtue ethics seems plausible (even if it isn't). *Review of Philosophy and Psychology*, 2:1, 121–36.

(2012). Extending the situationist challenge to responsibilist virtue epistemology. *Philosophical Quarterly*, 62: 223–49.

(forthcoming a). Extending the situationist challenge to reliabilism about inference. In Fairweather (ed.), *Virtue Scientia: Bridges Between Philosophy of Science and Virtue Epistemology*. Synthese Library.

(forthcoming b). Identifying and defending the hard core of virtue ethics. *Journal of Philosophical Research*.

(forthcoming c). Stereotype threat and intellectual virtue. In Flanagan and Fairweather (eds.), *Naturalizing Virtue*. Cambridge University Press.

Allen, C. (1982). Self-perception based strategies for stimulated energy conservation. *The Journal of Consumer Research*, 8:4, 381–90.

Allport, G. (1966). Traits revisited. *American Psychologist*, 21, 1–10.

Anderson, C., and Bushman, B. (2002). Human aggression. *Annual Review of Psychology*, 53, 27–51.

Andreoni, J., and Petrie, R. (2004). Public goods experiments without confidentiality: a glimpse into fund-raising. *Journal of Public Economics*, 88:7–8, 1605–23.

Annas, J. (1993). *The Morality of Happiness*. New York: Oxford University Press.

(2003). Virtue ethics and social psychology. *A Priori*, 2, 20–59.

(2011). *Intelligent Virtue*. Oxford University Press.

Anscombe, G. E. M. (1958). Modern moral philosophy. *Philosophy*, 33, 1–19.

Apsler, R. (1975). Effects of embarrassment on behavior toward others. *Journal of Personality and Social Psychology*, 32, 145–53.

Ariely, D. (2008). *Predictably Irrational*. New York: Harper Collins.

Aristotle (2000). *Nicomachean Ethics*. Translated by R. Crisp. Cambridge University Press.

(2000). *Rhetoric*. In *The Complete Works of Aristotle*, edited by Jonathan Barnes, translated by W. Rhys Roberts. Cambridge University Press.

Asch, S. (1951). Effects of group pressures upon the modification and distortion of judgment. In Guetzkow (ed.), *Groups, Leadership, and Men*, pp. 177–90. Pittsburgh: Carnegie Press.

(1952). *Social Psychology*. New York: Prentice Hall.

(1955). Opinions and social pressure. *Scientific American*, 193:5, 31–35.

(1956). Studies of independence and conformity: a minority of one against a unanimous majority. *Psychological Monographs*, 70:9, 1–70.

Ashby, F., Isen, A., and Turken, A. (1999). A neuropsychological theory of positive affect and its influence on cognition. *Psychological Review*, 106, 529–50.

Audi, R. (2001). Epistemic virtue and justified belief. In Fairweather and Zagzebski (eds.), *Virtue Epistemology: Essays on Epistemic Virtue and Responsibility*, pp. 82–97. Oxford University Press.

Aumann, R., and Brandenburger, A. (1995). Epistemic conditions for Nash equilibrium. *Econometrica*, 63:5, 1161–80.

Aviles, J., Whelan, S., Hernke, D., Williams, B., Kenny, K., O'Fallon, W., and Kopecky, S. (2001). Intercessory prayer and cardiovascular disease progression in a coronary care unit population: a randomized controlled trial. *Mayo Clinic Proceedings*, 76, 1192–98.

Axtell, G. (2010). Agency ascriptions in ethics and epistemology: or, navigating intersections, narrow and broad. In Battaly (ed.), *Virtue and Vice: Moral and Epistemic*, pp. 73–94. Oxford: Wiley-Blackwell.

Bacon, F. (1620). *Novum Organum*. Reprinted in Jones and Fogelin (eds.), *A History of Western Philosophy*, vol. III, 2nd edition (1969). Boston: Wadsworth.

Badhwar, N. (1996). The limited unity of virtue. *Nous*, 30:3, 306–29.

Baehr, J. (2006a). Character in epistemology. *Philosophical Studies*, 128, 479–514.

(2006b). Character, reliability, and virtue epistemology. *The Philosophical Quarterly*, 56, 193–212.

Barclay, P. (2004). Trustworthiness and competitive altruism can also solve the "tragedy of the commons." *Evolution and Human Behavior*, 25, 209–20.

Baron, M. (2003). Manipulativeness. *Proceedings and Addresses of the American Philosophical Association*, 77:2, 37–54.

Baron, R. (1997). The sweet smell of … helping: effects of pleasant ambient fragrance on prosocial behavior in shopping malls. *Personality and Social Psychology Bulletin*, 23, 498–503.

Baron, R. A., and Thomley, J. (1994). A whiff of reality: positive affect as a potential mediator of the effects of pleasant fragrances on task performance and helping. *Environment and Behavior*, 26, 766–84.

Bateson, M., Nettle, D., and Roberts, G. (2006). Cues of being watched enhance cooperation in a real-world setting. *Biology Letters*, 12, 412–14.

Batson, C. (1991). *The Altruism Question: Toward a Social-Psychological Answer.* Hillsdale, NJ: Lawrence Erlbaum Associates.

(2002). Addressing the altruism question experimentally. In Post, Underwood, Schloss, and Hurlbut (eds.), *Altruism and Altruistic Love: Science, Philosophy, and Religion in Dialogue*, pp. 89–105. Oxford University Press.

Batson, C., Coke, J., Chard, F., Smith, D., and Taliaferro, A. (1979). Generality of the "glow of goodwill": effects of mood on helping and information acquisition. *Social Psychology Quarterly*, 42, 176–79.

Batson, C., van Lange, P., Ahmad, N., and Lishner, D. (2003). Altruism and helping behavior. In Hogg and Cooper (eds.), *The Sage Handbook of Social Psychology*, pp. 279–95. London: Sage Publications.

Beebe, J. (2004). The *generality problem*, statistical relevance and the tri-level hypothesis. *Nous*, 38:1, 177–95.

Bem, D. (2011). Feeling the future: experimental evidence for anomalous retroactive influences on cognition and affect. *Journal of Personality and Social Psychology*, 100, 407–25.

Benson, H., Dusek, J., Sherwood, J., Lam, P., Bethea, C., Carpenter, W., Levitsky, S., Hill, P., Clem, D., Jain, M., Drumel, D., Kopecky, S., Mueller, P., Marek, D., Rollins, S., Hibberd, P. (2006). Study of the therapeutic effects of intercessory prayer (STEP) in cardiac bypass patients: a multi-center randomized trial of uncertainty and certainty of receiving intercessory prayer. *American Heart Journal*, 151:4, 934–42.

Bentham, J. (1995). *The Panopticon Writings.* London: Verso.

Bicchieri, C. (2006). *The Grammar of Society: The Nature and Dynamics of Social Norms.* Cambridge University Press.

Blackburn, S. (1998). *Ruling Passions.* Oxford: Clarendon Press.

Blass, T. (1999). The Milgram paradigm after 35 years: some things we now know about obedience to authority. *Journal of Applied Social Psychology*, 29:5, 955–78.

Bohnet, I., and Frey, B. (1999a). Social distance and other-regarding behavior in dictator games. *The American Economic Review*, 89:1, 335–39.

(1999b). The sound of silence in prisoner's dilemma and dictator games. *Journal of Economic Behavior and Organization*, 38, 43–57.

Boles, W., and Haywood, S. (1978). The effects of urban noise and sidewalk density upon pedestrian cooperation and tempo. *Journal of Social Psychology*, 104, 29–35.

Bovens, L., and Hartmann, S. (2003). *Bayesian Epistemology.* Oxford University Press.

Bowers, K. (1973). Situationism in psychology: an analysis and a critique. *Psychological Review*, 80, 307–36.

Boyce, C., Wood, A., and Brown, G. (2010). The dark side of conscientiousness: conscientious people experience greater drops in life satisfaction following unemployment. *Journal of Research in Personality*, 44, 535–39.

Brañas-Garza, P. (2007). Promoting helping behavior with framing in dictator games. *Journal of Economic Psychology*, 28, 477–86.

Brody, H. (2000). *The Placebo Response*. New York: Cliff Street Books.

Buchan, N., Johnson, E., and Croson, R. (2006). Let's get personal: an international examination of the influence of communication, culture and social distance on other regarding preferences. *Journal of Economic Behavior and Organization*, 60:3, 373–98.

Burger, J., and Caldwell, D. (2003). The effects of monetary incentives and labeling on the foot-in-the-door effect: evidence for a self-perception process. *Basic and Applied Social Psychology*, 25:3, 235–41.

Burnham, T. (2003). Engineering altruism: a theoretical and experimental investigation of anonymity and gift giving. *Journal of Economic Behavior and Organization*, 50, 133–44.

Burnham, T., and Hare, B. (2007). Engineering human cooperation. *Human Nature*, 18:2, 88–108.

Burnyeat, M. (1980). Aristotle on learning to be good. In Rorty (ed.), *Essays on Aristotle's Ethics*, pp. 69–92. University of California Press.

Cacioppo, J., Petty, R., Feinstein, J., and Jarvis, W. (1996). Dispositional differences in cognitive motivation: the life and times of individuals varying in need for cognition. *Psychological Bulletin*, 119, 197–253.

Camerer, C., and Thaler, R. (1995). Anomalies: ultimatums, dictators and manners. *Journal of Economic Perspectives*, 9, 209–19.

Carlsmith, J., and Gross, A. (1968). Some effects of guilt on compliance. *Journal of Personality and Social Psychology*, 53, 1178–91.

Centola, D., Willer, R., and Macy, M. (2005). The emperor's dilemma: a computational model of self-enforcing norms. *American Journal of Sociology*, 110:4, 1009–40.

Chaikin, A., Sigler, F., and Derlega, V. (1974). Nonverbal mediators of teacher expectancy effects. *Journal of Personality and Social Psychology*, 30, 144–49.

Charness, G., and Gneezy, U. (2007). What's in a name? Anonymity and social distance in dictator and ultimatum games. *Journal of Economic Behavior and Organization*, 63:1, 88–103.

Charness, G., Haruvy, E., and Sonsino, D. (2007). Social distance and reciprocity: the internet vs. the laboratory. *Journal of Economic Behavior and Organization*, 63:1, 88–103.

Chen, M., and Bargh, J. (1997). Nonconscious behavioral confirmation processes: the self-fulfilling consequences of automatic stereotype activation. *Journal of Experimental Social Psychology*, 33, 541–60.

Chwe, M. (2001). *Rational Ritual: Culture, Coordination, and Common Knowledge*. Princeton University Press.

Cimpian, A., Arce, H.-M., Markman, E., and Dweck, C. (2007). Subtle linguistic cues affect children's motivation. *Psychological Science*, 18:4, 314–16.

Clifford, W. (1987/1999). *The Ethics of Belief and Other Essays*. Amherst, NY: Prometheus Books.

Code, L. (1984). Toward a "responsibilist" epistemology. *Philosophy and Phenomenological Research*, 45, 29–50.

Cohen, A., Stotland, E., and Wolfe, D. (1955). An experimental investigation of need for cognition. *Journal of Abnormal and Social Psychology*, 51:2, 291–94.

Cohen, S. (1978). Environmental load and the allocation of attention. In Baum, Singer, and Valins (eds.), *Advances in Environmental Psychology*, vol. 1, pp. 1–29. Hillsdale, NJ: Erlbaum.

Cohen, S., and Lezak, A. (1977). Noise and inattentiveness to social cues. *Environment and Behavior*, 9, 559–72.

Cooper, J. (2007). *Cognitive Dissonance: Fifty Years of Classic Theory*. Los Angeles, CA: Sage.

Cornelissen, G., Dewitte, S., and Warlop, L. (2007). Whatever people say I am that's what I am: social labeling as a social marketing tool. *International Journal of Research in Marketing*, 24:4, 278–88.

Cornelissen, G., Dewitte, S., Warlop, L., Liegeois, A., Yzerbyt, V., and Corneille, O. (2006). Free bumper stickers for a better future: the long term effect of the labeling technique. *Advances in Consumer Research*, 33, 284–85.

Crisp, R. (1996). Modern moral philosophy and the virtues. In Crisp (ed.), *How Should One Live? Essays on the Virtues*, pp. 1–18. Oxford University Press.

Crutchfield, R. (1955). Conformity and character. *American Psychologist*, 10, 191–98.

Dalmiya, V. (2002). Why should a knower care? *Hypatia*, 17:1, 34–52.

Darley, J., and Batson, C. D. (1973). "From Jerusalem to Jericho": a study of situational and dispositional variables in helping behavior. *Journal of Personality and Social Psychology*, 27, 100–08.

Darley, J., and Fazio, R. (1980). Expectancy confirmation processes arising in the social interaction sequence. *American Psychologist*, 35, 867–81.

Darley, J., and Latané, B. (1968). Bystander intervention in emergencies: diffusion of responsibility. *Journal of Personality and Social Psychology*, 8, 377–83.

Darwin, C. (2009). *The Autobiography of Charles Darwin: 1809–1882*. New York: Classic Books.

Dawes, R., and Mulford, M. (1996). The false consensus effect and overconfidence: flaws in judgment or flaws in how we study judgment? *Organizational Behavior and Human Decision Processes*, 65:3, 201–11.

Dent, N. J. H. (1975). Virtues and actions. *The Philosophical Quarterly*, 25.

DeRose, K. (2005). The ordinary language basis for contextualism and the new invariantism. *The Philosophical Quarterly*, 55:219, 172–98.

DesAutels, P. (2004). Moral mindfulness. In DesAutels and Urban Walker (eds), *Moral Psychology: Feminist Ethics and Social Theory*, pp. 69–81. New York: Rowman and Littlefield.

Diogenes Laertius (1965). *Lives of Eminent Philosophers*, vol. 11. Translated by R. D. Hicks. Cambridge, MA: Harvard University Press.

Ditmarsch, H., Eijck, J., and Verbrugge, R. (2009). Common knowledge and common belief. In Eijck and Verbrugge (eds.), *Discourses on Social Software*, pp. 107–32. Amsterdam University Press.

Donnerstein, E., and Wilson, D. (1976). Effects of noise and perceived control on ongoing and subsequent aggressive behavior. *Journal of Personality and Social Psychology*, 34, 774–81.

Doris, J. (1998). Persons, situations, and virtue ethics. *Nous*, 32:4, 504–40.

(2002). *Lack of Character: Personality and Moral Behavior*. Cambridge University Press.

(2005). Replies: evidence and sensibility. *Philosophy and Phenomenological Research*, 71:3, 656–77.

(2010). Heated agreement: lack of character as being for the good. *Philosophical Studies*, 148, 135–46.

Doris, J., and Stich, S. (2005). As a matter of fact: empirical perspectives on ethics. In Jackson and Smith (eds.), *The Oxford Handbook of Contemporary Philosophy*, pp. 114–52. Oxford University Press.

Doris, J., and the Moral Psychology Research Group (2010). *The Moral Psychology Handbook*. Oxford University Press.

Dotter, D., and Roebuck, J. (1988). The labeling approach re-examined: interactionism and the components of deviance. *Deviant Behavior*, 9:19, 19–32.

Driver, J. (2003). The conflation of moral and epistemic virtues. In Brady and Duncan (eds.), *Moral and Epistemic Virtues*, pp. 101–16. Malden, MA: Blackwell.

Duckworth, A., and Seligman, M. (2005). Self-discipline outdoes IQ in predicting academic performance of adolescents. *Psychological Science*, 16:12, 939–44.

(2006). Self-discipline gives girls the edge: gender in self-discipline, grades, and achievement test scores. *Journal of Educational Psychology*, 98:1, 198–208.

Duckworth, A., Kirby, T., Tsukayama, E., Bernstein, H., and Ericsson, A. (2010). Deliberate practice spells success: why grittier competitors triumph at the National Spelling Bee. *Social Psychology and Personality Science*, 2, 174–81.

Duckworth, A., Peterson, C., Matthews, M., and Kelly, D. (2007). Grit: perseverance and passion for long-term goals. *Journal of Personality and Social Psychology*, 92:6, 1087–101.

Duckworth, A., Tsukayama, E., and May, H. (2010). Establishing causality using longitudinal hierarchical linear modeling: an illustration predicting achievement from self-control. *Social Psychological and Personality Science*, 1:4, 311–17.

Duncker, K. (1945). *On Problem Solving*. Psychological Monographs, 58. American Psychological Association.

Eckel, C., and Grossman, P. (1996). Altruism in anonymous dictator games. *Games and Economic Behavior*, 16, 181–91.

Epictetus *Letters to Lucilius*. Translated by Richard Sorabji.

Epicurus (1940). Fragments. In *The Stoic and Epicurean Philosophers*. Edited and translated by Whitney Oates. New York: Random House.

Epstein, S. (1983). Aggregation and beyond: some basic issues in the prediction of behavior. *Journal of Personality*, 51, 360–91.

Ernest-Jones, M., Nettle, D., and Bateson, M. (2011). Effects of eye images on everyday cooperative behavior: a field experiment. *Evolution and Human Behavior*, 32:3, 172–78.

Estrada, C., Isen, A., and Young, M. (1994). Positive affect influences creative problem solving and reported source of practice satisfaction in physicians. *Motivation and Emotion*, 18, 285–99.

(1998). Positive affect facilitates integration of information and decreases anchoring in reasoning among physicians. *Organizational Behavioral and Human Decision Processes*, 72, 117–35.

Feltz, A., and Zarpentine, C. (2010). Do you know more when it matters less? *Philosophical Psychology*, 23:5, 683–706.

Festinger, L., Riecken, H., and Schachter, S. (1956). *When Prophecy Fails*. Minneapolis: University of Minnesota Press.

Fields, J., and Schuman, H. (1976). Public beliefs about the beliefs of the public. *Public Opinion Quarterly*, 40, 427–48.

Foot, P. (1997). Virtues and vices. In Crisp and Slote (eds.), *Virtue Ethics*, pp. 163–77. Oxford University Press.

(2001). *Natural Goodness*. Oxford: Clarendon Press.

Forman-Barzilai, F. (2010). *Adam Smith and the Circles of Sympathy*. Oxford University Press.

Foucault, M. (1997). *Discipline and Punish*. Translated by Sheridan. New York: Pantheon Books.

Fox, J., and Guyer, M. (1978). Public choice and cooperation in *n*-person prisoner's dilemma. *Journal of Conflict Resolution*, 22:3, 469–81.

Frankfurt, H. (2001). The dear self. *Philosophers' Imprint*, 1:0.

Frey, B. S., and Bohnet, I. (1995). Institutions affect fairness: experimental investigations. *Journal of Institutional and Theoretical Economics*, 151:2, 286–303.

Frimer, J., Walker, L., Dunlop, W., Lee, B., and Riches, A. (2011). The integration of agency and communion in moral personality: evidence of enlightened self-interest. *Journal of Personality and Social Psychology*, 101:1, 149–63.

Frischer, B. (1982). *The Sculpted Word*. University of California Press.

Funder, D. (2006). Towards a resolution of the personality triad: persons, situations, and behaviors. *Journal of Research in Personality*, 40, 21–34.

Funder, D., and Ozer, D. (1983). Behavior as a function of the situation. *Journal of Personality and Social Psychology*, 44, 107–12.

Gächter, S., and Fehr, E. (1999). Collective action as a social exchange. *Journal of Economic Behavior and Organization*, 39:4, 341–69.

Geach, P. (1977). *The Virtues*. Cambridge University Press.

Geen, R., and O'Neal, E. (1969). Activation of cue-elicited aggression by general arousal. *Journal of Personality and Social Psychology*, 11, 289–92.

Gibbard, A. (2003). *Thinking How to Live*. Cambridge, MA: Harvard University Press.

Gigerenzer, G. (2007). *Gut Feelings*. New York: Viking.

Gigerenzer, G., Todd, P. M., and the ABC Research Group (2000). *Simple Heuristics That Make Us Smart*. New York: Oxford University Press.

Goldman, A. (1986). *Epistemology and Cognition*. Harvard University Press.

(1992). Epistemic folkways and scientific epistemology. In *Liasons: Philosophy Meets the Cognitive and Social Sciences*, pp. 155–75. Cambridge, MA: MIT Press.

(1993). Ethics and cognitive science. *Ethics*, 103, 337–60.

(1999). *Knowledge in a Social World*. Oxford University Press.

Good, T., and Brophy, J. (1973). *Looking in Classrooms*. University of California Press.

Graham, S. (1990). On communicating low ability in the classroom: bad things good teachers sometimes do. In Graham and Folkes (eds.), *Attribution Theory: Applications to Achievement, Mental Health, and Interpersonal Conflict*, pp. 17–36. Hillsdale, NJ: Erlbaum.

Greco, J. (1992). Agent reliabilism. *Nous*, 13, 273–96.

(1993). Virtues and vices of virtue epistemology. *Canadian Journal of Philosophy*, 23, 413–32.

(2000). *Putting Skeptics in Their Place: The Nature of Skeptical Arguments and Their Role in Philosophical Inquiry*. Cambridge University Press.

(2003). Knowledge as credit for true belief. In DePaul and Zagzebski (eds.), *Intellectual Virtue: Perspectives from Ethics and Epistemology*, pp. 111–34. Oxford University Press.

(2009). Knowledge and success from ability. *Philosophical Studies*, 142, 17–26.

(2010). *Achieving Knowledge: A Virtue-Theoretic Account of Epistemic Normativity*. Cambridge University Press.

Grusec, J., and Redler, E. (1980). Attribution, reinforcement, and altruism: a developmental analysis. *Developmental Psychology*, 16:5, 525–34.

Grusec, J., Kuczynski, L., Rushton, J., and Simutis, Z. (1978). Modeling, direct instruction, and attributions: effects on altruism. *Developmental Psychology*, 14, 51–57.

Guskin, S. (1978). Theoretical and empirical strategies for the study of the labeling of mentally retarded persons. In Ellis (ed.), *International Review of Research in Mental Retardation*, pp. 34–47. New York: Academic Press.

Hacking, I. (1999). *The Social Construction of What?* Harvard University Press.

(2006). Making up people. *London Review of Books*, 28:16.

Haidt, J. (2001). The emotional dog and its rational tail: a social intuitionist approach to moral judgment. *Psychological Review*, 108, 814–34.

Haley, K., and Fessler, D. M. T. (2005). Nobody's watching? Subtle cues affect generosity in an anonymous economic game. *Evolution and Human Behavior*, 26, 245–56.

Hamilton, D., Sherman, S., and Ruvolo, C. (1990). Stereotype-based expectancies: effects on information processing and social behavior. *Journal of Social Issues*, 46, 35–60.

Haney, C., Banks, W., and Zimbardo, P. (1973). Interpersonal dynamics of a simulated prison. *International Journal of Criminology and Penology*, 1, 69–97.

Harman, G. (1999). Moral philosophy meets social psychology: virtue ethics and the fundamental attribution error. *Proceedings of the Aristotelian Society*, New Series 119, 316–31.

(2000). The nonexistence of character traits. *Proceedings of the Aristotelian Society*, 100, 223–26.

(2001). Virtue ethics without character traits. In Byrne, Stalnaker, and Wedgwood (eds.), *Fact and Value*, pp. 117–27. Cambridge, MA: MIT Press.

(2003). No character or personality. *Business Ethics Quarterly*, 13:1, 87–94.

(2006). Three trends in moral and political philosophy. *The Journal of Value Inquiry*, 37.

Harris, M., and Rosenthal, R. (1985). The mediation of interpersonal expectancy effects: 31 meta-analyses. *Psychological Bulletin*, 97, 363–86.

Hartshorne, H., and May, M. (1928). *Studies in the Nature of Character*, vol. 1. New York: Macmillan.

Hatcher, R., Trussell, J., Nelson, A., Cates, W., Stewart, F., and Kowal, D. (2008). *Contraceptive Technology*. New York: Ardent Media.

Hawthorne, J. (2004). *Knowledge and Lotteries*. Oxford University Press.

Hebl, M., Foster, J., Mannix, L., and Dovidio, J. (2002). Formal and interpersonal discrimination: a field study of bias toward homosexuals. *Personality and Social Psychology Bulletin*, 28, 815–25.

Henderlong, J., and Lepper, M. (2002). The effects of praise on children's intrinsic motivation: a review and synthesis. *Psychological Bulletin*, 128:5, 774–95.

Hoffman, E., McCabe, K., Shachat, K., and Smith, V. (1994). Preferences, property rights, and anonymity in bargaining games. *Games and Economic Behavior*, 7, 346–80.

Hoffman, E., McCabe, K., and Smith, V. (1996). Social distance and other-regarding behavior in dictator games. In Plott and Smith (eds.), *Handbook of Experimental Economics*, vol. 1, pp. 429–35. Amsterdam: Elsevier.

Hoge, R., and Renzulli, J. (1993). Exploring the link between giftedness and self-concept. *Review of Educational Research*, 63:4, 499–65.

Hookway, C. (2003a). Affective states and epistemic immediacy. In Brady and Pritchard (eds.), *Moral and Epistemic Virtues*, pp. 75–92. Malden, MA: Blackwell.

(2003b). How to be a virtue epistemologist. In DePaul and Zagzebski (eds.), *Intellectual Virtue*, pp. 183–202. Oxford: Clarendon Press.

(2006). Epistemology and inquiry: the primacy of practice. In Heatheringon (ed.), *Epistemology Futures*, pp. 95–110. Oxford University Press.

Hudson, S. (1980). Character traits and desires. *Ethics*, 90, 539–42.

Hurka, T. (2001). *Vice, Virtue, and Value*. Oxford University Press.

(2006). Virtuous act, virtuous dispositions. *Analysis*, 66:1, 75.

Hursthouse, R. (1999). *On Virtue Ethics*. Oxford University Press.

Isen, A. (1985). Asymmetry of happiness and sadness in effects on memory in normal college students. *Journal of Experimental Psychology: General*, 114, 388–91.

(1987). Positive affect, cognitive processes, and social behavior. In Berkowitz (ed.), *Advances in Experimental Social Psychology*, vol. XX, pp. 203–54. San Diego: Academic Press.

Isen, A., and Daubman, K. (1984). The influence of affect on categorization. *Journal of Personality and Social Psychology*, 47, 1206–17.

Isen, A. M., and Levin, P. F. (1972). The effect of feeling good on helping: cookies and kindness. *Journal of Personality and Social Psychology*, 21, 384–88.

Isen, A., Clark, M., and Schwartz, M. (1976). Duration of the effect of good mood on helping: "Footprints on the sands of time." *Journal of Personality and Social Psychology*, 34, 385–93.

Isen, A., Daubman, K., and Nowicki, G. (1987). Positive affect facilitates creative problem solving. *Journal of Personality and Social Psychology*, 52, 1122–31.

Isen, A., Rosenzweig, A., and Young, M. (1991). The influence of positive affect on clinical problem solving. *Medical Decision Making*, 11, 221–27.

Isen, A., Shalker, T., Clark, M., and Karp, L. (1978). Affect, accessibility of material in memory, and behavior: a cognitive loop. *Journal of Personality and Social Psychology*, 36, 1–12.

J.R. (2012). *Women Are Heroes*. New York: Abrams.

Jacobs, R., and Campbell, D. (1961). The perpetuation of an arbitrary tradition through several generations of laboratory microculture. *Journal of Abnormal and Social Psychology*, 62, 649–58.

James, W. (1896/1979). The will to believe. In Burkhardt et al. (eds.), *The Will to Believe and Other Essays in Popular Philosophy*, pp. 291–341. Cambridge, MA: Harvard University Press.

Jennings, D., Amabile, T., and Ross, L. (1982). Informal covariation assessment: data-based vs. theory-based judgments. In Tversky, Kahneman, and Slovic (eds.), *Judgment Under Uncertainty: Heuristics and Biases*, pp. 211–30. New York: Cambridge.

Jensen, A., and Moore, S. (1977). The effect of attribute statements on cooperativeness and competitiveness in school-age boys. *Child Development*, 48, 305–307.

Jones, E. (1990). *Interpersonal Perception*. New York: Freeman.

Jones, E., and Harris, V. (1967). The attribution of attitudes. *Journal of Experimental Social Psychology*, 3, 1–24.

Jones, E., and Nisbett, R. E. (1971). *The Actor and the Observer: Divergent Perceptions of the Causes of Behavior*. New York: General Learning Press.

Jost, J., and Jost, L. (2009). Virtue ethics and the social psychology of character: philosophical lessons from the person-situation debate. *Journal of Research in Personality*, 43:2, 253–54.

Jussim, L. (1986). Self-fulfilling prophecies: a theoretical and integrative review. *Psychological Review*, 93, 429–45.

(1990). Social reality and social problems: the role of expectancies. *Journal of Social Issues*, 46:2, 9–34.

Kahneman, D., and Tversky, A. (1973). On the psychology of prediction. *Psychological Review*, 80, 237–51.

Kahneman, D., Slovic, P., and Tversky, A. (1982). *Judgment Under Uncertainty: Heuristics and Biases*. New York: Cambridge University Press.

Kamtekar, R. (2004). Situationism and virtue ethics on the content of our character. *Ethics*, 114, 458–91.

Katz, D., and Allport, F. (1931). *Student Attitudes*. Syracuse, NY: Craftsman.

Kelly, D. (2011). *Yuck! The Nature and Moral Significance of Disgust*. Cambridge, MA: MIT Press.

Keynes, J. M. (2009). *The General Theory of Employment, Interest, and Money*. New York: Classic Books America.

Khan, U., and Dhar, R. (2006). Licensing effect in consumer choice. *Journal of Marketing Research*, 43, 259–66.

Khatchadourian, R. (2011). In the picture: an artist's global experiment to help people be seen. *The New Yorker*, November 28 edition, 56–63.

Kilham, W., and Mann, L. (1974). Level of destructive obedience as a junction of transmitter and executant roles in the Milgram obedience paradigm. *Journal of Personality and Social Psychology*, 29, 696–702.

Konecni, V. (1975). The mediation of aggressive behavior: arousal level versus anger and cognitive labeling. *Journal of Personality and Social Psychology*, 32, 706–16.

Korte, C., and Grant, R. (1980). Traffic noise, environmental awareness, and pedestrian behavior. *Environment and Behavior*, 12, 408–20.

Korte, C., Ypma, A., and Toppen, C. (1975). Helpfulness in Dutch society as a function of urbanization and environmental input level. *Journal of Personality and Social Psychology*, 32, 996–1003.

Kraut, R. (1973). Effects of social labeling on giving to charity. *Journal of Experimental Social Psychology*, 9:6, 551–62.

Kristjansson, K. (2008). An Aristotelian critique of situationism. *Philosophy*, 83, 55–76.

Krucoff, M., Crater, S., Gallup, D., Blankenship, J., Cuffe, M., Guarneri, M., Krieger, R., Kshettry, V., Morris, K., Oz, M., Pichard, A., Sketch, M., Koenig, H., Mark, D., Lee, K. (2005). Music, imagery, touch, and prayer as adjuncts to interventional cardiac care: the monitoring and actualisation of noetic trainings (MANTRA) II randomized study. *Lancet*, 366, 211–17.

Krupka, E., and Weber, R. (2006). *The Focusing and Informational Effects of Norms on Pro-Social Behavior*. Working Paper, Carnegie Mellon University.

Kupperman, J. (1995). *Character*. Oxford University Press.

(2001). The indispensability of character. *Philosophy*, 76, 239–50.

Kuran, T. (1995). *Private Truths, Public Lies: The Social Consequences of Preference Falsification*. Cambridge: Harvard University Press.

Kuran, T., and Sunstein, C. (1999). Availability cascades and risk regulation. *Stanford Law Review*, 51:4, 683–768.

Kurzban, R., DeScioli, P., and O'Brien, E. (2007). Audience effects on moralistic punishment. *Evolution and Human Behavior*, 28, 75–84.

Lahroodi, R. (2007). Evaluating need for cognition: a case study in naturalistic epistemic virtue theory. *Philosophical Psychology*, 20:2, 227–45.

Lakatos, I. (1995). *The Methodology of Scientific Research Programmes*. Worrall and Currie (eds.). Cambridge University Press.

Latané, B., and Darley, J. (1968). Group inhibition of bystander intervention in emergencies. *Journal of Personality and Social Psychology*, 10, 215–21.

(1970). *The Unresponsive Bystander: Why Doesn't He Help?* New York: Appleton-Century-Crofts.

Latané, B., and Nida, S. (1981). Ten years of research on group size and helping. *Psychological Bulletin*, 89, 308–24.

Latané, B., and Rodin, J. (1969). A lady in distress: inhibiting effects of friends and strangers on bystander intervention. *Journal of Experimental Psychology*, 5, 189–202.

Lemert, E. (1972). *Human Deviance, Social Problems and Social Control*. New York: Prentice Hall.

Lepock, C. (2009). How to make the generality problem work for you. *Acta Analytica*, 24:4, 275–86.

(2011). Unifying the intellectual virtues. *Philosophy and Phenomenological Research*, 83:1, 106–28.

Levine, R., Norenzayan, A., and Philbrick, K. (2001). Cross-cultural differences in helping strangers. *Journal of Cross-Cultural Psychology*, 32, 543–60.

Lewis, D. (1986). Causal explanation. In *Philosophical Papers*, vol. II, pp. 214–40. Oxford University Press.

Loewenstein, G. (2000). Emotions in economic theory and economic behavior. *American Economic Review*, 90:2, 426–32.

MacIntyre, A. (1984). *After Virtue: A Study in Moral Theory*. University of Notre Dame Press.

Mack, A., and Rock, I. (1998). *Inattentional Blindness*. Cambridge, MA: MIT Press.

Malle, B. (2006). The actor-observer asymmetry in causal attribution: a (surprising) meta-analysis. *Psychological Bulletin*, 132, 895–919.

Malle, B., Knobe, J., and Nelson, S. (2007). Actor-observer asymmetries in explanations of behavior: new answers to an old question. *Journal of Personality and Social Psychology*, 93, 491–514.

Mantell, D. (1971). The potential for violence in Germany. *Journal of Social Issues*, 27, 101–12.

Marx, K. (1845/1998). *The German Ideology, Including Theses on Feuerbach*. New York: Prometheus Books.

Masclet, D., Noussair, C., Tucker, S., and Villeval, M.-C. (2001). *Monetary and Non-Monetary Punishment in the Voluntary Contributions Mechanism*. Working paper, Purdue University, Krannert Graduate School of Management.

Matthews, K. E., and Cannon, L. K. (1975). Environmental noise level as a determinant of helping behavior. *Journal of Personality and Social Psychology*, 32, 571–77.

McCrae, R., and John, O. (1996). An introduction to the five-factor model and its applications. *Journal of Personality*, 60:2, 175–215.

McDowell, J. (1979). Virtue and reason. *Monist*, 62, 331–50.

McNatt, B., and Judge, T. (2004). Boundary conditions of the Galatea effect: a field experiment and constructive reply. *The Academy of Management Journal*, 47:4, 550–65.

Mednick, M. (1963). Research creativity in psychology graduate students. *Journal of Consulting Psychology*, 27:3, 265–66.

Meichenbaum, D., Bowers, K., and Ross, R. (1969). A behavioral analysis of teacher expectancy effect. *Journal of Personality and Social Psychology*, 13, 306–16.

Merritt, M. (2000). Virtue ethics and situationist personality psychology. *Ethical Theory and Moral Practice*, 3, 365–83.

Merton, R. (1948). The self-fulfilling prophecy. *The Antioch Review*, summer, 193–210.

Meyer, W.-U., Bachman, M., Biermann, U., Hempelmann, M., Ploger, F.-O., and Spiller, H. (1979). The informational value of evaluative behavior: influences of praise and blame on perceptions of ability. *Journal of Educational Psychology*, 71, 259–68.

Mifune, N., Hashimoto, H., and Yamagishi, T. (2010). Altruism toward in-group members as a reputation mechanism. *Evolution and Human Behavior*, 31:2, 109–17.

Milgram, S. (1961). Nationality and conformity. *Scientific American*, December, 45–51.

(1974). *Obedience to Authority*. New York: Harper Collins.

Mill, J. S. (1859/2010). *On Liberty*. Cambridge University Press.

Miller, C. (2003). Social psychology and virtue ethics. *The Journal of Ethics*, 7:4, 365–92.

(2009). Empathy, social psychology, and global helping traits. *Philosophical Studies*, 142:2, 247–75.

(2010). Character traits, social psychology, and impediments to helping behavior. *Journal of Ethics and Social Philosophy*, 5, 1–36.

Miller, D., and McFarland, C. (1987). Pluralistic ignorance: when similarity is interpreted as dissimilarity. *Journal of Personality and Social Psychology*, 53:2, 298–305.

(1991). When social comparison goes awry: the case of pluralistic ignorance. In Suls and Wills (eds.), *Social Comparison: Contemporary Theory and Research*, pp. 287–313. Hillsdale, NJ: Erlbaum.

Miller, F. (2005). William James, faith, and the placebo effect. *Perspectives in Biology and Medicine*, 48:2, 273–81.

Miller, R., Brickman, P., and Bolen, D. (1975). Attribution versus persuasion as a means for modifying behavior. *Journal of Personality and Social Psychology*, 31:3, 430–41.

Mills, R. S., and Grusec, J. E. (1989). Cognitive, affective, and behavioral consequences of praising altruism. *Merrill-Palmer Quarterly*, 35, 299–326.

Mischel, W. (1968). *Personality and Assessment*. New York: Wiley.

Mischel, W., and Peake, P. (1982). Beyond déjà vu in the search for cross-situational consistency. *Psychological Review*, 89, 730–55.

Mischel, W., and Shoda, Y. (1995). A cognitive-affective system theory of personality: reconceptualizing the invariances in personality and the role of situations. *Psychological Review*, 102:2, 246–68.

Moerman, D., and Jonas, W. (2002). Deconstructing the placebo effect and finding the meaning response. *Annals of Internal Medicine*, 136, 471–76.

Mondaini, N., Gontero, P., Giubilei, G., Lombardi, G., Tommaso, C., Gavazzi, A., and Bartoletti, R. (2007). Finasteride 5 mg and sexual side effects: how many of these are related to the nocebo phenomenon? *The Journal of Sexual Medicine*, 4:6, 1708–12.

Monin, B., and Miller, D. (2001). Moral credentials and the expression of prejudice. *Journal of Personality and Social Psychology*, 81:1, 33–43.

Monin, B., Pizarro, D., and Beer, J. (2007). Deciding versus reacting: conceptions of moral judgment and the reason-affect debate. *Review of General Psychology*, 11, 99–111.

Montmarquet, J. (1987). Epistemic virtue. *Mind*, 96:384, 482–97.

(1993). *Epistemic Virtue and Doxastic Responsibility*. Lanham, MD: Rowman and Littlefield.

(2003). Moral character and social science research. *Philosophy*, 78:305, 355–68.

(2007). "Pure" versus "practical" epistemic justification. *Metaphilosophy*, 38:1, 71–87.

Mueller, C., and Dweck, C. (1998). Praise for intelligence can undermine children's motivation and performance. *Journal of Personality and Social Psychology*, 75:1, 33–52.

Nietzsche, F. (1997). *Daybreak*. Translated by R. J. Hollingdale, edited by Maudemarie Clark and Brian Leiter. Cambridge University Press.

(2001). *The Gay Science*. Translated by Josefine Nauckhoff, edited by Bernard Williams. Cambridge University Press.

(2002). *Beyond Good and Evil*. Translated by Judith Norman, edited by Rolf-Oter Horstmann and Judith Norman. Cambridge University Press.

(2005). *Ecce Homo*. Translated by Judith Norman, edited by Aaron Ridley and Judith Norman. Cambridge University Press.

(2006). *On the Genealogy of Morality*. Translated by Carol Diethe, edited by Keith Ansell-Pearson. Cambridge University Press.

Nozick, R. (1981). *Philosophical Explanations*. Cambridge, MA: Harvard University Press.

Nussbaum, M. (1995). *Poetic Justice: The Literary Imagination and Public Life*. Boston, MA: Beacon Press.

Oosterhof, N., and Todorov, A. (2008). The functional basis of face evaluations. *Proceedings of the National Academy of Sciences of the USA*, 105, 11087–92.

Ouellette, J., and Wood, W. (1998). Habit and intention in everyday life: the multiple processes by which past behavior predicts future behavior. *Psychological Bulletin*, 124:1, 54–74.

Page, R. (1974). Noise and helping behavior. *Environment and Behavior*, 9, 311–34.

Perugini, M., and Leone, L. (2009). Implicit self-concept and moral action. *Journal of Research in Personality*, 43, 747–54.

Phillips, D., Ruth, T., and Wagner, L. (1993). Psychology and survival. *Lancet*, 342, 1142–45.

Plato (1968). *The Republic of Plato.* Translated by Bloom. New York: Basic Books.

Plaza, J. (2007). Logics of public communications. *Synthese*, 158:2, 165–79.

Pollock, J. (1984). Reliability and justified belief. *Canadian Journal of Philosophy*, 14, 103–14.

Prentice, D., and Miller, D. (1993). Pluralistic ignorance and alcohol use on campus: some consequences of misperceiving the social norm. *Journal of Personality and Social Psychology*, 64:2, 243–56.

Prinz, J. (2009). The normativity challenge: cultural psychology provides the real threat to virtue ethics. *The Journal of Philosophy*, 13:2–3, 117–44.

Quine, W. (1969). *Ontological Relativity and Other Essays.* New York: Columbia University Press.

Rawls, J. (1971). *A Theory of Justice.* Cambridge, MA: Harvard University Press.

Regan, J. (1971). Guilt, perceived injustice, and altruistic behavior. *Journal of Personality and Social Psychology*, 18, 124–32.

Rege, M., and Telle, K. (2004). The impact of social approval and framing on cooperation in public good situations. *Journal of Public Economics*, 88:7–8, 1625–44.

Rigdon, M., Ishii, K., Watabe, M., and Kitayama, S. (2009). Minimal social cues in the dictator game. *Journal of Economic Psychology*, 30:3, 358–67.

Ring, K., Wallston, K., and Corey, M. (1970). Mode of debriefing as a factor affecting subjective reactions to a Milgram-type obedience experiment: an ethical inquiry. *Representative Research in Social Psychology*, 1, 67–85.

Rist, R. (1970). Student social class and teachers' expectations: the self-fulfilling prophecy in ghetto education. *Harvard Educational Review*, 40, 411–50.

  (1972). Social distance and social inequality in a kindergarten classroom: an examination of the 'cultural gap' hypothesis. *Urban Education*, 7, 241–60.

  (1973). *The Urban School: A Factory for Failure.* Cambridge, MA: MIT Press.

  (1977). On understanding the processes of schooling: the contribution of labeling theory. In Karabel and Halsey (eds.), *Power and Ideology in Education*, pp. 292–305. New York: Oxford University Press.

Roberts, R., and Wood, J. (2007). *Intellectual Virtues.* Oxford University Press.

Rohrer, J., Baron, S., Hoffman, E., and Swinder, D. (1954). The stability of autokinetic judgment. *Journal of Abnormal and Social Psychology*, 49, 595–97.

Rosenthal, R. (1974). *On the Social Psychology of the Self-Fulfilling Prophecy: Further Evidence for Pygmalion Effects and Their Mediating Mechanisms.* New York: MSS Modular Publications, Module 53.

  (1976). *Experimenter Effects in Behavioral Research.* New York: Irvington Press.

  (1985). From unconscious experimenter bias to teacher expectancy effects. In Dusek, Hall, and Meyers (eds.), *Teacher Expectancies*, pp. 37–65. Hillsdale, NJ: Erlbaum.

(1987). "Pygmalion" effects: existence, magnitude, and social importance. *Educational Researcher*, 16:9, 37–41.

(1994). Interpersonal expectancy effects: a 30-year perspective. *Current Directions in Psychological Science*, 3:6, 176–79.

(2002). Covert communications in classrooms, clinics, courtrooms, and cubicles. *American Psychologist*, 57, 839–49.

Rosenthal, R., and Jacobson, L. (1968). *Pygmalion in the Classroom: Teacher Expectations and Pupils' Intellectual Development*. New York: Holt Press.

Rosenthal, R., and Lawson, R. (1964). A longitudinal study of the effects of experimenter bias on the operant learning of laboratory rats. *Journal of Psychiatric Research*, 2, 61–72.

Rosenthal, R., and Rubin, D. (1978). Interpersonal expectancy effects: the first 345 studies. *The Behavioral and Brain Sciences*, 3, 377–86.

Ross, L. (1977). The intuitive psychologist and his shortcomings. In Berkowitz (ed.), *Advances in Experimental Psychology*, vol. x, pp. 174–214. New York: Academic Press.

Ross, L., and Nisbett, R. E. (1991). *The Person and the Situation*. Philadelphia: Cambridge University Press.

Ross, L., Greene, D., and House, P. (1977). The false consensus effect: an egocentric bias in social perception and attribution processes. *Journal of Experimental Social Psychology*, 13, 279–301.

Roth, A., Prasnikar, V., Okuno-Fujiwara, M., and Zamir, S. (1991). Bargaining and market behavior in Jerusalem, Ljubljana, Pittsburgh, and Tokyo: an experimental study. *American Economic Review*, 81, 1068–95.

Russell, D. (2009). *Practical Intelligence and the Virtues*. Oxford University Press.

Sabini, J., and Silver, M. (2005). Lack of character? Situationism critiqued. *Ethics*, 115, 535–62.

Sachdeva, S., Iliev, R., and Medin, D. (2009). Sinning saints and saintly sinners: the paradox of moral self-regulation. *Psychological Science*, 20:4, 523–28.

Salmon, W. (1984). *Scientific Explanation and the Causal Structure of the World*. Princeton University Press.

Samuels R., Stich, S., and Bishop, M. (2002). Ending the rationality wars: how to make disputes about human rationality disappear. In Elio (ed.), *Common Sense, Reasoning and Rationality*, pp. 236–68. New York: Oxford University Press.

Sarkissian, H. (2010). Minor tweaks, major payoffs: the problems and promise of situationism in moral philosophy. *Philosopher's Imprint*, 10:9, 1–15.

Schaller, M., and Cialdini, R. (1990). Happiness, sadness, and helping: a motivational integration. In Higgins and Sorrentino (eds.), *Handbook of Motivation and Cognition*, pp. 265–96. New York: The Guilford Press.

Schanck, R. (1932). A study of a community and its groups and institutions conceived as behaviors of individuals. *Psychological Monographs*, 43, 195.

Schelling, T. (1968). The life you save may be your own. In Chase (ed.), *Problems in Public Expenditure Analysis*, pp. 127–62. Washington DC: Brooking Institute.

Schrank, W. (1968a). The labeling effect of ability grouping. *The Journal of Educational Research*, 62:2, 51–52.

(1968b). A further study of the labeling effect of ability grouping. *The Journal of Educational Research*, 63:8, 358–60.

Schulz-Hardt, S., Frey, D., Lüthgens, C., and Moscovici, S. (2000). Biased information search in group decision making. *Journal of Personality and Social Psychology*, 78:4, 655–59.

Schulz-Hardt, S., Jochims, M., and Frey, D. (2002). Productive conflict in group decision making: genuine and contrived dissent as strategies to counteract biased information seeking. *Organizational Behavior and Human Decision Processes*, 88:2, 563–86.

Schwartz, S., and Gottlieb, A. (1991). Bystander anonymity and reactions to emergencies. *Journal of Personality and Social Psychology*, 39, 418–30.

Scott, C., and Yalch, R. (1980). Consumer response to initial product trial: a Bayesian analysis. *The Journal of Consumer Research*, 7, 32–41.

Searle, J. (1975). Indirect speech acts. In Cole and Morgan (eds.), *Syntax and Semantics, 3: Speech Acts*, pp. 59–82. New York: Academic Press.

(1995). *The Construction of Social Reality*. New York: Free Press.

Sheridan, C., and King, R. (1972). Obedience to authority with an authentic victim. In *Proceedings of the Eightieth Annual Convention of the American Psychological Association*, pp. 165–66. Washington DC: American Psychological Association.

Sherif, M. (1937). An experimental approach to the study of attitudes. *Sociometry*, 1, 90–98.

Sinnott-Armstrong, W. (ed.) (2008). *Moral Psychology*, vols. i–iii. Cambridge, MA: MIT Press.

Slonim, R., and Roth, A. (1998). Learning in high stakes ultimatum games: an experiment in the Slovak Republic. *Econometrica*, 66:3, 569–96.

Slote, M. (1992). *From Morality to Virtue*. Oxford University Press.

(2001). *Morals from Motives*. Oxford University Press.

Snow, N. (2009). *Virtue as Social Intelligence: An Empirically Grounded Theory*. New York: Routledge.

Snyder, M. (1984). When belief creates reality. In Berkowitz (ed.), *Advances in Experimental Social Psychology*, 31, pp. 64–67. San Diego, CA: Academic Press.

(1992). Motivational foundations of behavioral confirmation. In Zanna (ed.), *Advances in Experimental Social Psychology*, 20, pp. 67–114. San Diego, CA: Academic Press.

Snyder, M., and Swann, S. (1978). Behavioral confirmation in social interaction: From social perception to social reality. *Journal of Experimental Social Psychology*, 14, 148–62.

So, A. (1987). Hispanic teachers and the labeling of Hispanic students. *The High School Journal*, 71:1, 5–8.

Sosa, E. (1980). The raft and the pyramid: coherence versus foundations in the theory of knowledge. *Midwest Studies in Philosophy*, 5:1, 3–26.

(1991). *Knowledge in Perspective*. Cambridge University Press.

(2001). For the love of truth. In Fairweather and Zagzebski (eds.), *Virtue Epistemology: Essays on Epistemic Virtue and Responsibility*, pp. 49–62. Oxford University Press.

(2007). *A Virtue Epistemology*. Oxford University Press.

(2008). Situations against virtues: the situationist attack on virtue theory. In Mantzavinos (ed.), *Philosophy of the Social Sciences: Philosophical Theory and Scientific Practice*, pp. 274–91. Cambridge University Press.

(2011). *Knowing Full Well*. Princeton University Press.

Spitz, H. (1999). Beleaguered *Pygmalion*: a history of the controversy over claims that teacher expectancy raises intelligence. *Intelligence*, 27:3, 199–234.

Sreenivasan, G. (2002). Errors about errors: virtue theory and trait attribution. *Mind*, 111, 47–68.

(2008). Character and consistency: still more errors. *Mind*, 117, 603–12.

Stanley, J. (2005). *Knowledge and Practical Interests*. New York: Oxford University Press.

Stocker, M. (1976). The schizophrenia of modern ethical theories. *Journal of Philosophy*, 73:14, 453–66.

Strawson, P. F. (1960). Freedom and resentment. *Proceedings of the British Academy*, 48, 1–25.

Strenta, A., and DeJong, W. (1981). The effect of a prosocial label on helping behavior. *Social Psychology Quarterly*, 44:2, 142–47.

Sunstein, C. (2005). Moral heuristics. *Behavioral and Brain Sciences*, 28, 531–42.

Swanton, C. (2003). *Virtue Ethics: A Pluralist View*. Oxford University Press.

Tajfel, H. (1970). Experiments in intergroup discrimination. *Scientific American*, 5:223, 79–97.

(1973). The roots of prejudice: cognitive aspects. In Watson (ed.), *Psychology and Race*, pp. 76–95. Harmondsworth: Penguin.

(1981). *Human Groups and Social Categories*. Cambridge University Press.

(1982). Social psychology and intergroup relations. *Annual Review of Psychology*, 33, 1–30.

Taylor, E. (1957/1984). *Angel*. London: Virago.

Taylor, S., and Brown, J. (1988). Illusion and well-being: a social psychological perspective on mental health. *Psychological Bulletin*, 103, 193–210.

Thaler, R., and Sunstein, C. (2008). *Nudge: Improving Decisions about Health, Wealth, and Happiness*. New York: Penguin.

Thomas, W., and Thomas, D. (1929). *The Child in America*. New York: Knopf.

Thomson, J. J. (1996). Evaluatives and directives. In Harman and Thomson (eds.), *Moral Relativism and Moral Objectivity*, pp. 128–29. Oxford: Blackwell.

(1997). The right and the good. *Journal of Philosophy*, 94:6, 280–83.

Tronto, J. (1993). *Moral Boundaries: A Political Argument for an Ethic of Care*. New York: Routledge.

Tversky, A., and Kahneman, D. (1973). Availability: a heuristic for judging frequency and probability. *Cognitive Psychology*, 5, 207–32.

(2002). Extensional versus intuitive reasoning: the conjunction fallacy in probability judgment. In Gilovich, Griffin, and Kahneman (eds.), *Heuristics and Biases: The Psychology of Intuitive Judgment*. Cambridge University Press.

Tybout, A., and Yalch, R. (1980). The effect of experience: a matter of salience? *Journal of Consumer Research*, 6, 406–13.

Uleman, J. et al. (1996). People as flexible interpreters: evidence and issues from spontaneous trait inference. In Zanna (ed.), *Advances in Experimental Social Psychology*, vol. xxvii, pp. 211–80. San Diego: Academic Press.

Upton, C. (2009). The structure of character. *The Journal of Ethics*, 13, 175–93.

Vaidyanathan, R., and Praveen, A. (2005). Using commitments to drive consistency: enhancing the effectiveness of cause-related marketing communications. *Journal of Marketing Communications*, 11:4, 231–46.

Wallace, J. (1974). Excellences and merit. *The Philosophical Review*, 83:2, 182–99.

Walton, G., and Spencer, S. (2009). Latent ability: grades and test scores systematically underestimate the intellectual ability of stereotyped students. *Psychological Science*, 20:9, 1132–39.

Weyant, J. (1978). Effects of mood states, costs, and benefits on helping. *Journal of Personality and Social Psychology*, 36, 1169–76.

Williams, B. (1985). *Ethics and the Limits of Philosophy*. Cambridge: Harvard University Press.

Zagzebski, L. (1996). *Virtues of Mind*. Cambridge University Press.

(2010). Exemplarist virtue theory. In Battaly (ed.), *Virtue And Vice: Moral and Epistemic*, pp. 39–55. West Sussex: Wiley-Blackwell.

Zanna, M., Sheras, P., Cooper, J., and Shaw, C. (1975). Pygmalion and Galatea: the interactive effect of teacher and student expectancies. *Journal of Experimental Social Psychology*, 11, 279–87.

Zhong, C.-B., Bohns, V., and Gino, F. (2010). Good lamps are the best police: darkness increases dishonesty and self-interested behavior. *Psychological Science*, 21:3, 311–14.

Index

Adams, Robert Merrihew, 31, 66, 126
Annas, Julia, 22, 68,
Anscombe, Elizabeth, 8, 17, 22, 76
Ariely, Dan, 39, 48
Aristotle, 65, 103, 106
Asch, Solomon, 133
attention, 42, 45, 47, 49
attribution errors, 54–58
Autrey, Wesley, 1, 69, 75
availability cascade, 59

Baron, Robert, 45
Batson, Daniel, 35, 49, 72
Bentham, Jeremy, 189
bias
    availability, 59
    confirmation, 60
    false consensus effect, 55
    fundamental attribution error, 53, 54, 56, 60,
        131, 156
    selection, 58
Bicchieri, Cristina, 92, 97, 132, 193
Big Five, *see* Five Factor model
Bohnet, Iris, 52, 191, 197
Burnham, Terrance, 198
bystander apathy, 41–42

CAPS, *see* cognitive-affective personality system
Charness, Gary, 52, 198, 201
Code, Lorraine, 111, 115, 116, 122, 135
cognitive-affective personality system, 78
construal, 6, 42, 53, 56, 57, 74, 76, 93, 94, 100,
    126
Cornelissen, Gert, 90, 91

Darley, John, 35, 41, 50, 72, 170
demand characteristics, 40, 41–43, 63, 74, 139, 146
deviance, 95
Doris, John, 3, 8, 31, 33, 37, 58, 64, 65, 71, 79,
    112, 126, 152, 176
Duckworth, Angela, 77, 170

Duncker, Karl, 121
Dweck, Carol, 159, 165, 167

egalitarianism, 23, 32, 34, 35, 37, 40, 53, 63
elitism, 32
empathy, 24, 48
Epicurus, 10, 186, 188–89, 200, 201, 203
ethics of care, 76
exhortation, 23, 88, 97, 106

Five Factor model, 52, 137
Frey, Bruno, 52, 191, 197
Funder, David, 77

generality problem, 118–19, 125, 140
Gigerenzer, Gerd, 58, 152
Goldman, Alvin, 49, 113, 140, 177
Greco, John, 113, 117, 155
Grusec, Joan, 90

Hacking, Ian, 107, 168, 177
Harman, Gilbert, 3, 38, 54, 55
heuristic
    availability, 141–43
    disgust, 155
    disposition, 156
    representativeness, 143–48
    social distance, 190–201
Hoffman, Elizabeth, 72, 190, 198, 201
Hookway, Christopher, 111
Hurka, Thomas, 20, 64, 158

Isen, Alice, 36, 46, 50, 52, 71, 120–25

J.R., 204–5
Jussim, Lee, 168

Kahneman, Daniel, 58, 141–48, 152

Latané, Bibb, 41
looping kinds, 107, 168, 177

MacIntyre, Alasdair, 8, 23, 30, 63
Malle, Bertram, 55
Mednick, Martha, 121
Mischel, Walter, 53, 56, 60, 61, 76, 78
Montmarquet, James, 103, 115, 128, 137, 158
mood elevators and depressors, 46,
     118–26
moral credentialing, 98, 100, 177
moral schizophrenia, 20, 64

need for cognition, 137
nocebo, 84

placebo, 84, 85, 88, 90, 91, 102
pluralistic ignorance, 131–36
portability of context, 77, 79
prayer, 85, 92
principle of charity, 103

Rist, Ray, 159, 167, 169
Rosenthal, Robert, 158–65
Ross, Lee, 53, 54, 55, 56, 58, 163
Russell, Daniel, 7, 20, 28, 33, 78

saints, 25, 28, 32, 34, 35, 37
self-concept, 88–105, 161–78
self-fulfilling prophecy, 85–94, 161–76
Sherif, Muzafer, 132
social ontology, 190–201
Sosa, Ernest, 111–17, 158

Sreenivasan, Gopal, 54, 69–76
stereotype threat, 185

Tajfel, Henri, 201
Tversky, Amos, 59, 141–48

vice
   dishonesty, 2, 20, 38, 56, 102, 161, 175
   factitious, 96
   manipulativeness, 12, 102, 175
   overconfidence, 161, 176, 177
virtue
   act-based theory of, 64, 158
   as triadic relation, 106, 177
   creativity, 120–26
   de, 81
   factitious, 161–79
   grit, 77, 170
   high-fidelity/low-fidelity distinction, 31, 32,
        34, 72, 73, 76, 77, 79, 82, 136
   honesty, 2, 27, 31, 38, 39, 65, 67, 73, 77, 82, 93,
        105, 119, 179, 185, 187, 199, 202
   intellectual courage, 115, 126–36
   magnificence, 65
   modesty, 101
   thick/thin distinction, 20
   unity of, 33

Zagzebski, Linda, 28, 112, 115–19, 129
Zimbardo, Philip, 37, 43, 72, 200

Made in the USA
San Bernardino, CA
21 December 2015